THE WITCHER
AND PHILOSOPHY

The Blackwell Philosophy and Pop Culture Series
Series editor: William Irwin

A spoonful of sugar helps the medicine go down, and a healthy helping of popular culture clears the cobwebs from Kant. Philosophy has had a public relations problem for a few centuries now. This series aims to change that, showing that philosophy is relevant to your life—and not just for answering the big questions like "To be or not to be?" but for answering the little questions: "To watch or not to watch *South Park*?" Thinking deeply about TV, movies, and music doesn't make you a "complete idiot." In fact, it might make you a philosopher, someone who believes the unexamined life is not worth living and the unexamined cartoon is not worth watching.

Already published in the series:

THE WITCHER AND PHILOSOPHY

TOSS A COIN TO YOUR PHILOSOPHER

Edited by

Matthew Brake and Kevin S. Decker

WILEY Blackwell

Published by John Wiley & Sons, Inc., Hoboken, New Jersey.
Published simultaneously in Canada.

For general information on our other products and services or for technical support, please contact our Customer Care Department within the United States at (800) 762-2974, outside the United States at (317) 572-3993 or fax (317) 572-4002.

Wiley also publishes its books in a variety of electronic formats. Some content that appears in print may not be available in electronic formats. For more information about Wiley products, visit our web site at www.wiley.com.

Library of Congress Cataloging-in-Publication Data

Names: Brake, Matthew, 1984– editor. | Decker, Kevin S., editor.
Title: The witcher and philosophy : toss a coin to your philosopher / edited by Matthew Brake and Kevin S. Decker.
Description: Hoboken : John Wiley & Sons, Inc., 2025. | Series: The Blackwell philosophy and pop culture series | Includes index.
Identifiers: LCCN 2024010499 (print) | LCCN 2024010500 (ebook) | ISBN 9781394168736 (paperback) | ISBN 9781394168743 (adobe pdf) | ISBN 9781394168750 (epub)
Subjects: LCSH: Witcher (Television program)
Classification: LCC PN1992.77.W54 W58 2024 (print) | LCC PN1992.77.W54 (ebook) | DDC 791.45/72–dc23/eng/20240319
LC record available at https://lccn.loc.gov/2024010499
LC ebook record available at https://lccn.loc.gov/2024010500

Cover Design: Wiley
Cover Images: © Nastassia/Adobe Stock, © Marcus Lindstrom/Getty Images, © geen graphy/Shutterstock

Set in 10/12pt SabonLTStd by Straive, Pondicherry, India
SKY10085166_091924

Contents

Contributors

Walter Barta is a graduate student and special projects grant-holder at the University of Houston. Lately he has been researching witcherbility studies in the department of monstro-biology. In his free time he is a philosopher-for-hire, wandering the world, searching for and fighting off the many errors, falsehoods, fallacies, misunderstandings, and other monstrosities that plague popular culture. Please remember to "toss a coin to your philosopher."

Matthew Brake is an Assistant Professor of Philosophy at Northern Virginia Community College. He is also the series editor for the Theology, Religion, and Pop Culture series from Fortress Academic. As the co-editor of this book, he would like to thank all of you who have bought it. Please tell your friends to buy it, too, so that they can also "toss a coin to your witcher [volume editor]."

Gerald Browning is an Instructor of English and Self-Defense at Grand Valley State University. He also teaches English at Muskegon Community College. However, when he isn't tipping a coin to his local witcher, he is training in martial arts and buying tickets to Jaskier concerts. Much like Jaskier, Gerald is a published storyteller. His novel, *Demon in My Head,* is his only horror novel, and he has contributed to other Popular Culture and Philosophy publications.

Yael Cameron is a Senior Lecturer at Auckland University of Technology and on Tuesday evenings occasionally dresses as a Vengerbergian acolyte. Her research is interdisciplinary, crossing between continental philosophy, religion, and occasional chaotic forays into forbidden fire magic. While she doesn't have superhuman senses, she does make up for this by being inhumanly beautiful and publishes widely in this guise on mythology and its relation to contemporary literature and film. So there's that talent in her bag of forgotten bones, and like horses, whores, and mages, a talent that's only useful 'til it's not.

Like a rambling minstrel, **Matthew Crippen** is a wandering professor who has plied his trade on four continents, taking up other jobs as well, such as performing music, coaching gymnastics, and sword (machete) work on tree farms. His publications parallel the hybrid monstrosities in

The Witcher. They mix cognitive science, history of Western and non-Western philosophy, environmental philosophy, ethics, politics, aesthetics, and philosophy of technology and science, also discussing other stuff like the intelligence of slime mold or gut bacteria influencing our brains.

Kevin S. Decker is Professor of Philosophy at Eastern Washington University and does odd jobs around the college like burying bodies and wrangling alligators. He is the editor or co-editor of 15 books in philosophy and popular culture, most recently *Dune and Philosophy* and *Star Wars and Philosophy Strikes Back* (with Jason T. Eberl), and the author of *Who is Who? The Philosophy of Doctor Who*. He giggles every time he hears the name "Mousesack."

Paul Giladi is a Lecturer in Philosophy at SOAS University of London. One of Paul's areas of research and teaching expertise is critical social theory, specifically topics at the intersection of the literature on epistemic injustice and on recognition theory. If Paul were a mage in the Witcherverse, he would probably be deemed too "woke" by the likes of Stregobor. Paul also tends to giggle inanely whenever he hears the word "Ragamuffin"—c'mon, you know why ...

In the realm of academia, **Corey R. Horn** roams the halls of Tulane University as a PhD candidate in the Department of Philosophy. A sorcerer specializing in the intricate dance of international relations and human rights, Corey's work seeks to push the realms closer together, toward a more just and prosperous world. When Corey isn't writing as fast as Geralt wields his sword, you can find him in a coffee shop, consuming caffeine potions—forever fueling intellectual conquests.

John P. Irish is an educator and independent researcher specializing in the works of John Locke and John Adams. He has earned master's degrees in Philosophy and Humanities, with a Doctorate in Humanities from Southern Methodist University. He wrote his dissertation on the intriguing and lesser-known mid-nineteenth-century Irish American speculative fiction writer Fitz-James O'Brien, often called the "Irish Poe." He is currently editing a three-volume collection of O'Brien's weird tales in collaboration with Swan River Press. Contributing regularly to the magazine *Philosophy Now: A Magazine of Ideas*, he also published an article in the edited volume *Asimov's Foundation and Philosophy: Psychohistory and Its Discontents*. An interesting facet of his teaching philosophy is his belief that literature only becomes truly captivating when vampires appear, which explains his immediate fascination with *The Witcher*. Residing in Bridgeport, Texas, he shares a lakeside home with his wife Elizabeth and their five children: Tom, Annie, Teddy, Lucy, and Holly—otherwise known as their pets.

Ceádmil! **Andriy Ivanchenko** is originally from the Eastern city of Kharkiv in Ukraine, where he is currently residing having spent 20 or so years abroad. He got his master's degree in English and Applied Linguistics from the University of Cambridge, then wrote a doctoral dissertation discussing some ways linguistic methods can be applied to interpreting literary (more specifically, dramatic) conversation. Afterwards, he spent some years teaching academic English in Japan, including a well-beloved seminar on cultural and linguistic aspects of fantasy literature and fantasy magic in particular. His appreciation of all things *Witcher* goes back many years—in fact, quite a while before the very first *Witcher* game was unleashed upon the world. He's currently gearing up to study other linguistic aspects of the Witcherverse, but let that remain a mystery for now, nell'ea?

Steven Kammerer is a writer, director, composer, and independent scholar of the encounters between East and West down through the ages, from Herodotus to Heidegger. His master's degree in German Studies is from Queen's University in Kingston, Ontario, while doctoral studies at Queen's and Simon Fraser University helped launch him on stints of archive research in Germany and Egypt. Since then he's led a fairly Witcheresque life of high adventure. During the "Arab Spring," he covered the million-strong demonstrations in Tahrir Square, Cairo, while his trips up and down the Nile saw him sometimes as the lone tourist in an ancient temple, village, or oasis. He put in three seasons of mineral exploration in the mountains of northeastern Yukon Territory, where he had many—all too many!—encounters with bears, bees, thick clouds of mosquitoes, and once or twice saw what he could have sworn was a leshen. A season as deck-hand on a salmon trawler in the rough waters off the craggy shores of the Alaskan panhandle (very Skellige!) seasoned him into something of a sailor. Among other film projects, he's the award-winning writer-director of *Ada* (2019), a biopic of Countess Ada Lovelace, daughter of Lord Byron and the world's first computer programmer. His moody piano compositions can be found on Spotify.

Graham Lee has undergraduate and graduate degrees in philosophy, which he appreciates is only slightly more relatable than having gone to mage school. He is newer to *The Witcher* than many of his colleagues, admittedly having been introduced to it through the television series (shame, shame). While it took him to the fourth episode to understand there were different timelines (and still longer to understand that the guard was more breaking the fourth wall than busting Jaskier's balls), it only took him to the fourth page of *Blood of Elves* to understand that the books aren't as confusing.

Wulf Loh is Assistant Professor at the University of Tübingen, Germany, where he leads a small research group on the ethics of AI and robotics.

When he is not boring his students with questions of algorithmic bias and discrimination, he still loves to go chasing after Ciri or explore the Skellige Isles on his PS4.

Victoria Lyle is a senior undergraduate completing degrees in English and in Religion/Philosophy. Much like those studying at the temple of Melitele, Victoria spends her time reading, studying, and trying to avoid the strife of life. Finishing up her undergraduate studies isn't quite as intense as undergoing the Trial of Grasses, but she may emerge as an entirely different creature in the end.

Tim Miechels is a PhD student and lecturer at the Radboud University Nijmegen. He mainly teaches courses in the field of metaphysics and philosophical anthropology and is writing a dissertation on the concept of "naturalism" in the works of Edmund Husserl and Martin Heidegger. He once aspired to become a witcher in the School of the Bear, but his constitution makes him unfit for any practical activity whatsoever.

Raised in the southern kingdom of Darwen, Fortunio Fang served the Serpent Clan as a formidable spearman. But after Merwyn's coup, Fortunio Fang fled to the forests, living as a spear-for-hire until the Conjunction of the Spheres thrust him to a place called Earth. Finding an earthling woman to mate with (producing two hybrid offspring), Fortunio Fang assumed the identity of **Edwardo Peréz**, setting aside his warrior ways to teach rhetorical and critical theory as a Professor of English.

Shane J. Ralston is the Dean of Wright College, Woolf University, and a scholar of philosophical pragmatism. He's authored two books, one on the philosopher John Dewey and the other on environmentalism. He also edited a collection of essays on international relations and pragmatism. In addition, he's composed over 50 articles and book chapters on topics as wide-ranging as gardening activism and distracted caregiving. Before joining the dark side of higher education administration, he was a tenured Philosophy Faculty member at Pennsylvania State University, a human resources director at the American University of Malta, a grant writer at the City of Santa Clarita, and a mechanic at too many bicycle shops to list. He's had so many jobs inside and outside of academia that he sometimes daydreams about living in the *Witcher* world, where he'd have a singular motivation: to kill demons. Similar to a witcher, being a college dean makes people think he's a freak, but that doesn't stop him from doing his job!

Corry Shores teaches philosophy at the Middle East Technical University in Ankara, Turkey. He works primarily on Gilles Deleuze and phenomenology, at times in relation to film and painting. He recently authored the book, *The Logic of Gilles Deleuze: Basic Principles*. Easily startled, he asks that you observe the Law of No Surprises when you meet him.

Darian J. Shump is an independent scholar, a fledgling game developer, and the Administrative Coordinator for the Center of Excellence in Digital Game Development at Rensselaer Polytechnic Institute. Outside of his work at RPI, his research focuses on visual culture in contemporary Japan, including representations of shape-shifting *yōkai* in print and digital media, and informs his broader approach to game development and narrative design. Through fall 2021, Darian pursued an MA in East Asian Languages and Cultures at Florida State University. He also previously earned an MA in Religion from Florida State University and a BA in History and Religious Studies from Stetson University.

Ryan Smock is from a rural town in Arizona and has taught both English and philosophy in higher education for 14 years. He currently teaches at Arizona State University, sometimes moonlighting at the Oxenfurt Academy when Dandelion is on leave. The last time they met, disagreement over Girardian perspectives on theater ended in a duel. Dandelion, wielding a rubber chicken, won.

Julie Loveland Swanstrom is an Associate Professor of Philosophy and Religion at Augustana University in Sioux Falls, South Dakota. She received her PhD in philosophy from Purdue University. She teaches a range of courses across philosophy of religion, historical philosophy and theology, philosophy of science, and ethics. In her research, she explores medieval theories of causation, using odd and curious cases of causation to help understand causal presumptions people hold. Creation, witchcraft, and early medicine are helpful odd or curious cases, and her familiarity with medieval Jewish, Islamic, and Christian philosophy and theology (including especially Ibn Sina and Aquinas) undergirds such research. She also uses philosophical and theological methods and ideas to explore science fiction and fantasy works. The Brotherhood suspects her of witchcraft, which, given her studies, is understandable.

Fiona Tomkinson graduated from Oxenfurt and then saddled up Roach with the aim of traveling to the far reaches of the Eurasian Continent. Delayed for over 20 years in Istanbul, where she taught literature in Asia whilst studying to become a Doctor of Philosophy in Europe, she finally made it to Japan in 2017. She encountered numerous monsters on the way, but now chiefly battles with jellyfish in the Pacific Ocean.

Zoe L. Tongue is a Lecturer in Law at the University of Leeds, where she researches reproductive rights. She also works on law and feminism in speculative fiction, mostly as an excuse to write about her favorite movies and television shows. She has published on representations of reproduction within mainstream and feminist science fiction works. When she was younger she was kicked out of Aretuza for failing to master her inner chaos, and now seeks her revenge by working to free the demon Voleth Meir.

Cisil Vardar is a second-year master's student in philosophy at the University of Utah. She works on the ways to approach the philosophy of action via imagination in Kant and Fichte. As a devoted follower of art and extremity in every possible form, she values Nouvelle Vague, Giallo movies, and Denpa visual novels. If the truth in fiction may refer to beliefs, she believes that bending chaos would be possible for her in the next conjunction of spheres.

Emily Vega is an educator, writer, and folklorist from Houston, Texas. Her grandmother was a *curandera* (a Mexican folk healer), which introduced her to the world of magic, witches, and the stories we tell about them. This led her to eagerly researching (and poorly practicing) witchcraft and eventually writing her dissertation on the subject. Her love of folklore and all things witchy also led her to *The Witcher*. Given the chance, she would most definitely listen to one of Jaskier's/Dandelion's songs, and perhaps even applaud.

By day, **Zachary Vereb** is a professor at the University of Mississippi, where he instructs courses in ethics, critical thinking, and public policy. By night, he practices martial arts and enjoys fantasy role-playing games. This is prepara-tion for becoming a witcher, though Zach's long hair will take several more years to acquire the characteristic white color. Luckily, Zach's voice isn't as intimidating as Geralt's, since that would scare off his students!

Erin Williams is an editor and writer with RTI International, a large research nonprofit. She earned her master's in Religion at Duke University where she focused on religion and world-building in science fiction and fantasy novels, short stories, and video games. Her two thesis papers explored religion and technology in Margaret Atwood's *MaddAdam* trilogy and J.B. Rhine's research into parapsychology, which means she was really fun to talk to at parties. She just played *The Witcher 3* for at least the fifth time and made a point to discover every question mark on the map, which took about 118 hours.

Florian R.R. van der Zee obtained his bachelor's and research master's degrees in philosophy at Radboud University in Nijmegen, the Netherlands. He specialized in social and political philosophy, and when he wasn't studying Kalkstein's *Transmutations and Metamorphoses*, he usually pored over Carl Schmitt's treatises. Since writing his chapter, he has become a PhD candidate working on issues in medical ethics, philosophy, and his-tory at Erasmus MC in Rotterdam, the Netherlands. Now he'd like a word with Vesemir about consent forms.

Introduction
Toss a Coin to Your Witcher ... and Your Philosopher

Matthew Brake

Thank you, dear readers, for picking up this volume! Some consider philosophers to be relics of a bygone era, creatures who live apart from society, with a moral code and way of speaking that might make them seem as, well ... as monstrous as the topics they attempt to tackle. With their ivory towers, and tweed jackets, and steel swords ... whoops! Did I mix up philosophers with witchers? My mistake.

But is this such a strange mistake to make? Anyone who has read the books by Andrzej Sapkowski (to say nothing of having played the video games or watched the Netflix series) knows that there are extended philosophical treatments of the nature of the world, meditations on monstrosity, and musings about the moral decisions that a person ought to make in such a world ... if they even have a choice in those decisions at all!

My own journey into the world of *The Witcher* is backwards compared to many other fans. I began by watching the Netflix series. One day I walked into the living room and asked a friend what they were watching: "A new show called *The Witcher*" was the reply. It was near the end of the very first episode, right before Geralt's fight with Renfri's men. After watching that first fight scene, I was hooked, and my plans for the day were cancelled so I could sit and binge the entire first season. Then I read the books. Finally, I played the video games, and I would consider *Witcher 3* one of the best games I've ever played.

The fantasy world Sapkowski created is perfect for the Blackwell Philosophy and Popular Culture series. In this book, you'll find the work of a number of philosophers seeking answers to the questions asked in the various adaptations of *The Witcher*. How do we navigate a world of imperfect moral choices? Should a person really avoid picking the "lesser evil"? If destiny exists, can we really speak of the existence of free will? What can the racism on the Continent show us about our own world? What does it mean to be a woman in the world of *The Witcher*—and in our world?

As you read this book, I hope you will be inspired to go back and engage with the world of Geralt of Rivia. If you play the video games, I hope you appreciate the complex moral world that has been fashioned, and if you haven't read the books, then I hope you will go back to the source material and spend time thinking about the philosophical quandaries that Sapkowski has filled his books with. *The Witcher* is a philosophical text in its own right. I hope this book makes that apparent.

ETHICS

1

A Friend of Humanity
On Mercenaries, Mutants, and Morals

Zachary Vereb

> Monsters do bad things to people ... humans do bad things to everybody.
>
> "A Grain of Truth"[1]

Geralt is a witcher, and witchers are mutants. They are inhuman monsters, so why would anyone want to become one? Andrzej Sapkowski takes the word "witcher" from the Polish *wiedźmin*. But a better way to think about the word is to see its parallel with "wiccan," a person believed to practice magic. And of course, many such persons were really burned alive out of the thought that they were inhuman, satanic monsters.

In "Dear Friend" (season 2, episode 6) Geralt and his adopted daughter Ciri argue. Ciri wants to gain the power of the witchers to acquire their strength and magic. Geralt doesn't like the idea. To become a witcher means to undergo harsh medical trials, trials that might kill, or worse. If witchers are monsters, they certainly aren't born so. *They are made into monsters.* Ciri protests, imploring Geralt to let her partake of the Trial of the Grasses. Her motive is not strength and magic, but vengeance. "You want to kill yourself trying to become a mutant so if you survive, you can kill yourself trying to get revenge." Ciri responds: "You don't give a shit about what I want ... all you care about is damn duty!" Wait a second. If witchers like Geralt are *monsters*, what is this talk of "duty"? Aren't duties a matter of ethics, of morals? Do monsters have morals? Witchers are not only mutants, but mercenaries that kill other monsters. Do mercenaries have morals?

Scenes like this in the Netflix series pull us in and make us question what we would do in the place of Geralt or Ciri. If Geralt worries about Ciri's humanity, what does that tell us about his humanity? *The Witcher* prompts us to ask important questions about why we should do the right thing in a world where evil often trumps virtue, where the good guys don't always win in the end. It turns out that these questions about ethics tell us a lot about what it means to be human. By depicting mutants like Geralt, *The*

The Witcher and Philosophy: Toss a Coin to Your Philosopher, First Edition.
Edited by Matthew Brake and Kevin S. Decker.
© 2025 John Wiley & Sons, Inc. Published 2025 by John Wiley & Sons, Inc.

Witcher actually teaches us about *our* humanity. But it can only do so if we gather the courage to engage in a little moral philosophy.

Since Geralt is often portrayed as a heroic exemplar of the moral philosophy of Stoicism, we can start there. We will then see, however, that he is better appreciated as a representative of the Kantian ethical view. The Kantian view is the ideal philosophical frame to help us make sense of what a duty to be a friend of humanity means, even though Geralt himself has much to learn about becoming a true friend of humanity. Finally, as we compare Yennefer's selfish worldview with Geralt's evolution as a Kantian exemplar, we grapple with important questions of who we want to be. Whether we are mutants, mercenaries, or mediocre members of the human race, we must question the sort of lives we should live. Do we have a duty to become a friend of humanity? While the Stoic view has answers, the Kantian one helps us to better understand Geralt's progress as a moral mutant and the nature of this duty. This, in turn, gives us the opportunity to philosophize about how we see ourselves in the series, or even in Geralt.

The Mercenary with a Moral Compass?

In the Netflix series, Geralt of Rivia is portrayed, at first glance, as a stoic role model full of humility, courage, and trustworthiness. Yet the people of the Continent often stereotype witchers as emotionless and inhuman.

Historically, Stoicism is an introspective philosophy with a cosmopolitan perspective. It asks us to reflect on things in our control, and to see ourselves as citizens of the world rather than as representatives of nations or races. While its roots are in ancient Greece and the Roman period, it's currently popularized by websites like *Modern Stoicism* and *The Daily Stoic*.[2] Yet Geralt is also motivated by coin and self-preservation and indeed cares little for the plight of humans across the Continent—and these are very un-Stoic traits. Should witchers like Geralt be viewed as Stoic mercenaries?[3] A better and more basic question, however, is this: Can witchers like Geralt be true moral agents who freely choose to abide by ethical duties? Geralt lives according to the motto that "evil is evil.... Lesser, greater, middling ... it's all the same" ("The End's Beginning," season 1, episode 1), but we might wonder if such a simple slogan makes sense in an increasingly complicated and brutal world.

Though Geralt undoubtedly evolves in season 3, the opening scenes of the show's first episode paint a compelling moral picture. After killing the wretched Kikimora, Geralt heads to a tavern to claim his reward. We learn that he, like all witchers, kills monsters for cash. But because of this, he is rejected by the community, as evidenced by how he's treated in the tavern. As the episode continues, we meet Princess Renfri Vellga, who attempts to convince Geralt to assist in her vengeance on Stregobor. He refuses to help, insisting on principled neutrality instead of giving in to her inclinations. In the end, he recommends that she move on, to end the cycle of violence. We are thus introduced to Geralt as a kind of honorable mercenary, strong-willed, principled, and independent—all important Stoic virtues. Yet if he is a Stoic, his exploits have taught him little about how to be a friend of humanity, even as he helps humans. We even begin to notice resentment in Geralt's eyes. At best, Geralt is a superficial Stoic. Later in the series, Geralt does learn how to become a true friend of humanity, to see this as his ethical duty. However, it becomes hard to make sense of his character evolution from the Stoic perspective. Instead, we need a different ethical perspective.

Is Geralt a Stoic, and If So, Is He a Bad One?

It's natural to view Geralt as a Stoic seeking inner tranquility, evading the turmoil of politics in a world he can't control. Stoic philosophers, like the slave Epictetus (c. 50–c. 135 CE) and the Roman Emperor Marcus Aurelius (121–180 CE), teach us to focus on the things that are under our control.[4] Things that we cannot control, like the opinions of others, the world of politics, and the luxuries of food, drink, lust, and comfort, should be of no concern to us. The Stoics enjoin us to pursue justice and wisdom when it's in our power, but they remind us of our limitations. If you can't understand why the ills of the world exist (or that we can't change them), the Stoic thinks, you just need to expand your perspective, "zoom out" to see how the evils make sense in the context of the whole. This leads the Stoics to an optimistic view of the world; they adopt a *teleological* view, in which nature is organized for reasons and structured by purposes, around a logical center, or *Logos*. Geralt tries to act stoically. But if he's a Stoic, he's bad at it.

In the beginning of the series, Geralt's life centers around coin: he hunts monsters for the reward, caring little for the well-being of those he saves or for the monsters themselves (which is odd, since people often consider *him* to be a monster, too!).[5] In other words, contrary to the usual injunction of Stoicism to promote cosmopolitan justice within your control, Geralt's interactions with others early on in the series end up being largely contractual. Neither friendship with humanity nor Stoic concern for justice or wisdom factor into his work as a witcher. Coin is the main goal, and he follows these inclinations for some time in the series. Further, Geralt does not view others in the world as the Stoics do, as "citizens of the world." This less-than-Stoic sentiment is echoed by others in season 2, with the dark and hardly stoic observation that "Monsters do bad things to people ... humans do bad things to everybody" ("A Grain of Truth," season 2, episode 1). Geralt is not really interested in two of the four main Stoic virtues, namely wisdom and justice. Yet, he does try to live up to Stoic virtues of moderation and courage. We might say that Geralt is Stoic-like, and this helps to explain the popular appeal of his character in the series as an exemplar of Stoicism. By the same token, Geralt's decisions—especially given his philosophizing about the lesser evil—set him up to be more of a Kantian, as we will soon see. Even if Geralt lines up more with Kant's philosophical view, he still has a long way to go in the series to understand how this moral philosophy encourages friendship with humanity as a moral duty. But before we get to this, let's talk about evil.

Philosophizing the Lesser Evil

Returning to the Renfri–Stregobor conflict from the first episode of the Netflix adaptation, we see Geralt tell Stregobor, "Evil is evil, Stregobor. Lesser, greater, middling ... it's all the same. I'm not judging you. I haven't only done good in my life either. But now, if I have to choose between one evil and another, then I prefer not to choose at all." This scene tells us that there are certain boundaries Geralt will not cross, even for coin.

Though Geralt is no philosopher, he shares the concerns of the ethical theory of Immanuel Kant (1724–1804), who was inspired by the Stoics but goes beyond them.[6] Kant's ethical theory is "deontological." *Deon* means "duty" in Greek. A deontological ethic bases right and wrong on correct principles for action rather than on the results of actions—as, say, utilitarianism does. Utilitarianism, a moral philosophy sharpened by John Stuart Mill (1806–1873), suggests that we should pursue actions that produce the greatest good for the greatest number of people. On Mill's view, the only thing that matters for ethics at the end of the day is the final result of our actions. Utilitarianism is referred to by philosophers as a *consequentialist* theory rather than a deontological one. Kant's moral philosophy differs greatly from Mill's, and Kant argues that the consequences of our actions are irrelevant to their true moral worth. What really matters, he claims, is that we do the right thing for the right reason, consequences be damned.

For Kant, as he writes in his *Groundwork of the Metaphysics of Morals* (1785), we have certain duties by virtue of our nature as rational beings.[7] *The Witcher*'s hedonistic sorceresses and the Redanian Prince Radovid provide examples of Kant's idea that, in acting, we are often led astray by our desires. These include the desire to pursue our self-interest even when it conflicts with what we know to be right. For Kant, reflecting on our nature as rational beings, we find within ourselves a moral law that guides us in the face of bad choices. The key to finding this law is the *categorical imperative* ("act only according to that maxim [rule] through which you can at the same time will that it become a universal law"). Kant refers to the categorical imperative as the supreme principle of morality, and he observes that this principle has similar counterparts in other cultures and religions. He refers to the golden rule from the

Christian tradition, as well as the more negatively phrased silver rule from the Confucian tradition.[8]

In one respect, Geralt embodies the categorical imperative in that he must do his duty, and that no duty can compel him to violate the rights of others, even if those actions could be rationalized as "lesser evils."[9] Humanity, on the Kantian view that Geralt represents, is deserving of dignity and respect. To be a friend of humanity involves respecting the humanity in others. Geralt realizes that killing Renfri, even to better the world (which is doubtful, since Stregobor is trying to manipulate Geralt), violates his moral duty to treat others as *ends in themselves*. Upon further reflection on the categorical imperative, Kant says, "Now I say: a human being and generally every rational being *exists* as an end in itself, *not merely as a means* for the discretionary use for this or that will, but must ... always be considered *at the same time as an end*."[10] This means that as moral beings, we are *sources of value*: we choose ends and goals. We are invaluable *persons*, not things that have more or less value depending on circumstances. On the Kantian view, we have a duty to refrain from treating humans as objects to manipulate like Stregobor does. Wrong is wrong. Treating others as mere means (except acting in self-defense) is evil for both Kant and Geralt. A true friend of humanity would never do this. So as a witcher, Geralt doesn't pursue his own happiness or pleasure, as do other characters on the Continent. Rather, he adopts an ethical way of living in line with Kant's ethical philosophy.

Even if Geralt is unhappy, Kant would say that he is *worthy of happiness* and retains the dignity of being a moral agent. And moral agents, as Kant argues, have duties to promote the happiness of others, to do good to them when it is in their power. This duty holds, Kant thinks, even if we do not like those people: "To *do good* to other human beings insofar as we can is a duty, whether one loves them or not; and even if one had to remark sadly that our species, on closer acquaintance, is not particularly lovable, that would not detract from the force of this duty."[11] Geralt of course dislikes many humans, but this doesn't stop him—as the series progresses—from pursuing his duty, attempting to help others in need. A true friend of humanity understands the duty to love their neighbors. As Kant refers to this, the "maxim of benevolence (practical love of human beings), is a duty of all human beings toward one another, whether or not one finds them worthy of love."[12] Geralt might dislike the political strife on the Continent—the selfishness of humans, mages, and elves—but he nonetheless strives to do his duty.

An exchange between Yennefer and Ciri in "Unbound" (season 3, episode 2) confirms Geralt's deontological focus on duty rather than on weighing outcomes. Yennefer asserts, "In all those lessons, I should have taught you that sometimes, discretion is more important than valor.... We should have taught you about consequences." Ciri answers, "Consequences are just an excuse not to act." At this point in the series, Yen has not taken on a motherly role toward Ciri: she's still shrewd and unprincipled. She sees things transactionally, not ethically. But as Kant warns us—and which helps to explain why Geralt and Yen's first attempt at a relationship fails— "friendship cannot be a union aimed at mutual advantage but must rather be a purely moral one."[13] Ciri's retort suggests that she has taken many of Geralt's Kantian teachings on duty, reciprocity, and respect to heart. It's obviously inhuman, Ciri realizes, to treat others as objects. Yet paradoxically, it also seems inhuman to let people die just because of moral scruples.[14] As the dialogue continues, Yen seems to reveal the monstrous underbelly of Kant's ethics: "You saved one, and the consequence has likely damned a hundred others in exchange."

Hard Upbringings and Harder Wits with Foxes and Ravens

Geralt believes in keeping promises, no matter the consequences. "But a promise must be honored," says Geralt, "as true for a commoner as for a queen" ("Of Banquets, Bastards, and Burials," season 1, episode 4). Yet there are problems with that approach. Kant would understand Geralt's hesitation to forgive Yen for selfishly betraying them, just to regain her magic ("Shaerrawedd," season 3, episode 1). It is a duty, Kant says, "of human beings to be *forgiving. ...* But this must not be confused with *meek toleration* of wrongs ... for then a human being would be throwing away his rights and letting others trample on them, and so would violate his duty to himself."[15] Let's explore the contrast between Geralt's Kantian outlook and Yennefer's egoism.

Yennefer of Vengerberg, like Geralt, is a complicated character. She's torn between a desire for the approval of others and her own self-realization. As a result, her interests and desires often come into conflict with those around her. Later in the series, she finds herself in complex political entanglements. Deeper tensions abound: *love vs. power, duty vs. control, friendship vs. egoism.* She cannot harmonize the ends of others with her own, as Kant's duty implores, nor does she want to. Yen cares little, at least early in the series, to respect the humanity of others. She is out for herself. At the end of the day, her egoistic worldview is antithetical to Geralt's duty to be a friend of humanity. It is unsurprising that Geralt and Yen end up providing dramatic contrasts that bring the series to life. After all, they represent very different ethical worlds, and very different takes on how we should relate to humanity.

Yennefer acts as if guided by the political theorist Niccolò Machiavelli (1469–1527), who enjoins the wise leader to pursue manipulative means, to be a cunning fox when necessary. Machiavelli says, "a prudent ruler cannot keep his word, nor should he, when such fidelity would damage him ... those best able to imitate the fox have succeeded best."[16] This Machiavellian view appears to be the polar opposite of the Stoic and Kantian ones, leading us to question the attraction between Yennefer and Geralt in the first place.[17] Yen had a difficult upbringing. It comes as little surprise that she begins her adult life as an egoist: "There is no us, only me" ("Bottled Appetites," season 1, episode 5). Her selfishness is expressed in a calculating way, like Machiavelli's fox. Yennefer's symbol is the Black Kestrel. Later in the same episode, Yen reveals her way of seeing the world in terms of the slogan, "Nobody smart plays fair." The clever Kestrel is only out for herself. This Machiavellian Kestrel has no care for the worth of humanity. Friendship with humanity, on this view, is only important if it helps us to better exploit others. Yen's early view of the world clashes with Geralt's Kantian one, even if he still has much learning to do on what it means to be a friend of humanity.

Geralt's animal, the White Wolf, is symbolic of loyalty. Geralt is a realist about political struggles on the feudalistic Continent, but he doesn't conclude that the depravities of others justify joining them in doing evil. A stark contrast to the White Wolf, Yen prefers cunning over honor, for example, using mages as catapult fodder in season 1's finale. Her harnessing of the element of fire is meant to strike fear in the hearts of others. As Machiavelli argues, this makes sense, since "it is much safer to be feared than loved."[18] This egoistic and manipulative worldview is imported into her view of the Continent's politics: "Politics is just the personal wrapped up in a different package" ("Reunion," season 3, episode 3). Nothing could be more different than Geralt's selfless commitment to duty, as when he firmly states, "I won't abandon Ciri, even if it costs me my life," in the same episode.

Yennefer, unlike others in the Brotherhood of Sorcerers, becomes less Machiavellian over time. Whether this is due to the cultivation of family with Geralt and Ciri or her exposure to Geralt's deontological ethics is not for us to say. But in seeing her growth, we as viewers are confronted with our own relation to others, and we must ask: Is it possible to be a principled individual in a selfish world?

Becoming a True Friend of Humanity

In the first episode of the Netflix series, Queen Calanthe, the "Lioness of Cintra," provides a gem of wisdom on this question. "In the face of the inevitable," she declares, "good leaders should always choose mercy. In the future, you will be wise to do the same" ("The End's Beginning"). There's a bit of irony here, as Machiavelli suggests not only being a fox, but also sometimes being a lion.[19] Perhaps Calanthe balances out the contradictions between Geralt and Yen, but in doing so, she loses her life, her city, and her people. Kant himself reminds us of the humility required to be a friend of humanity, and Calanthe seems to meet the challenge by sacrificing her crown. As Kant says,

> A *friend of human beings* as such (i.e., of the whole race) is one who takes an effective interest in the well-being of all human beings (rejoices with them) and will never disturb it without heartfelt regret. ... Taking to heart the duty of being benevolent as a friend of human beings (a necessary humbling of oneself) serves to guard against the pride that usually comes over those fortunate enough to have the means for beneficence.[20]

Like Calanthe, the bard of *The Witcher*, Jaskier, mediates between the principled concerns of Kant's deontology and the material desires of Machiavelli. Jaskier, rather than Yennefer or Geralt, best reflects what it means to be a real, ethical human who seeks to become a friend of humanity in Kant's sense. Fragile, Jaskier is not a fighter. He creates songs rather than fighting battles. Still, Jaskier gathers courage to fight and to forgive, and he helps us remember that we must *choose* to act. By contrast, Geralt sometimes behaves as if he were unfree: his one-sided pursuit of duty paints him as a shackled monster, and it reminds us that he is a mutant. One criticism of Kant's ethics is that when we act purely from our rational-moral nature, we are all the same. But where is our humanity without our individuality? Where is good without creation and choice? By the same token, Yen's political machinations encourage her to think ahead of herself, anxiously. She can't live in the moment, as Jaskier teaches. If we are always projecting into the future, always worried about the not-yet, how can we ever live as good humans? Jaskier too grapples with selfish political dilemmas, but he succeeds in putting the happiness of others as his end (we call these "imperfect duties of virtue" for Kant). Jaskier's actions help both Geralt and Yen see that being ethical is not simply a matter of obeying formal duties or overcoming self-interest. It is also a matter of actively cultivating friendship and love. What else could it mean to be a friend of humanity?

Both Geralt and Yennefer are incomplete characters—by blindly pursuing duty or desire, they miss something. Geralt is the White Wolf and Yen is the Black Kestrel. What is Jaskier? His name in Polish translates as "Buttercup" (or, roughly, as "Dandelion"). As others have observed, the buttercup flower, hearkening back to Shakespeare, is symbolic of *lovers and innocence*.[21] The dandelion, in addition, is commonly viewed as a symbol of *hope*. Our bard fleshes out the missing human elements with the human heart and ear. Without love, we remain immature Machiavellian egoists, unable to truly understand what it means to be human or do right. Without hope, doing right is hard to understand, and we once again remain unable to make sense of who we should become. Kant himself recognized this.[22] At the end of the day, if we equip ourselves with philosophical eyes (or, like good bards, philosophical ears), *The Witcher* teaches us a lot about our own world, our choices, and ourselves. To absorb these lessons, even by exploring the trials of mercenaries, mutants, and mages, let's first learn to listen to those imperatives, *O' Valley of Plenty* ♪, and become friends of humanity.

Notes

1. "A Grain of Truth," season 2, episode 1.
2. *Modern Stoicism*: https://modernstoicism.com; *The Daily Stoic*: https://daily stoic.com. For a good overview of Stoicism and its popularity, see Matthew Sharpe, "Stoicism 5.0: The Unlikely 21st Century Reboot of an Ancient Philosophy," *The Conversation*, July 13, 2017, https://theconversation.com/stoicism-5-0-the-unlikely-21st-century-reboot-of-an-ancient-philosophy-80986. Ask yourself if Geralt really seems to be a stoic or not.
3. Jamie Ryder, in "Stoicism And Geralt Of Rivia's Philosophy Of Life" (*Medium.com*, February 22, 2022, https://medium.com/@Jamie_ryder/stoicism-and-geralt-of-rivias-philosophy-of-life-e4c96a35e1ef), reflects on whether Geralt should be seen as a stoic.
4. Classic texts to read include Marcus Aurelius, *The Meditations*, trans. G.M.A. Grube (Indianapolis: Hackett, 1983) and Epictetus, *The Handbook (The Encheiridion)*, trans. Nicholas P. White (Indianapolis: Hackett, 1983).
5. Dragons are an interesting exception for Geralt, as seen in "Rare Species," season 1, episode 6.
6. Martha C. Nussbaum connects the philosophical views of Immanuel Kant and the Roman Stoics well in "Kant and Stoic Cosmopolitanism," *The Journal of Political Philosophy* 5 (1997), 1–25.
7. See Immanuel Kant, *Groundwork of the Metaphysics of Morals*, trans. Mary Gregor (New York: Cambridge University Press, 2012).
8. Kant, *Groundwork of the Metaphysics of Morals*, 34, 40, and 42.
9. In a later philosophical treatise on religion, Kant argues that we all rationalize (or make excuses for) ignoring what we know to be right to meet the demands of our self-interested desires. See Immanuel Kant, *Religion within the Boundaries of Mere Reason*, trans. George di Giovanni, in *Religion and Rational Theology* (New York: Cambridge University Press, 1996).
10. Kant, *Groundwork of the Metaphysics of Morals*, 40; emphasis original.
11. Immanuel Kant, *Metaphysics of Morals*, trans. Mary J. Gregor, in *Practical Philosophy* (New York: Cambridge University Press, 1996), 530; emphasis original.
12. Kant, *Metaphysics of Morals*, 570.
13. Kant, *Metaphysics of Morals*, 586.
14. This is a dilemma Kant himself was pressed to address, now known as "Kant's Axe." Kant's response can be found in the essay, "On the Supposed Right to Lie from Benevolent Motives," trans. Mary J. Gregor, in *Practical Philosophy* (New York: Cambridge University Press, 1996), 612.
15. Kant, *Metaphysics of Morals*, 578; emphasis original.
16. Niccolò Machiavelli, *The Prince* (New York: Cambridge University Press, 2019), 60.

17. For an example of how *The Prince* is adapted for today, see Chris Taylor, "The Machiavellian Way: How 'The Prince' Can Help Women at Work," *Reuters.com*, May 3, 2022, https://www.reuters.com/business/machiavellian-way-how-the-prince-can-help-women-work-2022-05-03.
18. Machiavelli, *The Prince*, 57.
19. Machiavelli, *The Prince*, 60; emphasis original.
20. Kant, *Metaphysics of Morals*, 587.
21. Gretchen Scoble and Ann Field, *The Meaning of Flowers: Myth, Language & Lore* (San Francisco: Chronicle Books, 1998), 19.
22. In his later works, Kant would build in the importance for practical hope with his postulate of immortality. Fans of *The Witcher* books may continue on this philosophical thread, making sense of Geralt and Yennefer's journey to an afterlife realm later on. Unfortunately, we must save those reflections for another time. This chapter has not been concerned with the beyond, but with the here and now.

2

The Witcher's Dilemmas
Genuine or Apparent?

Walter Barta and Graham Lee

Contrasting with the simplistic moral reasoning of fairy tales, the stories of Andrzej Sapkowski's *The Witcher* series are complicated with conflicting duties, interests, and values, forcing Geralt of Rivia to choose amidst complexity and uncertainty. Moreover, these choices often involve trade-offs because no one option is clearly better than the others. Throughout the books, television shows, and video games, moral conundrums and quandaries abound. Should Geralt side with Renfri or Stregobor, and by which standards should he make such a choice? Should Geralt take the easy way out and kill a monster, take the hard way and break a curse, or just opt not to intervene at all? Must he obey orders from a corrupt lord or can he decline?

Geralt's difficult decisions raise a more general philosophical question about moral dilemmas: Are they truly irreconcilable conflicts of value? Or do they just appear to be so? Do they actually involve priorities that, upon reflection, are easily weighed against each other?

On the Trolley and the Idr

As moral philosophers have long lamented, moral duties often conflict, making for moral dilemmas: cases with two mutually exclusive options either (a) that cannot both be chosen but that both appear to be the right thing to do, or (b) that both appear to be the wrong thing to do but one of which must be chosen. As far back as ancient Athens, Socrates (469–399 BCE) was discussing moral dilemmas. In Plato's *Republic* he asks: Can we break a promise to prevent harm? More recently, Phillipa Foot (1920–2020) popularized the study of moral dilemma, which she defined as "the general question of what we may and may not do where the interests of human beings conflict."[1] Following Foot's lead, Judith Jarvis Thomson coined the term "trolley problem" for the type of moral decision in which one moral value is pitted against another.[2] For most of these problems, we're asked to

The Witcher and Philosophy: Toss a Coin to Your Philosopher, First Edition.
Edited by Matthew Brake and Kevin S. Decker.
© 2025 John Wiley & Sons, Inc. Published 2025 by John Wiley & Sons, Inc.

imagine a forced scenario with two bad outcomes. Imagine, for example, that Geralt is hunting an Idr—a ferocious, man-eating, insectoid monster—and in the monster's path is a village of poor peasants. If Geralt baits the beast to change its trajectory just a bit, it will spare the village but head toward a lone peasant (who was not originally under threat) instead.[3] Roughly speaking, this is a version of a trolley problem, with the trolley replaced by a monster. The trolley driver (in our case, monster hunter) can either let five die and one live or kill one and save five. In the former case, he saves fewer lives; in the latter case he directly causes a death. What should he choose? People's intuitions differ regarding the decision, and so a dilemma emerges.

Geralt's adventures are replete with such dilemmas. Sometimes Geralt even reflects on them philosophically in the novels, describing dilemmas as "sacrificing one good in order to save another one."[4] Similarly, the plots of the video games often turn upon such dilemmas. Gameplay involves making critical decisions for Geralt which sometimes result in drastically different in-game outcomes, forcing players themselves to grapple with Geralt's moral difficulties firsthand as an essential element of the experience. Far from merely slaughtering beasts, the players must make choices for, and as, the Witcher. The player is able to both embody the hero and live out the consequences of their choices, engaging moral thought experiments through gaming. But if both sides of a dilemma are (or seem) moral, how should Geralt choose? Indeed, how should we choose for Geralt? And *are* these truly irreconcilable conflicts? Or do they just *seem* to be?

Genuine Dilemmas

Many of Geralt's moral dilemmas seem genuine, pitting one true moral duty against another true moral duty in a zero-sum way.

The conflict in the story "The Lesser Evil" presents one of the most painful and controversial of Geralt's decisions, where he finds himself reluctantly forced to choose between two seeming evils.[5] On one side is Stregobor, an elder sorcerer in the city of Blaviken who is hiding from an (allegedly) cursed princess he has been hunting; on the other side is Renfri (a.k.a. Shrike), the princess, who intends to punish Stregobor for the indignities she's suffered at his hands. Geralt is hired by Stregobor to kill Renfri and by Renfri to kill Stregobor. Both parties feel justified killing the other in self-defense. This calls to mind the "Plank of Carneades" thought experiment, a philosophical dilemma in which two drowning, shipwrecked sailors attempt to get hold of a floating plank that can only carry one of them. At first Geralt attempts to opt out: "If I'm to choose between one evil and another, then I prefer not to choose at all."[6] But when Geralt later returns to town, Renfri's goons interpret this as siding with Stregobor, and they confront Geralt in the streets, saying, "It's an ultimatum!" These circumstances force Geralt's hand, and blood is shed. In the conflict, Geralt attempts to negotiate with Renfri until the final blow, but she never relents, and he kills her in self-defense. Geralt's role in the situation earns him both lingering regret and the dishonorable moniker, "The Butcher of Blaviken." On first glance this case seems to be a *genuine* moral dilemma in the sense that two irreconcilable and irreducible moral requirements are pitted against each other:

1. Side with Renfri to protect her.
2. Side with Stregobor to protect him.

Bernard Williams (1929–2003), among many other philosophers, argued that there are *genuine* moral dilemmas, truly tragic scenarios with no right answer because there are moral values, neither of which can reasonably be seen to override the other. According to Williams,

> It may well be, then, that moral conflicts are in two different senses ineliminable. In a particular case, it may be that neither of the *ought*'s [sic] is eliminable. Further, the tendency of such conflicts to occur may itself be ineliminable.... Moral conflicts are neither systematically avoidable, nor all soluble without remainder.[7]

Indeed, in Blaviken, Geralt tries his hardest to come to a solution to avoid the dilemma, rejecting both offers from Stregobor and Renfri in the hopes that the situation would resolve itself. But, failing at this, Geralt must act as he does and accept the consequences—including his regret. The existentialist philosopher Jean-Paul Sartre (1905–1980) famously discussed a similar dilemma in which his student must make an important personal decision: either go off to fight the Nazis or stay home to care for his mother.[8] Asked for advice, Sartre ultimately gave the student no authoritative answer, telling him that the choice is his and that he must live with it. As Geralt puts it, Sartre forced his student, as Geralt puts it, "to suffer the agony of choice."[9] In other words, and consistent with Williams's worries, moral decisions may not have easy ways out.

The pessimistic view proposed by Williams seems to have some roots in the polytheistic tradition of Greek tragedy, popularized in more recent times by Friedrich Nietzsche (whom *Witcher* author Sapkowski himself also quotes).[10] Nietzsche seems committed to a view of the human condition as deeply conflicted, writing,

> The misery in the essence of things—which the contemplative [Greek philosopher] is not disposed to explain away—the antagonism in the heart of the world, manifests itself.... With the heroic effort made by the individual for universality, ... he experiences in himself the primordial contradiction concealed in the essence of things, i.e., he trespasses and suffers.[11]

In other words, the goal of discovering universally correct moral responses in complex, multifaceted situations is perhaps too much to ask of us. According to Nietzsche, neither Geralt nor a video-game player should expect every moral problem to have a solution. This may simply be a constraint on moral decisions. Like Renfri, who may have been born under a bad moon, to play as Geralt may be to play a rigged game.

Another poignant *Witcher* case highlighting this tragic human condition comes in "A Grain of Truth," a story involving Geralt's old friend Nivellen, a repentant former rapist cursed for his crimes to take the form of a beast, and Nivellen's lover Vereena, who happens to be a bruxa, a blood-thirsty monster with a human form.[12] As the situation unfolds, Nivellen realizes that Vereena cannot control the monstrous impulses that drive her to feed upon innocent townsfolk. Yet, when Vereena is killed, Nivellen's curse is broken by Vereena's true love for him. In short, Vereena had two inner imperatives that tragically and inevitably conflicted: feeding herself and loving another. Geralt and Nivellen face a moral conflict as well:

1. Let Vereena continue feeding on peasants, so that she may survive.
2. Kill Vereena, though she is Nivellen's true love, in order to save the peasants.

The occurrence of such conflicts within the core of the human psyche indicates the deep truth that Nietzsche points to: not all desires, and perhaps not all duties, are capable of being brought into harmony.

Another example comes from the story "The Last Wish," in which Geralt becomes the master of a djinn and is granted three wishes. He inadvertently curses his friend, the bard Dandelion (Jaskier), with one wish. Meanwhile, the sorceress Yennefer of Vengerberg attempts to capture the djinn to obtain the wishes for herself.[13] In the end, with Yennefer and the djinn in mortal conflict, Geralt realizes his dilemma:

1. If he doesn't make his last wish, he and Dandelion may lose their lives.
2. If he does make his last wish, the liberated djinn may kill Yennefer.

Geralt knows that the djinn cannot harm its former master. So, in order to avoid these two equally bad options, Geralt attempts to trick the djinn:

3. If he frames his last wish in a manner that spiritually binds Geralt and Yennefer together, then the djinn can never harm one without harming the other.

Geralt thus manages to rescue everyone involved from the djinn's wrath. However, this is done at great personal cost, since Geralt and Yennefer are trapped together forever in an unintended form of magical matrimony. Such are the tradeoffs in the magical world of *The Witcher*: just like in Newtonian physics—no action without an opposite reaction—the scales of karmic justice for the djinn dictate that nothing is saved without something paid.

Other examples abound throughout *The Witcher* video games. In these cases, the decisions faced by the player are genuine dilemmas because the player can choose only from among the limited set of programmed options. Worse still, many of these decisions have no good outcomes, just greater or lesser evils. The moral world in the games challenges and even conspires against the player's desire for a clean conscience. Consistent with Williams's grim diagnosis, dilemmas are embedded in the fabric of the human condition, the contingencies of the moral situation, and even the software of video games.

Apparent Dilemmas

However, after finding himself between a rock and a hard place one too many times, Geralt seems to reject genuine dilemmas as genuine. Geralt's consistent characteristics include his integrity, his neutrality, and his resolve to resist forced choices. In most cases, when tempted by an immoral option, Geralt refuses. For instance, when Prince Xander promises great riches to assassinate his father, the king of Kerack—"Decide. Yes or no."—the posed dilemma is revealed to be a fake-out by the prince, a test of the witcher's integrity. Geralt passes the test by refusing, even in the face of pressure, earning him the prince's favor.[14] In other cases, when faced with two equally unappealing options, Geralt instead attempts a third option. These choices are often difficult and not always successful, but are often more morally rewarding. For example, in the story "The Witcher," Princess Adda, infant daughter of King Foltest of Temeria, is cursed to become a Striga, a man-eating monster that terrorizes Foltest's kingdom by eating his innocent subjects.[15] When Geralt is hired to resolve the situation, he seemingly has two options:

1. Let the monster-princess, Striga-Adda, continue her killing spree.
2. Kill her, thus sacrificing Foltest's only daughter.

However, as Geralt notes, this is not really a dilemma in the first place because rescuing innocents is straightforwardly the "lesser evil" over sparing a blood-thirsty monster, at least by most moral standards—except perhaps King Foltest's. Even so, Geralt rejects this "lesser evil," instead choosing a third option:

3. Break the curse, turning the monster-princess back into a human and saving everyone.

This third option is better than the other two because it means killing no one, even though it is more difficult for Geralt personally. In this case and others, Geralt's situation is only an *apparent* dilemma, not really a dilemma at all, because there are clearly better and worse options, and sometimes third options.

Similarly, many philosophers have argued that moral dilemmas are always apparent, never genuine, some for theological reasons. For example, Peter Geach (1916–2013) believed that a benevolent God who is either omnipotent or rational would not allow dilemmas to exist. Geach suggests, "If God is rational, he does not command the impossible; if God governs all events by his providence, he can see to it that circumstances in which a man is inculpably faced by a choice between forbidden acts do not occur."[16] In other words, if God is omnipotent, completely controlling events that occur, then he can prevent all dilemmas; and, even if God is merely rational, then he would not issue conflicting sets of commandments because a rational being would never create mutually exclusive requirements for moral behavior. Geach's view seems to derive from the moral traditions of monotheistic religions, in which God's demand that we face a genuine moral dilemma would be theologically inconsistent.

The case of Adda the Striga suggests that the magic of the *Witcher* world seems arranged to avoid genuine dilemmas. First, the entire situation arises only because King Foltest commits an initial transgression—incest with his sister, for which he is punished by a curse—creating the Striga in the first place. Thus, as Geach might say about this case, Foltest is not "inculpably faced by," but may indeed be culpably faced by, the problem. Second, the situation permits Geralt a better option, to kill the Striga, and even a still better option, to reverse the curse. Under a specific set of magical conditions—stop the Striga from returning to her coffin before morning—an escape from the dilemma is available.[17] Indeed, one might wonder whether the very magical metaphysics itself is structured, the spheres are so conjoined, and God—or whatever supernatural entity or entities govern destiny on the Continent—is so benevolently disposed as to foreclose the possibility of a moral agent facing a genuine dilemma, so long as that agent is up to the task.

However, since Geralt himself seems relatively agnostic for much of the narrative, perhaps we shouldn't appeal to divine providence and should instead just appeal to logic. Moral systems that allow for genuine dilemmas seem to be logically inconsistent, and in at least one case Geralt deduces his way out of such a set of contradicting duties. In the story "Voice of Reason," two knights of the Order of the White Rose, Count Falwick and Sir Tailles, challenge Geralt to a seemingly impossible set of commands.[18] These are:

1. That Geralt must defeat Sir Tailles in a duel to first blood or else be killed.
2. That Geralt must not harm Sir Tailles or else be killed.

Geralt realizes that win or lose, either way he will be killed. However, Geralt finds a logical loophole:

3. Repel Sir Tailles's own sword back into his face, thus winning the duel without harming anyone according to the rules of the duel.

This third option makes the commands compatible: Geralt must defeat but not harm Sir Tailles. This permits Geralt to satisfy both requirements while avoiding direct contradiction—Geralt defeats the knight at his own game and logic with a clever ricochet.

Still, it is possible to imagine scenarios in which no third option is available—for example, a conflict in which Sir Tailles specifies the rules airtightly. In such a scenario, Geralt must defeat and must not defeat Sir Tailles. This would make for a straightforward logical contradiction, requiring both a specific event to happen, and for that event not to happen.

Unlike Bernard Williams, many other philosophers have accepted that, in cases of contradiction, one of the two moral requirements—one of Geralt's apparent "oughts"—can simply be rejected.[19] In order to avoid moral contradictions, W.D. Ross (1877–1971) suggested we think of the obligation of moral duties as "prima facie" duties that can be overridden depending on relevant circumstances. Ross writes, "*'[P]rima facie* duty' or 'conditional duty' [is] a brief way of referring to the characteristic (quite distinct from that of being a duty proper) ... of being an act which would be a duty proper if it were not at the same time of another kind which is morally significant."[20] Accordingly, when genuine dilemmas seem to arise, they are only apparent dilemmas. This is because in the conflict between prima facie duties, one of them, upon reflection, overrides the other. For example, in the conflict between Renfri and Stregobor, Ross might say what we have is only an apparent dilemma between Geralt's prima facie duty to Renfri and his prima facie duty to Stregobor. Providing more information about the competing interests at stake could show that one interest might override the other, resolving the dilemma. Was Stregobor lying to Geralt? Was Renfri lying to Geralt? Were Stregobor's fears of Renfri founded? Were Renfri's grievances against Stregobor founded? Answers to any of these questions could have shed more light on the nature of the situation, enabling Geralt to weigh the competing duties properly. Ross does not guarantee that every such situation will be clarified—indeed, in Geralt's case, he will "never be sure," but Ross assures us that in principle there would be an answer if we just knew all of the relevant facts.

If we are to trust Peter Geach's reasoning, there are always possibilities for resolutions to our dilemmas that do not require compromising our moral principles. If we are to trust W.D. Ross's reasoning, one of two irreconcilable options may be overridden by the other. But, if genuine dilemmas don't exist, why do they so often seem to? Perhaps when we conceive of any given decision between two bad options, we're just committing the "either/or" fallacy like Sir Tailles: making the error of assuming that there are just two options—either win or lose—and no more. Or perhaps we're committing the "false equivalency" fallacy like King Foltest: making the error in reasoning of assuming two things to be equal—my daughter's life and the peasants' lives—that are truly unequal.

Resolved Dilemmas?

Even here, though, is a meta-dilemma: Should we believe that there are genuine dilemmas or not? Certainly, some dilemmas are merely apparent, as many examples from Geralt's adventures make clear. Interestingly, Geralt's actions after killing Renfri seem to bear upon this. Stregobor attempts to perform an autopsy on Renfri's body in order to confirm that his suspicions about her being cursed are true, but he's prevented from doing so by Geralt, who does not want her to undergo further indignity. There are several ways to interpret Geralt's actions:

1. Perhaps Geralt is reeling over a genuine dilemma and knows he will feel regret regardless of the autopsy's results.
2. Perhaps Geralt believes this was merely an apparent dilemma and doesn't want to know the results, lest he regret that he made the wrong choice.
3. Or perhaps Geralt does not think the results matter either way because they'll come too late to make any difference for poor Renfri, and he does not want to give Stregobor the satisfaction of being right.

This last answer is perhaps the most satisfactory for at least two reasons. First, regardless of the results, Geralt seems to be committed to resolving the irresoluble. For him and for us, *even if a dilemma turns out to be genuine*, the only way to properly approach one is *as if it is apparent*, since prematurely treating dilemmas as genuine would shorten the full moral reflection that a dilemma demands. Second, as made clear in Geralt's resistance to taking either side, it is Stregobor's and Renfri's conflicting self-righteousness that seems to have caused the moral dilemma in the first place. So maybe righteousness should not really be reaffirmed, but rather a lingering residue of regret is appropriate, so as to temper the sense of absolute certainty that might create such conflicts between parties. Either way, Geralt's approach toward dilemmas, treating them with seriousness and openness, is an admirable method that any conflict of human values demands. So then, as a reader, viewer, or player, what do you choose:

1. Genuine?
2. Apparent?

Notes

1. Phillipa Foot, "The Problem of Abortion and the Doctrine of the Double Effect," in *Virtues and Vices: And Other Essays in Moral Philosophy* (Oxford: Clarendon Press, 2003), 19.
2. Judith Jarvis-Thomson, "Killing, Letting Die, and the Trolley Problem," *The Monist* 59 (1976), 204–217.
3. Andrzej Sapkowski, *The Season of Storms*, trans. David French (London: Orbit Books, 2018), chap. 1.
4. Sapkowski, *The Season of Storms*, chap. 9.
5. Andrzej Sapkowski, *The Last Wish*, trans. Danusia Stok (London: Gollancz, 2007), 86–129.
6. Sapkowski, *The Last Wish*, 115.
7. Bernard Williams, "Ethical Consistency," in *Problems of the Self* (New York: Harvard University Press, 1986), 179.
8. Jean-Paul Sartre, "Existentialism Is a Humanism," in Walter Kaufman ed., *Existentialism from Dostoyevsky to Sartre* (New York: New American Library, 1975), 345–368.
9. Sapkowski, *The Season of Storms*, 27.
10. Sapkowski, *The Season of Storms*, 1.
11. Friedrich Nietzsche, *The Birth of Tragedy; or, Hellenism and Pessimism*, ed. Oscar Levy, trans. William A. Haussmann (Delhi: Lector House, 2019), 78–79.
12. Sapkowski, *The Last Wish*, 45–79.
13. Sapkowski, *The Last Wish*, 245–309.
14. Sapkowski, *The Season of Storms*, chap. 8.
15. Sapkowski, *The Last Wish*, 3–37.
16. Peter Geach, *God and the Soul* (London: Routledge & Kegan Paul, 1969), 128.
17. Sapkowski, *The Last Wish*, 3–37.
18. Sapkowski, *The Last Wish*, 310–352.
19. Williams, "Ethical Consistency," 171.
20. W.D. Ross, *The Right and the Good*, ed. Philip Stratton-Lake (Oxford: Clarendon Press, 2002), 19.

3

Lesser of Two Evils
Deliberation and the Witcher's Moral Dilemma

Corey R. Horn

Evil is evil, Stregobor. Lesser, greater, middling, it's all the same. I'm not judging you. I haven't only done good in my life, either. But now, if I have to choose between one evil and another, then I prefer not to choose at all.

"The End's Beginning"[1]

Geralt of Rivia—aka the Witcher—finds himself in a string of moral dilemmas throughout his travels. In the first episode of the Netflix series, Geralt is thrust straight into a conflict between Stregobor, a sorcerer, and Renfri, a former princess, in which he's asked to choose the lesser of two evils. Making such a choice is a hallmark of moral dilemmas and thought experiments in moral philosophy. Geralt's position as the middleman in a feud between Stregobor and Renfri allows viewers to put themselves in his shoes. The conflict offers only two solutions to Geralt—kill one of them or the other. Yet, Geralt does not see the same black-and-white picture that Stregobor and Renfri paint, and many times throughout the episode he tries to convince them that there may be alternative solutions. This sort of moral deliberation allows Geralt to escape the dilemma of the lesser of two evils and provides us with a novel lens through which to view our own moral dilemmas.

Runaway Trolley, a Wizard, and a Former Princess

When we first meet Geralt, he is returning to the town of Blaviken, seeking the bounty for a slain monster. The alderman's daughter tells Geralt she knows someone who may take the beast off his hands. She brings him to what appears to be an ordinary castle, but upon entering transforms into the opulent oasis of Stregobor, the sorcerer who protects the town. Stregobor explains that it is foretold that a coming plague will kill the

The Witcher and Philosophy: Toss a Coin to Your Philosopher, First Edition.
Edited by Matthew Brake and Kevin S. Decker.

human race, and it will be caused by a woman born during the black sun. Stregobor has been tracking and locking up women born during the black sun, and he performs autopsies after they die to confirm his suspicions that they carry the mutation connected to the plague. Stregobor justifies these heinous actions by claiming that this path is the "lesser evil." He is comparing the two possible outcomes that have been provided: either he finds, captures, and keeps these women locked away until they die, or the human species ends. Both options involve killings—either the women born or the human species—so both involve evil actions. We should note that killing the women is an evil action brought about by Stregobor, and not killing the women is an evil omission of action, given Stregobor's knowledge. So though both options are evil, the nature of evil action is different in the two scenarios. However, according to Stregobor, killing the women born during the black sun is justified because the alternative is so much worse. In other words, it is better to sacrifice the women born during the black sun than to allow them to live and end the entire human race.

Choosing between lesser evils is a hallmark of moral dilemmas. Which choice we make and how we justify our choices when faced with these dilemmas depends on the ethical view we subscribe to. One such view is *utilitarianism*, put forth by Jeremy Bentham (1748–1832), which says that the correct moral choice would be the one that maximizes the greatest amount of happiness for the greatest number of people. Happiness does not necessarily mean the emotion we feel but the overall well-being of those involved. The opposite of happiness, unhappiness, is not the same as suffering—a point that will be important for our later discussion. To better understand this difference, let's first return to our wizard and discuss maximizing happiness before turning to a princess who seeks to minimize suffering.

According to utilitarianism, Stregobor's actions are morally permissible, and according to some forms of utilitarian reasoning, his actions may be morally required. He justifies his actions as choosing between lesser evils, and so by choosing, he maximizes the greatest amount of possible happiness. One of the criticisms offered by opponents of utilitarianism is that this happiness is often generated at the expense of others' suffering. But utilitarians say that allowing—or even causing—suffering is morally permitted so long as the happiness generated outweighs the suffering.

To illustrate the point, consider the thought experiment of the runaway trolley, first described by Philippa Foot (1920–2010). Imagine you are the driver of a trolley car and that the brakes on the car have failed. You have only two options: steer to the left or continue on the right. On the left track is a single rail worker, and on the right are five workers in the trolley's path. Whichever track you choose, the worker(s) on that track will die. Which way do you steer?[2] Following the principles of utilitarianism, the right course of action would be to steer the train left, killing the one rail worker and sparing the five. The outcome of steering left would maximize happiness for the greatest number of people, five over one. Some may object that they are not responsible for the trolley's brake failure, so they would not be responsible for the deaths of the five workers if they stayed on the track; yet, they would be responsible for the one rail worker if they switched the tracks. We could respond to this objection by stating that responsibility is inescapable. Doing nothing when you are aware of the situation and could reasonably change tracks, is itself a choice. So you become responsible for the deaths of the five workers by staying on the righthand-side track. This is the same logic Stregobor relies on. His argument for capturing and keeping women born during the black sun rests on maximizing happiness for the greatest number of people: humanity over a handful of captured women. He does so because he knows about the prophecy that tells of humanity's end, and so by abstaining from action, Stregobor would be responsible for a bad outcome he believes he can prevent.

This takes us to Stregobor's reason for bringing Geralt to his tower: the wizard needs help finding and killing Renfri—one of the women born during the black sun. After recounting Renfri's crimes, such as killing and stealing, he justifies his request by appealing to the lesser evil argument: killing some—*especially* someone like Renfri— is less evil than letting everyone perish. Here, Stregobor goes so far as to call Renfri "worse than a monster" because monsters kill out of hunger, whereas she kills for pleasure. So killing Renfri is justified because it will save humanity from the plague as well as save any possible future victims of Renfri's crimes— just like killing monsters protects their potential future victims. Geralt is not swayed and refuses Stregobor's offer. As he leaves Stregobor's tower, he tells the wizard, "evil is evil ... if I have to choose between one evil and another, then I prefer not to choose at all."[3] Geralt's refusal to choose means more than refusing the wizard's offer. His refusal is indicative of the way he deliberates during moral decision-making. But before unpacking our Witcher's moral approach, we first need Renfri's side of the story.

Geralt comes to understand Renfri's views when she comes across him in the neighboring woods. In direct contrast to Stregobor's description, Renfri claims she kills and steals for survival—placing herself at least on par with the monsters Geralt hunts. Further, she says that Stregobor's men raped her while she was young and were sent to hunt her down after she fled home. Renfri then asks for Geralt's help in killing the wizard, making the same kind of appeals to the lesser evil as Stregobor did. Like Stregobor, she compares two options: letting Stregobor live despite the evils he has committed and will likely continue to commit in the future or killing Stregobor. Renfri argues that the lesser evil would be to kill Stregobor— ending the cycle of suffering he brings about. Renfri's appeal to the lesser evil takes on a different form of utilitarianism than the happiness-based version we saw earlier.

As proposed by Karl Popper (1902–1994), *negative utilitarianism* says that we ought to minimize suffering before maximizing happiness. On the negative utilitarian view, the right choice is the one that leads to minimizing the immediate suffering of those affected by our actions, even if we sacrifice possible happiness that could be created. Even though the negative utilitarian is committed to minimizing suffering over maximizing happiness, their conclusions are often the same as those in Bentham's classical utilitarian view. For example, confronting the trolley problem, the negative utilitarian would still choose to direct the train toward the one rail worker, but for different reasons than Bentham's utilitarianism would recommend. The goal of the negative utilitarian is to reduce overall suffering, so directing the trolley to one worker compared to the five would reduce the number of individuals that suffer. Thus, while Renfri and Stregobor can agree on killing one rail worker over the five, their reasoning for doing so differs.

Renfri uses negative utilitarian reasoning when trying to convince Geralt of her position. By killing Stregobor, Geralt would reduce the number of individuals suffering at the wizard's hands. As grounds for reducing suffering, she relies on Stregobor's actions in the past and his firm commitment to continue his work in the future. By contrast, Stregobor uses prophecies—expected outcomes—to calculate how to maximize the total happiness of the greatest number of individuals. By killing Renfri—and any subsequent women born during the black sun—Stregobor has determined that the greatest possible amount of happiness can be generated.

Nevertheless, Geralt rejects both Renfri and Stregobor's offers. As he explained to Stregobor in his castle and again—admittedly in fewer words—to Renfri in the woods, he does not pick sides when it comes to lesser evils.

The Lesser Evil of Omelas

Renfri appeals to the moral principle that you ought to minimize suffering. Stregobor justifies his support for admittedly evil actions by appealing to the moral principle that you ought to do what generates the greatest possible good. Following these principles, however, can lead us to justify terrible actions. For example, what if you could bring into existence a perfectly just utopia at the expense of the life or happiness of one person? The story "The Ones Who Walked Away from Omelas" by Ursula K. Le Guin (1929–2018) asks precisely this question.[4] Le Guin describes Omelas as a utopian city: everyone is happy, and there is no poverty, crime, or hunger. Omelas enjoys great happiness and peace. However, Omelas keeps a dark secret from its citizens, revealed only when they come of proper age.

In a basement within the city is a locked room, no bigger than a broom closet. Inside this closet is a child, naked and alone. Le Guin explains that this child has not always been inside the closet and can remember what daylight looks like and the sound of their mother's voice. Occasionally, someone comes around to ensure the child stands up, and they replenish the food and water. The child screams and pleads but, over time, stops speaking altogether. The other children of Omelas learn about the child in the basement when they come of age. They learn of the child's torture and that, in some way, this child's misery keeps Omelas beautiful, just, and peaceful. Terminating the child's suffering would also end Omelas's utopian existence. Like the children of Omelas, Le Guin invites her readers to choose: end Omelas's perfect life for its citizens or continue that life in mute acceptance of the child's suffering.

The case of Omelas closely resembles that of Stregobor and Renfri. Both seek to sacrifice the other for the sake of humanity: Stregobor is doing this for humanity's continued existence; Renfri seeks to end Stregobor's witch hunt and prevent future harm. The case of Omelas exhibits the extremes of Renfri and Stregobor's moral reasoning. If we could create a world in which everyone would be maximally happy, at the expense of one person's well-being, shouldn't we take that deal? Stregobor and Renfri certainly think so, but this view entails deliberately sacrificing one person for the benefit of many others. With stakes so high, it is no wonder that Geralt decides not to choose at all in cases of lesser evils. To choose would itself be to bring about some sort of evil—so, to choose one horn of the dilemma is to affirm that bringing about evil is necessary. In pushing against the demand to choose, Geralt prompts us to consider why we do, or whether we should, think that bringing about evil is ever necessary.

Moral Deliberation: The Witcher's Way

Geralt's rejection of both Renfri and Stregobor's offers was not merely a rejection of their reasoning (in which case better reasoning on their parts might have convinced him); he was also rejecting the idea that any moral choice could be between simple matters of fact. Instead of treating these dilemmas as a choice between two different descriptions of the world, Geralt deliberates and makes his decisions based on the facts of the situation and the values he holds. To illustrate the moral position of Geralt, consider the following thought experiment by contemporary philosopher Raff Donelson.[5]

Imagine a being that looks like us and claims to be all-knowing. Donelson calls this being "Delphi." Delphi demonstrates its all-knowing nature by giving various facts and accounts of history. Try as they might, the people fail to ask Delphi an unanswerable question, so Delphi wins their trust. Delphi provides cures to diseases, technological advances that propel society centuries into the future, and solutions to historical mysteries. Donelson further explains that Delphi's initial pronouncements about morality align with many deep-seated and shared commitments. However, Delphi also begins to advocate for things we hold as morally wrong, saying, for example, that enslaving people is always permissible and that killing your firstborn child is mandatory. The people try to argue with Delphi, but Delphi can justify his judgments and refute the people's objections. Donelson says that while some people doubt Delphi's all-knowing status, others accept these pronouncements as true. However, none are moved to act on the questionable principles.

Donelson's story attempts to show that certain moral claims (killing your firstborn is mandatory, etc.) demand deliberation, not just automatic compliance. Delphi demonstrated its all-knowing status—its factual claims proved true—so we might take it that its moral claims must also be true. It seems as though Delphi's moral pronouncements must be followed lest we risk being immoral. Yet, it is a perfectly reasonable response to these pronouncements to deliberate and think about what they entail rather than to take unthinking action. Likewise, during Geralt's discussions with Stregobor and Renfri, he listens to their reasons for wanting to kill the other and enlisting his help. The facts of the situation remain relatively the same: women born during the black sun may threaten human existence, and it seems something must be done. While Renfri is seeking revenge and Stregobor is seeking to prevent the deaths of millions, both accept that moral principles tied to these facts ought to be acted upon. Geralt, conversely, does not.

Instead, Geralt chooses to deliberate in moments that allow for reflection and contemplation. Rather than accepting the logic of utilitarianism as embodying moral truth, Geralt accepts the facts of the matter, yet deliberates on his values and the available options. Geralt's deliberation becomes more evident when he justifies his refusal to Stregobor and Renfri. When Geralt claimed that he preferred not to choose at all if he had to choose between one evil or another, he did so with the benefit of moral deliberation. Geralt explains that he only kills monsters and does not get involved with the affairs of humans.

Geralt is what Donelson calls an *ethical pragmatist*. Instead of appealing to moral truths, Geralt grounds his moral deliberation in facts and shared values. As a witcher, Geralt operates on the "Witcher's Code," which constrains some of his actions and provides a set of shared values to evaluate moral situations.[6] One such value is killing not out of fear but instead only to save lives. Stregobor and Renfri's "lesser evil" proposals are made out of fear and desire for revenge. It is no wonder why Geralt would refuse their requests once he deliberated on the situation's facts and realized these requests were contrary to a value system shared by witchers.

Facing Lesser Evils Pragmatically

Moral dilemmas force thinkers into making difficult choices based on their preferred moral system. Utilitarians like Stregobor seek to maximize the greatest amount of happiness for the greatest number of people, which can come at the expense of other people. As we saw in Le Guin's example, the flourishing utopia of Omelas is built on the shoulders of a suffering child. Utilitarians like Bentham would accept the conditions for this utopia, admitting that the child's suffering is terrible, but this lesser evil would prevent the suffering of all the other people of Omelas. When the children of Omelas are informed about the suffering child and the implications of ending the torture, they're afforded the opportunity to deliberate. In "The End's Beginning," Geralt is in a similar position to the informed children of Omelas. Yet, these children tend to affirm the received moral truths of Omelas's society and continue the cycle of utilitarian torture. Geralt's deliberation is different: if given a choice, he would take the facts of Omelas's existence—utopia at the expense of a child—and make a determination based on shared values rather than appealing to some moral truth.

Deciding to hunt and kill a monster is easy for Geralt. Monsters harm and kill people and should be stopped: he kills monsters to protect others. Moral dilemmas are far greater foes. When faced with two choices, both sure to bring about some sort of evil, we try to justify our choice by appealing to a moral system. "I ought to change the course of the trolley, unfortunately killing the one worker," the utilitarian would say, "because it creates the greatest amount of happiness (or lowest amount of suffering) for six workers potentially at risk." Yet as we saw above, these kinds of appeals can justify horrific scenarios. As Donelson's thought experiment shows, if a moral system can justify pronouncements like "you must kill your firstborn child" or "you should torture one child for the sake of the whole city," then appealing to these systems to justify our actions may not be the best method for choosing to act.

Instead, Geralt adopts the ethical pragmatist position of moral deliberation. When faced with moral dilemmas, Geralt takes the facts and evaluates the possible actions against a value system shared with other witchers. This sort of moral deliberation makes it possible for Geralt to justify his actions to the community of his peers and opens further possibilities for addressing the dilemma at hand. Armed with a sword for monsters and pragmatic deliberation for moral dilemmas, Geralt seeks to protect the people around him and rid the world of monsters of all kinds.

Notes

1. "The End's Beginning," season 1, episode 1, 18:20.
2. Philippa Foot, "The Problem of Abortion and the Doctrine of the Double Effect," in *Virtues and Vices: And Other Essays in Moral Philosophy* (Oxford: Oxford University Press, 2002), 23.
3. "The End's Beginning," 18:20.

4. Ursula K. Le Guin, "The Ones Who Walk Away from Omelas," in *The Wind's Twelve Quarters* (New York: Harper Perennial, 1997).

5. Raff Donelson, "Ethical Pragmatism," *Metaphilosophy* 48 (2017), 383–403.

6. I will note the existence of the Witcher's Code is controversial. While Geralt denies its existence in the books, in the Netflix series, Geralt gives glimpses of a shared code. See for example, "Kaer Morhen," season 2, episode 2, 20:45.

4

Friendship in the Wild
Kant, the Witcher, and Curiosity

Cisil Vardar

Geralt of Rivia's story gained immense popularity with the release of *The Witcher 3: Wild Hunt* in 2015. Part of the game's appeal is that, as players, we're responsible for Geralt's actions and decisions, which in turn shape Ciri's destiny. In fact, the choices players make in interactions with Ciri determine her fate at the end of the game. Three endings are possible for Ciri: she becomes a witcher, she becomes the empress of Nilfgaard, or she dies. Many fans prefer the ending in which Ciri becomes a witcher.[1] One reason for this may be that Geralt and Ciri come close to having an ideal friendship in this version of events. Such a friendship requires respect for a friend's wishes and it requires players to curb their curiosity in game decisions impacting Ciri. As we'll see, what is true about friendship in the game is true in real life as well.

You've Got a Friend in Kant

Curiosity about our friends is understandable, but prying into every little matter in order to support them would damage our friendship. For this reason, Immanuel Kant (1724–1804) argues that, in an ideal friendship, we should limit our love by exercising respect. Friends should be careful to avoid hurting each other's pride by giving excessive help or criticism. In his book *The Metaphysics of Morals*, Kant links this idea to the importance of equality of love and respect. While love brings friends together through a strong bond, respect keeps them at a safe distance from each other. By balancing love and respect, we can prevent "blinding emotion" that could cause us to hurt the pride of our friend when love overtakes respect.[2] Kant draws our attention two different kinds of respectful attitudes. The first requires the friends to limit their criticism of each other. Thus friends should be careful about pointing out each other's mistakes even though it might be in their best interests to be criticized.[3] The second requires us to

The Witcher and Philosophy: Toss a Coin to Your Philosopher, First Edition.
Edited by Matthew Brake and Kevin S. Decker.
© 2025 John Wiley & Sons, Inc. Published 2025 by John Wiley & Sons, Inc.

limit helping friends, as well as to limit how much help we expect from them, because any kind of excessive help can place a burden on the mutual respect friends must hold for each other.[4]

Kant's notion of ideal friendship rests on two conditions. First, associates ought to feel mutual love toward each other, and their feelings of respect ought to be equal. Second, their love ought to be equally limited by respect. The first condition implies that ideal friendship is "practically unattainable,"[5] because we can't know a friend's mind, and so we don't know whether they love and respect us as much as we do them. With his second condition, though, Kant wants to make the ideal friendship relationship more practically achievable by saying we have to balance our love with respect. Curiosity initiates love, and we can't be friends with someone who doesn't express any curiosity about us.

In *The Witcher* 3 the relationship between Geralt and Ciri fluctuates between parental love and friendship. Parents often love their children more than their children love them back. Parents accept the life choices of their children when they're becoming adults by respecting their values, and by expecting the same respect in return. This is crucial not only in real life, but in Geralt's effort to form an ideal friendship with Ciri. In fact, his success or failure in this regard impacts the ending of the game.

In his *Lectures on Ethics*, Kant describes three different kinds of friendships: friendships of need, friendships of taste, and moral friendships. Friendships of need are about the survival goals of each party, who show concern for each other in managing food and shelter.[6] Friendships of taste exist between two associates from different occupations who likely differ from each other in their perspectives on life. Such friends have a desire to obtain a "second opinion" on art and culture. These first two types of friendship are both based on mutual giving and receiving. Finally, in a moral friendship, friends open up to each other about their ideas and feelings, sharing private thoughts and forming mutual respect.[7] So moral friendship is the closest friendship to the ideal.

Moral friendship occupies a very important place in Kant's understanding of society. He claims that human beings are marked by our "unsocial sociability." While we need others in life, we also need to hide some parts of ourselves from others, and this makes us lonely. Moral friendship delivers an opportunity to relate more closely. But Kant also wonders if we can ever be sure that a friend has the same attitudes as we have, since we can't enter into their private thoughts?[8]

The Witcher 3 enables us to use technology to get around this limitation, experiencing the adventures from the perspective of both Ciri and Geralt. The developers could have used flashbacks to allow us to understand Ciri, but they wanted gamers to play Ciri as an independent person. What distinguishes our playing Ciri from interactive flashbacks is that we can make decisions *as* Ciri rather than simply observe her from Geralt's perspective. The importance of this point of view is reflected in the thinking of George

Herbert Mead (1863–1931), who argues that our self-consciousness develops only through interactions with others. Mead calls this "taking the role of the other." In these crucial interactions, one person offers a gesture, and in turn the gesture is contemplated by, and responded to, by another person. The first person remembers this entire gesture–action sequence, and sees it duplicated in society.[9] In moments of reflection, a person has to gauge how to square these responses with those they have learned from others. So Mead thinks that taking the role of others and developing multiple perspectives is crucial to the development of our sense of self. In *The Witcher 3*, by playing Ciri, we're able to occupy her private thoughts and experience her reactions to game events, giving us a new perspective to reflect on our own private thoughts.

Playing, at different times, two characters and witnessing their private thoughts causes the player to become a kind of conduit between Ciri and Geralt. Since we don't play Ciri at the same time as we play Geralt, we may still be uncertain about Ciri's private thoughts toward Geralt and vice versa. In video games, the player's curiosity is encouraged, and with a good game we want to explore every possible situation and reaction that the game offers us. But if we play Geralt as wanting an ideal moral friendship with Ciri, that means we ought to limit "his" curiosity toward her. Fittingly, players are only able to reach the Ciri-as-witcher ending by limiting their curiosity about her.

"Running into dilemmas all the time"

In *The Witcher 3*, the Ciri-as-witcher ending and the Ciri-as-empress ending result from making multiple positive choices in the player's interaction with Ciri, whereas the Ciri-dies ending comes from making three negative choices. Since the choices for reaching the positive endings are limited in number, the player needs to be careful about making these decisions. Some ambiguous choices in the game can only be understood as contributing to a positive outcome if we think of them as cases of limiting love and curiosity by respect.

The first choice occurs when Ciri repeatedly fails to control her powers for the upcoming battle against the Wild Hunt and is close to giving up. Ciri signals that she needs to brush off her anxiety about the battle. She asks for advice from Geralt: "How do you do it? Always manage to pull yourself together, focus, no matter what's happening?" The player can either choose to say, "Think I know what might lift your spirits" (positive choice) or "Relax, you don't have to be good at everything" (negative choice). Ciri needs the positive advice to help her muster her courage, but from our perspective, the advice isn't obviously the most positive: relaxing could also lift the spirits. A closer look at the second choice, however, reveals a slightly undermining attitude: Geralt would be telling a friend that she doesn't need to be good at something that she actually wants to be good at. This could hurt his friend's pride. But it seems like an act of love to accept our friend as she is, even if this diminishes her aspirations. Here, demonstrating love for Ciri without limiting it out of respect for her desires should be avoided. After picking the less respectful option, Ciri and Geralt drink together, and a cat, which symbolizes magic in the world of *The Witcher*, consumes a swallow. We're meant to read this as a sign that magic has consumed Ciri: she's lost her chance to be good at it, and what's worse, it was a result of our choice. After the more respectful choice is made, Ciri and Geralt have a snowball fight, and then Ciri leaves for training with a renewed belief in her abilities. The better, more respectful choice doesn't just follow Geralt's desires. Rather, Geralt's memories from his own childhood point the way to friendship, as he states that Ciri is part of a tradition that Vesemir taught him. Valuable shared activity blossoms between the characters.[10]

The second ambiguous choice determining Ciri's future occurs when Philippa and Margarita, manipulative sorcerers of the Lodge of Sorceresses, want to talk to her. The player-as-Geralt must make a decision to accompany her or not. Going with Ciri is the choice that leads to worse outcomes, whereas letting her handle the talk alone leads to the positive outcome. Players are understandably curious about what will occur in the meeting, and they expect a pay-off for their efforts after all the trouble they go through to find the Lodge. Accompanying Ciri can be interpreted as a choice made out of love: the player wants to extend help to a friend, knowing that Philippa uses people for her own interests and has some plans for Ciri. However, if we limit our love according to Kant's notion of ideal friendship, we see that genuinely helping Ciri means not playing the part of the overprotective father figure. Making this choice leads to a cutscene emphasizing that Geralt trusts Ciri, whereas the cutscene following the less respectful choice has Geralt intervening in the conversation. This seems to undermine Ciri's autonomy, and it exhibits a disrespectful attitude. Following this urge can actually doom Ciri in the end.

The final ambiguous choice occurs when Geralt, Yennefer, and Ciri explore the secret lab of Avallac'h the Aen Saevherne. A she-elf says that Avallac'h was only interested in Ciri in order to continue his experiments on the Elder blood. Ciri is a half-elf, and Avallac'h considers her a disgrace to their race. After a conversation between Ciri and Avallac'h's lover, Ciri becomes angry, remembering how Avallac'h used her and then betrayed her trust. When she wants to destroy the lab, the player-as-Geralt gets two choices: to say "Calm down" (the negative choice), or "Go for it" (the positive choice). One way to interpret the positive choice is that it values Ciri's wishes, rather than allowing Geralt to impose his attitudes on her. Encouraging Ciri to "go for it" helps Geralt form a more ideal friendship with her. In the ensuing cutscene, Geralt and Ciri share the enjoyment of destroying the lab together.

"Traveled half the world to find you, but I never intended to force anything on you"

Ciri-as-witcher is the ending to *Witcher 3* most preferred by players. We should understand this preference as coming from the satisfaction that Geralt's and Ciri's developing moral friendship gives the player. In this ending, they come to share the same stances in life and come close to achieving Kant's ideal friendship: Geralt comes to respect Ciri's wish to be free. Events leading up to the Ciri-as-witcher or Ciri-as-empress endings diverge from each other at one choice, when Geralt is planning his next move with Ciri, and she asks if she should visit the emperor, her real father. Clues derived from the player's first conversation with the emperor tell us this meeting won't be a happy reunion between father and daughter, but rather will be about his plans to use Ciri as a pawn. But Ciri thinks of Geralt as her genuine father and wants to stay close to him. The choice regarding whether to visit the emperor or not ignites a familiar curiosity in the player: How will this dramatic reunion play out? Many players will limit their curiosity out of respect for Ciri's values and so refuse to visit the emperor. In making a decision, they might see a clash between their natural instincts and Geralt's friendship commitments. But the player needs to make Geralt adopt attitudes of moral friendship, as well as working toward the Kantian ideal of friendship. To do so, the player must partly push their own interests and presuppositions aside and instead ask, "What would I do if I were Geralt?"

The Witcher 3 allows the player to move between the minds and private thoughts of Geralt and Ciri, and it encourages players to achieve positive endings by limiting excessive love and curiosity with respect in the way Kant says we must in order to form ideal friendships. Most players prefer the Ciri-as-witcher ending because Ciri and Geralt are able to share moral feelings, commitments, and worldview. To get to this ending, with its realistic sense of moral friendship, these players need to resist their curiosity about the results of other choices.

In real life, our friendships aren't tested by this strong curiosity. Thus, we aren't always aware of this need to strike the right balance between curiosity about and respect for others. Yet the game challenges our curiosity, and helps us realize the importance of limits in our friendships. As a result, we can learn a lot from the challenges of the game in shaping our real-life friendships as well.

Notes

1. A Reddit poll from 2018 shows that 71.6% of players went with the Ciri-as-witcher ending. While some fans consider the empress ending as the best one, this ending depends particularly on the choices of the players. If we think about the ending in terms of what Ciri wants for herself rather than what would be

best for her in the player's eyes, the witcher ending makes the most sense in that context.

2. Immanuel Kant, *The Metaphysics of Morals*, trans. Mary J. Gregor (Cambridge: Cambridge University Press, 1991), 470.
3. Kant, *The Metaphysics of Morals*, 470.
4. Kant, *The Metaphysics of Morals*, 470.
5. Kant, *The Metaphysics of Morals*, 471.
6. See Stijn Van Impe, "Kant on Friendship," *International Journal of Arts and Sciences* 4 (2011), 127–139.
7. Kant, *The Metaphysics of Morals*, 472.
8. Kant, *The Metaphysics of Morals*, 472.
9. See Agnes E. Dodds, Jeanette A. Lawrence, and Jaan Valsiner, "The Personal and the Social: Mead's Theory of the 'Generalized Other,'" *Theory & Psychology* 7 (1997), 483–503.
10. Robert Nozick believes that shared activities between friends should be based on mutual understanding. For instance, if we're going to see an opera, we should do so for the sake of sharing the experience rather than the fact that I prefer to see the opera over any other activity. I see the snowball fight as a genuine shared activity, as it gives equal pleasure to Ciri and Geralt. See Robert Nozick, "Love's Bond," in *The Examined Life* (New York: Simon & Schuster, 1989), 68–86.

FREE WILL
AND EXISTENTIALISM

5

Destiny, Fate, and the Law of Surprise
Determinism, Free Will, and *The Witcher*

Graham Lee

In *The Witcher*, the Law of Surprise dictates that if a person saves a man, that person is to be offered a blessing unknown to either or both. The blessing in most cases is the saved man's firstborn child, when the offspring is born or conceived without that man's knowledge. The Law impacts the interconnected fates of Ciri and Geralt, among others. But what is fate? Is it different from destiny? And is there room for free will in the *Witcher* world?

Fate and the Path of Destiny

The terms "destiny" and "fate" are often used interchangeably, but not in *The Witcher*.[1] The philosopher Robert Solomon (1942–2007) offers the following explanation of destiny:

> Destiny is not so much a necessary outcome (it could easily be imagined otherwise) as it is an outcome that is necessary given some larger sense of purpose. This may well include consideration of the character and abilities of the person or ... a people. One cannot understand destiny just by understanding how (causally) the outcome came about, although a person or people's self-conscious awareness of purpose is surely one of the most important causal facts in the explanation.[2]

Here, Destiny is an outcome that is necessary given a larger sense of purpose of a person or a people, perhaps on account of their character or abilities.

The Witcher and Philosophy: Toss a Coin to Your Philosopher, First Edition.
Edited by Matthew Brake and Kevin S. Decker.
© 2025 John Wiley & Sons, Inc. Published 2025 by John Wiley & Sons, Inc.

"Fate" often is used interchangeably with "fatalism," as it is with "destiny." Hugh Rice says:

> Though the word "fatalism" is commonly used to refer to an attitude of resignation in the face of some future event or events which are thought to be inevitable, philosophers usually use the word to refer to the view that we are powerless to do anything other than what we actually do.[3]

So, fatalism involves the individual's belief that what happens is inevitable. This includes people's actions.[4] This is how Solomon defines fate, with the caveat that it involves "a peculiar sense of necessity."[5] Lisa Raphals equates fate with destiny:

> By fate or destiny I mean the notion that there is a set or immutable pattern to the world. It may be understood as humanly knowable or ultimately inscrutable, personified as (or under the power of) a God or independent of any divine will. At the level of individual agency, a conscious agent is apt to consider the "fate" she is "given" in life, and ask what can be changed and what is unalterable.[6]

Combining these definitions, we get that fate is the course and outcome of a person's life, *regarded by* them as inevitable and usually determined by supernatural forces. If a person sees their life as "fated," then that life is seen to be, but need not actually be, beyond their control. Similarly with "determined by supernatural forces"—what a person sees is not necessarily the truth. Given this definition, supernatural forces seem to at least influence (if not determine) the course and outcome of lives in *The Witcher*.

In the series, fate is treated as subordinate to destiny, a fact borne out in the "Destiny" entry in the Glossary of the original *Witcher* computer game:

> Many people believe in the existence of Destiny, a mysterious force which binds certain people together, determining their fates. According to believers, one can either follow the path of Destiny of one's free will or try to resist it, although the latter can bring grim consequences. On the other hand, some feel that Destiny is not everything. These people say that something more is needed in order to bind two lives together, even if the rules of fate decide otherwise.
>
> The poet Dandelion contemplates whether human life is ruled by Destiny. Dandelion mentions the Law of Surprise—when a witcher demands from a man rescued on the road that which he does not expect once he returns home. It turns out to be a child born during the father's absence. Witchers take the Unexpected Children to their fortresses and train them to be their successors. Dandelion also wonders whether love can bind people with bonds of destiny. In no ballad does he provide a clear answer to the questions posed.[7]

Several things are worth noting here. First, Destiny is commonly seen as a supernatural force determining the events of people's lives. Second,

Dandelion puts into question whether human life is ruled by Destiny so that a person's future may be beyond their control. Fate, according to this definition, is the course and outcome of a person's life, albeit considered by them in a certain way, and perhaps accurately so.

The "path of Destiny," then, is the course and outcome a fated person's life *should* take and have, the fate intended by Destiny. So, can a person's fate fail to follow the path of Destiny? This depends, according to the Glossary definition above, on whether the person follows the path (or resists the path) by exercising their free will. But what exactly could it mean to follow the path (or to act at all) of your own free will, and what would it mean to resist the path? Dandelion/Jaskier also wonders whether people are bound with "bonds of destiny" by love. Dandelion gives no clear answer to this question in any ballad, but philosophy is more help than ballads in this case.

Determinism, Freedom, and the Law of Surprise

Now let's unpack some other relevant concepts—in this case, determinism and freedom. The entry on the Law of Surprise in *The Witcher* game's Glossary says:

> When a witcher saves a man's life and the man says, "In gratitude, I will give whatever you desire," the witcher then answers, "You will grant me whatever unexpected thing you encounter when you return home." In rare instances, the surprise proves to be an infant, born during its father's absence. Based on the Law of Surprise, the child belongs to the witcher, becoming the Unexpected Child to whom the witcher is bound by Destiny. Many Unexpected Children were brought to Kaer Morhen, where they were then raised and trained to be witchers.[8]

So, a witcher can and will become "bound by Destiny" to an Unexpected Child provided the Law is properly invoked. This glossary entry seems to provide an answer to our central question, that the fates of people *can* follow the paths of Destiny through the exercise of their free will.

But two things might stop us from accepting this interpretation. First, the entry on the Law of Surprise says what *must* happen if a witcher's claimed reward turns out to be an Unexpected Child (namely, the child comes to be the witcher's) and suggests what must happen if the claimed reward turns out to be something else unexpected (this *thing* becomes the witcher's). The glossary entry also indicates that the *fate* of many Unexpected Children is to be raised and trained to be witchers. On the face of it, the entry notes what *will* happen in certain cases when the Law is invoked, but without indicating that any person in the scenario could have acted otherwise than they did. The idea that someone could do otherwise than what they did, in fact, do is at the heart of what we usually mean by free will. In philosophy, this understanding of free will is called "libertarianism" (not in the political sense). Peter van Inwagen explains it this way:

> When I say of a man that he "has free will" I mean that very often, if not always, when he has to choose between two or more mutually incompatible courses of action—that is, courses of action that it is impossible for him to carry out more than one of—each of these courses of action is such that he can, or is able to, or has it within his power to carry it out.[9]

In other words, "libertarian freedom" is the ability to freely act in different ways in a given set of circumstances. This freedom makes us morally responsible for our actions. Libertarians reject "determinism," the idea that all events in the world necessarily follow from prior events, conditions, and physical laws.[10] By contrast with libertarians, "hard" determinists argue for a deterministic world where we don't have "the sort of free will required for moral responsibility."[11] Libertarianism and hard determinism are called "incompatible," because the two views say that determinism and free will cannot coexist.

A third view about determinism and free will argues that they actually are compatible and can coexist. Harry Frankfurt (1929–2023), an advocate of "compatibilism,"[12] writes:

> The following may all be true: there were circumstances that made it impossible for a person to avoid doing something; these circumstances actually played a role in bringing it about that he did it, so that it is correct to say that he did it because he could not have done otherwise; the person really wanted to do what he did; he did it because it was what he really wanted to do, so that it is not correct to say that he did what he did only because he could not have done otherwise. Under these conditions, the person may well be morally responsible for what he has done.[13]

According to compatibilism, a person has free will, even if determinism is true, as long as she is able to do what she desires.[14] This is the essence of "compatibilist freedom." And because there can be a kind of free will according to compatibilism, the view is sometimes called "soft determinism."

The Law and Freedom

Now let's reconsider the glossary entries for Destiny and the Law of Surprise. Does a libertarian, a hard determinist, or a compatibilist interpretation of them make the most sense? And assuming that the Law of Surprise situation they reference is more or less the situation everywhere else in *The Witcher* world, which interpretation of that world makes the most sense?

Recall that the Destiny glossary entry says, "Witchers take the Unexpected Children to their fortresses and train them to be their successors."[15]

Recall also that the Law of Surprise glossary entry indicates that the fate of many Unexpected Children is to be raised and trained to be witchers. Taking these two passages at face value *alone*, both entries seem to indicate that no person in the sort of scenario has any free will whatsoever. That suggests a hard determinist world.

But this is to read things out of context in at least two ways. Let's first remind ourselves of the immediate context, of what else is said in the Destiny entry (the Law of Surprise entry only provides more details about the situation in question): "According to believers, one can either follow the path of Destiny of one's free will or try to resist it, although the latter can bring grim consequences."[16] According to believers in Destiny, a person can try to resist the path of Destiny—the course their life ought to take, but does not necessarily take. Built into the very notion of the path of Destiny, it seems, is the idea that the course and outcome of a person's life—their fate—is not (or at least need not be) determined. If this is so, then the hard determinist interpretation is ruled out.

Notice also that trying to resist the path of Destiny can bring grim consequences. Let's think about this for a moment. The path of Destiny for an individual can be happy or mediocre (not totally grim). We know this because the fates of many characters in *The Witcher* world are not grim, while the fates of others are not *totally* grim. Even if the course of a character's life is by and large grim, there may be some happy times here and there, and the outcome may still be happy. So the path of Destiny for a person's life can be happy, while their fate turns out to be at least partly grim because they try to resist the path by their own free will. In other words, the course and outcome of a person's life can deviate from what Destiny has in store for them. So a person's fate can stray from the path of Destiny—their fate is not determined. Things are looking up for the libertarian interpretation, but not so for the hard determinist and the compatibilist interpretations.

The hard determinist and compatibilist interpretations also do not seem to fit significant situations in the narrative. There doesn't seem to be any evidence indicating that everything in *The Witcher* world is determined by prior events, conditions, and *physical laws*, so to think that this fictional world is deterministic seems to rely on presupposing that it is. Even the Glossary entries we have considered appear to try to resist the (hard and soft) deterministic interpretations.

And we haven't even gotten to perhaps the best evidence against the hard determinist interpretation *in* the entries:

> On the other hand, some feel that Destiny is not everything. These people say that something more is needed in order to bind two lives together, even if the rules of fate decide otherwise.... Dandelion *also* wonders whether love can bind people with bonds of destiny. In no ballad does he provide *a clear answer to the questions posed.*[17]

"On the other hand" prefaces a nondeterministic interpretation of *The Witcher* world—by certain individuals, "some," at least, *in* that world. "These people" "feel ... that *something more is needed* in order to bind two lives together, *even if* the rules of fate decide otherwise." This something more might be *love*, which arguably makes no sense if it doesn't come from free will. That Dandelion "also wonders" about love as outside of Destiny's control reinforces the idea that human lives in *The Witcher* world are not ruled by Destiny.

There is further reason to doubt that compatibilism applies here. Let's take another look at the scenario described in the Law of Surprise entry. In it, a man tells the witcher who saves him that he will give the witcher whatever he desires. To this the witcher replies, even demands, that the man will give him the unexpected thing the man encounters upon returning home. If this turns out to be an unexpected child, the child will become the witcher's, "becoming the Unexpected Child to whom the witcher is bound by Destiny." The compatibilist sees this scenario in terms of the witcher demanding and receiving the unexpected thing of necessity, given the circumstances, and becomes bound to it by Destiny if it turns out to be an Unexpected Child. The witcher cannot do otherwise, but, as long as he does what he wants, he acts freely.

However, the witcher (and Duny) don't seem to get what they want at all. Because the witcher demands something whose nature he doesn't even know could mean that his act of demanding it was arbitrary, and this in turn could mean that he did not desire to demand it in the first place. In that case, he would not have acted freely even according to compatibilism. Now, this wouldn't mean that he and others in *The Witcher* world tend to act this way. So even if compatibilism doesn't pan out in this sort of scenario, it might in others—in other sorts of situations in *The Witcher* world, perhaps in a piecemeal way. But as we noted earlier, *The Witcher* world doesn't seem to be deterministic, and the best candidates for such evidence—the Glossary entries—say it is not.

Meanwhile, the entries seem to detail what happens, or usually happens, during situations in which the Law of Surprise is invoked, rather than what Destiny dictates must happen. Alternatively, they could be read as detailing (i) what must happen *when* the Law is invoked—that the one invoking it receives their unexpected reward—but also (ii) what isn't bound to happen and is freely done apart from such auspicious circumstances. Even if the entries were read as detailing (i), despite all the evidence we have considered against such a reading, this would still leave room for libertarian freedom to be part of the process. For, the reward's manner of reception—that is, when, where, and how it is to be received—and nature (e.g., the personality and character of the Unexpected Child when received) could be significantly influenced by the choices of many people, including the child, in a libertarian way. All this is to say that the two entries *can* be seen as evidence that libertarian freedom is employed—and possessed.

Invocations of the Law

Let's now turn to some instances of the Law's fulfillment in *The Witcher*, seeing them as case studies against which to test the libertarian freedom interpretation.[18]

Case I: Roegner's invocation of the Law
Through invocation of the Law of Surprise, Pavetta is promised to Duny. King Roegner is saved by Duny after becoming injured and stranded at the bottom of a ravine. Invoking the Law, Roegner promises Duny as reward "whatever [the former] had left at home without knowing or expecting it." This is revealed to be Pavetta, who is born to Roegner and Queen Calanthe later that year. Duny later seeks to claim his reward, his beloved as his bride, after she comes of age.[19]

This can be interpreted in terms of libertarian freedom: Roegner exhibits it in making the promise and Duny shows it in seeking, years later, to obtain what was promised. Even if his attainment of it is determined by the Law, the manner of its attainment and what precisely is obtained (i.e., Pavetta's personality and character as it is at that time) could still be influenced by choices that need not have been made—by Roegner, Calanthe, Duny, Pavetta, and many others.

Case II: Geralt's first invocation of the Law
It also is through invocation of the Law of Surprise that Ciri is initially promised to Geralt. Coming to Duny's aid and being instrumental in the lifting of his curse—effectively saving his life—during the events of Pavetta's 15th birthday feast, Duny asks Geralt to name his reward. Geralt asks for "that which you [Duny] already have but do not know," invoking the Law. Since Ciri was conceived by Pavetta and Duny prior, she is to later become Geralt's ward.[20]

This case also seems to involve libertarian freedom: Duny exhibits it in asking Geralt to name his reward and Geralt shows it by invoking the Law. Even if his attainment of it is in some way determined by the Law, the manner of its attainment and the nature of what's obtained (i.e., Ciri's personality and character) could still be influenced by choices that need not have been made—by many others, just as in Case I.

Case III: Geralt's second invocation of the Law
Ciri is later promised to Geralt a second time as well by means of the Law's invocation, this time by the merchant Yurga. After saving Yurga's life, in reward Geralt asks for what Yurga finds at home but does not expect, again invoking the Law of Surprise. Unknown to both, Yurga's wife took in Ciri— thought by the former to be an orphan—while the latter is on the run, amounting to Geralt's naming of Ciri as reward a second time.[21]

Libertarian freedom seems present here as well: Yurga's wife exhibits it in taking in Ciri as a runaway and Geralt shows it by saving Yurga and invoking the Law. Again, even if his reward is in some way determined by the Law, details about the reward could still be influenced by choices that need not have been made—by Yurga's wife, Ciri, Yurga, Geralt, and others.

Freedom Under the Law

Ultimately, the Law of Surprise might in some ways bind its invokers and the Unexpected Children claimed through it, but they and others in *The Witcher* world still are unbound by Destiny—other than when they choose to bind themselves to each other—through love, perhaps. That may settle the question concerning *The Witcher* world, but philosophers continue the dispute concerning the real world, where different laws apply.

Notes

1. See section 1 in Carl Hoefer, "Causal Determinism," in *The Stanford Encyclopedia of Philosophy* at https://plato.stanford.edu/archives/spr2023/entries/determinism-causal.
2. Robert C. Solomon, "On Fate and Fatalism," *Philosophy East & West* 53 (2003), 439.
3. Hugh Rice, "Fatalism," in *The Stanford Encyclopedia of Philosophy* at https://plato.stanford.edu/archives/spr2023/entries/fatalism (foreword).
4. For a similar definition of fatalism, see David Hunt and Linda Zagzebski, "Foreknowledge and Free Will," in *The Stanford Encyclopedia of Philosophy* at https://plato.stanford.edu/archives/sum2022/entries/free-will-foreknowledge (foreword). For a corresponding definition of a fatalist, see Richard Taylor, "Fatalism," *The Philosophical Review* 71 (1962), 56.
5. Solomon, "On Fate and Fatalism," 435.
6. Lisa Raphals, "Fate, Fortune, Chance, and Luck in Chinese and Greek: A Comparative Semantic History," *Philosophy East & West* 53 (2003), 537.
7. CD Projekt Red, *The Witcher*, CD Projekt, PC/Mac, 2007.
8. CD Projekt Red, *The Witcher*.
9. Peter van Inwagen, *An Essay on Free Will* (Oxford: Clarendon Press, 1983), 8.
10. Hoefer, "Causal Determinism."
11. Derk Pereboom, *Living without Free Will* (Cambridge: Cambridge University Press, 2003), xiv (see also xviii).
12. Michael McKenna and D. Justin Coates, "Compatibilism," in *The Stanford Encyclopedia of Philosophy* at https://plato.stanford.edu/archives/fall2021/entries/compatibilism (foreword).
13. Harry G. Frankfurt, "Alternate Possibilities and Moral Responsibility," *The Journal of Philosophy* 66 (1969), 839.
14. McKenna and Coates, "Compatibilism," sec. 2.1.
15. CD Projekt Red, *The Witcher*; emphasis added.

16. CD Projekt Red, *The Witcher*; emphasis added.
17. CD Projekt Red, *The Witcher*; emphasis added.
18. A work that helped popularize this method more than perhaps any other, and which is also one of the most famous (and shortest) papers of contemporary philosophy, is Edmund L. Gettier, "Is Justified True Belief Knowledge?," *Analysis* 23 (1963), 121–123.
19. Andrzej Sapkowski, *The Last Wish* (London: Gollancz, 2007), chap. 5.
20. Sapkowski, *The Last Wish*, chap. 5; see also subsequent chapters.
21. Andrzej Sapkowski, *Sword of Destiny* (London: Gollancz, 2015), chap. 6.

6

Compatibilism and the Law of Surprise

Myth, Free Will, Destiny, and Hedgehogs

Shane J. Ralston

> The Law of Surprise is a law as old as humanity itself. The law dictates that a man saved by another is expected to offer his savior a boon whose nature is unknown to one or both parties. In most cases, the boon takes the form of the saved man's firstborn child, conceived or born without the father's knowledge.[1]

One of the most bewildering concepts in *The Witcher* television series is the so-called "Law of Surprise"—a concept with philosophical implications as massive as Geralt's biceps! For new fans of *The Witcher* TV show, episode flashbacks and flashforwards combine with the Law to make for a steep learning curve. The Law of Surprise befuddles viewers at several points in the series, especially during the betrothal banquet scene. It begs for a helpful explanation. This chapter offers that, plus a novel account of the Law tied to "compatibilism," an alternative position in the debate about free will and determinism.

Determinism is the position that anything that occurs at any given moment in time necessarily occurs the way it does because of what occurred the moment before. If determinism is true, then given the laws of physics and causation, we should be able to predict all future events. Libertarianism is the exact opposite: humans possess free will and so can choose to do something differently than what they did, so not all events are determined in advance.[2] Compatibilism is the view that libertarianism and determinism are both true, so despite the fact that most events have been determined in advance, humans can choose to act, to freely will outcomes or even to behave unpredictably.

The Law of Surprise is based on a Polish and Slavic myth stating that a great deed—for example, saving someone's life or doing God's work—must be repaid with a future windfall, something the indebted person

The Witcher and Philosophy: Toss a Coin to Your Philosopher, First Edition.
Edited by Matthew Brake and Kevin S. Decker.
© 2025 John Wiley & Sons, Inc. Published 2025 by John Wiley & Sons, Inc.

doesn't yet even have (or even know that he will have)—for example, a child. The windfall is literally called the "Child of Surprise." In the *Witcher* world, the character Ciri is the Child of Surprise. Given the intervention of destiny—a close relative of determinism—morality, which presumes free will and autonomy, might play little or no part in whether the Child of Surprise or windfall is acceptable to either the beneficiary or the Child. Failing to welcome the windfall, as Geralt discovers, forecloses future possibilities for free choice, binding Geralt's destiny with even greater certainty to Ciri, his Child of Surprise. If he had instead dutifully adopted her, he might have had greater opportunities for exercising free will. Here, the Law of Surprise suggests a novel form of compatibilism, which, in the fictional world of *The Witcher*, could be used to help explain why the Law of Surprise dictates specific outcomes (or shared destinies), but permits some degree of latitude or free choice by the characters in how these outcomes (or shared destinies) come about!

The Plot Thickens

In "Of Banquets, Bastards, and Burials" (season 1, episode 4), Geralt is recruited by the bard Jaskier to attend a banquet, a betrothal feast for Princess Pavetta, daughter of Queen Calanthe. A knight by the name of Lord Urcheon upsets the joyous festivities to claim Pavetta's hand based on the Law of Surprise. With his face hidden under a helmet and body covered with armor, it's difficult to see Lord Urcheon's true form. Eist knocks the helmet from the lord's shoulders—to reveal that he's a hedgehog! Queen Calanthe orders Geralt to attack Lord Urcheon, but he refuses, realizing that Urcheon isn't a monster, but a man cursed. With Geralt's help, Lord Urcheon disarms the guards. He explains again to Queen Calanthe that Pavetta is his future wife in virtue of the Law of Surprise. After a larger fight breaks out, Queen Calanthe commands the fighting to cease.

But the drama isn't over yet:

> Duny [Lord Urcheon] hugged Pavetta and explained he was cursed as a young boy. He lived his whole life in misery until the day he saved Queen Calanthe's husband, King Roegner, from certain death. By tradition, he chose the Law of Surprise as payment. Eist pushed Queen Calanthe to honor the tradition, driven by the belief destiny had determined the surprise be Pavetta and, should she resist, chaos would surely ensue. Duny abandoned all hope of claiming the Law of Surprise when he heard the king returned to find a child on the way. He knew no woman could accept him as he is. So, he waited until the twelfth bell when the curse broke. He never intended to meet Pavetta. Only watch from afar. But destiny intervened and they fell in love. Queen Calanthe seemed to accept destiny, handing over her sword and extending her hand to Duny. She pulled him close, whispered "here is your

destiny," and then pulled out a knife and aimed it at his throat. Pavetta screamed out, suddenly awakening her abilities, sending everyone flying across the room.[3]

Queen Calanthe agrees to honor the Law of Surprise. Pavetta and Duny kiss, ending the curse and transforming Duny back into his human form. Duny wants to repay Geralt for saving his life, and while Geralt at first refuses, he agrees to take his repayment according to the Law of Surprise. Pavetta immediately vomits with morning sickness, revealing that she's pregnant with a child. So, we immediately know that Geralt's Child of Surprise, his reward for saving Duny, will be Ciri, Pavetta's daughter.

Geralt initially resists taking his reward. Watching out for Princess Ciri's safety would put a damper on his adventures slaying monsters and witches and bedding tavern wenches. Eventually, though, he must accept his fate as her protector, defending against the Nilfgaardians and those who see her as the fulfillment of Ithlinne's Prophecy, a prediction that the world will freeze to death once elven blood is spilled. Questions arise: Does the Law of Surprise dictate that Geralt must follow a rigid path toward claiming his Child of Surprise, or is there some latitude in how Geralt interprets his obligations here? By delaying acceptance of his responsibility for Ciri, does Geralt become less free?

The Free Will–Determinism Debate

Discussions about whether our choices in life are ultimately free or determined have a long history in philosophical discourse. Questions about the extent to which life decisions are bounded or unbounded, restricted or free, often revolve around two discrete positions mentioned earlier: libertarianism and determinism. Libertarians claim that humans have free will because they can always choose to do otherwise. Indeed, judgments about moral and legal responsibility depend on the assumption that people were at liberty to choose another option than the one they did. Otherwise, how could they be said to be accountable for their actions?

Determinists, on the other hand, insist that all events occur within a web of causes and effects ultimately governed by the laws of physics. If we accept this scientific view, and we concede that all prior causes that could condition a human choice are in principle knowable, then we could ideally predict how a person chooses to act, and do so with absolute certainty. *Ergo*, no human choice is truly the product of free will. The problem with determinism is that it undermines moral and legal judgments that a person is responsible for the consequences of their actions, since it's impossible for them to ever choose to do otherwise. Our future is already sealed or determined in advance. So, we're ultimately responsible for nothing we do! And although "destiny" and "fate" aren't scientific concepts, they can substitute, especially in fantasy stories, for the laws of physics, fixing our future path and defeating the possibility of freely choosing an alternate path.

Compatibilism is a third rail between support for libertarianism or determinism. It holds that a person's actions can be both free and determined. There are at least three arguments that are fairly representative of why people might find compatibilism attractive. First, in the *paradigm case argument*, there are some standard instances in which we feel that we're acting freely but know our choices are determined in advance. An example is when you have to choose between chocolate and vanilla ice cream. While you don't feel forced to choose one over the other, your choice actually reflects prior events and experiences, such as developing a preference for one flavor over the other or a bad past experience with one flavor that makes you detest it.

The second is the *epistemic or knowledge-based argument*: I know what freedom feels like, even though I can't be certain that I'm entirely free. While I don't know all the events that determine my actions—even though in principle I could—I do nevertheless feel that my choices are constrained by both outside and inside forces. External influences (environment, history, laws of nature) and internal predispositions (habits, preferences, mental states) control my choices, but this doesn't mean I'm deluding myself when I say that I feel free or that I could have chosen otherwise. So, both free will and determinism must be true. In other words, they're perfectly compatible.

The last is the *best possible world argument*: nobody would want to live in an indeterministic universe (that is, the opposite of determinism), a chaotic world ungoverned by physical laws. Likewise, no rational being would wish to live in a universe lacking freedom (that is, the opposite of free will), a world populated by slavish creatures, each bound to its already determined future by metaphorical chains and shackles. So, if we want to live in the best of all possible worlds, we ought to embrace compatibilism. Whichever of these three arguments we appeal to, free will and determinism prove to be consistent. So, compatibilism is probably true.

Compatibilism is also roughly equivalent to what Sara Bizarro calls "Polythetic Free Will," the idea that free will and responsibility aren't absolutes, but that each exists along a spectrum or continuum of more or less freely chosen, and greater or lesser responsibility-generating actions. In Bizarro's words:

> One of the aspects of the polythetic view of free will is the point of origin of the action. A free action comes from us, which makes us somewhat responsible. A non-free action does not come from us, which makes us somewhat not responsible. If we are to be mechanisms, we want to be self-winding mechanisms, as opposed to other-winding mechanisms.[4]

Emerging from Bizarro's polythetic view of free will are a number of fascinating implications for compatibilism: *free will is voluntary*—it "originates in the person, it is not a result of manipulation" like forcing or deceiving someone to choose; *free will is responsive to reasons*—actions aren't random but thought out, "choices are considered, and reasons are used to make these choices"; *free will relies on knowledge*—"information and knowledge regarding the possible consequences of the action" are readily available to the person; *free will presumes no defects*—the person suffers no difficulties "outside of their awareness and control" such as limitations on their ability to think or perceive; *free will presumes the existence of alternatives*—there are two or more options, so the person possesses multiple paths from which to choose; and *free will is self-constrained*—a person can limit themselves and their options, "but if that constraint is irreversible and they want to reverse it, then they may become less free as a result."[5]

Destiny and Freedom in the *Witcher* World

In the *Witcher* world, why does the Law of Surprise dictate the futures of characters like Duny and Geralt? The short answer: nobody wants to screw with destiny, because fate always has the last word. In the case of Duny and Pavetta, it seems perverse that Duny might've claimed someone's daughter as a bride in exchange for a heroic deed. So, the writers maneuver around that shocking implication of the Law by noting that Duny and Pavetta developed feelings for each other months earlier, and the Law of Surprise only cemented those feelings in a future marriage. Duny and Pavetta were free to fall in love, but even if they hadn't, Pavetta would have eventually been his. According to the Law of Surprise, Pavetta is payback for Duny saving King Roegner's life. However, this is not a reward that's *chosen*: it's fated that Pavetta shall be Duny's. She is destined to become his Child of Surprise. Within the narrative, there is latitude for free action, but the outcome is nonetheless determined in advance.

So, how does the Law of Surprise function in Geralt's case? Why does it bind him to Ciri, the daughter of Pavetta, as her protector but not her betrothed? The Law manifests in different ways and its manifestation to some degree depends on the interpretation given to it by the beneficiary. So, while Duny understands his windfall as Pavetta's hand in marriage, Geralt appreciates his as an obligation of another sort: the duty to protect Ciri against the many forces that want her dead. Free will enters the picture in how that interpretation is rendered. Geralt tried to evade responsibility, but fate guides him back to it, until finally he must accept his fate. The Child of Surprise also has a part to play in interpreting how the Law of Surprise conditions her and the beneficiary's future choices and dictates their shared destiny. In this way, the Law has a consensual element. Its execution depends on agreement between the beneficiary and the Child of Surprise about the terms of their future relationship or fated bond.

Besides the banquet scene from season 1, episode 4, two other sequences demonstrate how freedom and fate prove compatible in the world of *The Witcher*. One is the dragon hunt sequence ("Rare Species," season 1, episode 6), when Geralt reveals to Yennefer that his third wish to the djinn joined their fates together. (Previously, when Jaskier discovers the djinn's bottle and releases the evil spirit, it attacks him. In the book, Geralt recalls an old incantation to send the djinn away. In the television show, Geralt wishes for peace and quiet, so that Jaskier loses his voice. His second wish causes the guard to burst. The third and final wish Geralt makes is that he'll never lose Yennefer.) This news of their intertwined fates angers Yennefer, who quickly reminds Geralt that he is bound to Ciri by the Law of Surprise. Why is she mad? She believes both that he's robbed her of her freedom and that with two competing fated paths, it's possible that Geralt will neglect his duty to protect Ciri to be with her. Yennefer chooses to abandon Geralt, believing this will allow him to fulfill his obligation to Ciri. Of course, fate will have a hand in bringing all three together in the near future. Another sequence of scenes occurs only days prior to Nilfgaard invading Cintra. Geralt arrives in Cintra to claim his Child of Surprise, hoping to take Ciri away from the city and protect her from the Nilfgaardian army. However, Geralt's plan is frustrated by Ciri's grandmother, Queen Calanthe. She doesn't want to hand Ciri over, so she tricks him into waiting and then imprisons him. Geralt leaves Cintra, thinking he's failed in his duty. Ciri later escapes Cintra ("The End's Beginning," season 1, episode 1) and then discovers Geralt in a farmhouse recovering from his wounds ("Much More," season 1, episode 8). As fate would have it, she asks Geralt, "Who is Yennefer?" The Law of Surprise plus the djinn's third wish tie the three characters' fates together, but that doesn't mean that each must follow a rigidly fixed course to a common destination. Indeed, Ciri, Yennefer, and Geralt each make their own path toward their shared destiny.

A Witcher Compatibilist?

Is the *Witcher* world governed by determinism or does it allow for free will? The Law of Surprise dictates fated outcomes (or shared destinies), but in the process of reaching those destinies, the involved parties can freely choose how to pursue and interpret their paths. Of course, when the beneficiary of the Law tries to evade his destiny, fate intervenes, drawing him back to his Child of Surprise with even greater restrictions on his free choice. Freedom and unfreedom, indeterminism and determinism, chaos and order are simultaneously at work in the Law of Surprise. In other words, compatibilism is the name of the game!

If we return to Bizarro's polythetic free will, a close cousin of compatibilism, we can say with greater precision how compatibilism operates in the *Witcher* world. While Geralt can be seen as a "mechanism" determined to protect his Child of Surprise, Ciri, he is what Bizarro calls a "self-winding" rather than an "other-winding" mechanism. A self-winding mechanism has its own motivations, intentions, and reasons, and acts accordingly, even though the alternatives it selects are constrained in advance by fate or physics. An other-winding mechanism, on the other hand, is entirely controlled by forces outside of itself, so that it is almost wholly determined, not freely choosing. Geralt voluntarily chose for Duny to compensate him according to the Law of Surprise. Geralt had reasons for making his choice. He knew what the Law of Surprise entailed and that he'd be bound to accept his fate as guardian of his Child of Surprise. Here, we would say that the sliding scale of Geralt's freedom is high: he suffers from no cognitive defects, other than weaknesses of the will for beautiful women and wine! Plus, Geralt had alternatives: he didn't have to choose to be repaid via the Law of Surprise. Lastly, and most importantly, Geralt's choices were self-constrained, since he initially freely rejected an irreversible or fated constraint (i.e., his role as Ciri's protector), but by resisting it he actually became less free. Only by accepting his fate does Geralt truly embrace his freedom to act within fated constraints. This sounds utterly self-contradictory, but that's the beauty of compatibilism!

As the ancient Greeks professed, when a sacred prophecy is decreed, there's no sense fighting the gods' will! Think of the example of Oedipus: he did everything in his power to thwart his destiny, as foretold by the Oracle at Delphi, to kill his father and marry his mother, and yet everything the Oracle predicted came true! "Know thyself!" here means submit to fate and accept the path chosen for you. Within the parameters of a predetermined future, the traveler can at least choose to make the path their own, a path punctuated by surprise and wonder, yet a path nevertheless constrained by fate. That's compatibilism. And that's the path of the witcher!

Notes

1. Fandom Games Community, "The Law of Surprise," *Witcher Wiki*, October 9, 2016, at https://witcher.fandom.com/wiki/Law_of_Surprise.
2. Libertarianism in the free will debate means something different than political libertarianism. Political libertarianism is the idea that government should have minimal influence over people's lives, other than to protect private property. Consequently, personal liberty is maximized. Free will libertarianism states that humans do in fact have free choice, while political libertarianism prescribes less government as a way to expand opportunities for humans to exercise free choice.
3. Fandom Games Community, "Duny," *Witcher Wiki*, at https://witcher.fandom.com/wiki/Duny_(Netflix_series).
4. Sara Bizarro, "Free Will and *A Clockwork Orange*: A Polythetic View of Free Will," *Ethical Perspectives* 29 (2022), 191.
5. Sara Bizarro, "Free Will and *A Clockwork Orange*," 192.

7

Silver or Steel?
Rethinking Rational Choice in an Irrational World

Erin Williams and Darian J. Shump

You have only a limited time to make some dialogue choices.
Choose quickly, or else chance will decide for you.

The fate of individual characters and at times even entire
communities depends on the choices you make.

The Witcher 3: Wild Hunt

Although an emphasis on player choice is nothing new to digital gaming, developers have increasingly taken advantage of innovations in late-generation hardware in an attempt to grant players greater agency. Immersive sims, for example, claim to provide players with the freedom to choose their own paths; in doing so, they rely heavily upon emergent gameplay mechanics designed to respond to the player's decisions in complex situations. The only problem is that even some of the most popular entries in the genre, including the *BioShock* series (2007–2013), *Dishonored* (2012) and *Dishonored 2* (2016), and *Prey* (2017), still ultimately funnel players toward one of two categories of ending: "good" or "bad." Any agency players appear to be given at the start seems illusory by the end—their choices rooted firmly in following the path most likely to bear greater fruit.

The Witcher 3: Wild Hunt (2015) subverts this illusion of rational choice often found in modern video games.[1] Unlike so-called "immersive" sims, *The Witcher 3* emphasizes that an individual's decisions are never inconsequential, but the repercussions of players' actions tend to be random at best. Acts of kindness are just as likely to embroil Geralt in open conflict or unleash a plague as they are to result in a handful of coin. In much the same way, even the most straightforward of decisions, the choice between silver (for monsters) or steel (for humans and nonhumans) in combat, reinforces the moral ambiguity and unpredictability of life on the Continent. For players, identifying an in-game monster might seem relatively easy—but in a world of monsters, some of whom are human or human-like in appearance, the "right" choice is rarely so clear.

The Witcher and Philosophy: Toss a Coin to Your Philosopher, First Edition.
Edited by Matthew Brake and Kevin S. Decker.
© 2025 John Wiley & Sons, Inc. Published 2025 by John Wiley & Sons, Inc.

Immersive Sims and the Illusion of Choice

Known colloquially as "immersive sims" or "imsims," immersive simulation games are tricky to define. The roots of the term can be traced through the works and words of Warren Spector, a game designer and producer whose early credits include *Ultima VI: The False Prophet* (1990), *Ultima Underworld: The Stygian Abyss* (1992), and *System Shock* (1994). Each of these games marks a stage in the evolution of immersive sims; typically, the last of the three is most popularly cited as the first "true" entry in the genre. According to Spector, gameplay in immersive sims is not "scripted— we're using rules and physics and [artificial intelligence] to remove the barriers to belief, so that players are not constantly being reminded that they're playing a game."[2] This game design forces the player to become an active part of the gameworld, and success means that the lines between the real and the digital seem to collapse.

However, the ways by which immersive sims do this aren't set in stone. Immersive sims collectively emphasize emergent gameplay as a means of creating the feeling of a living and responsive world. They reject the notion of a single, linear path through the game by granting players the freedom to solve problems in unexpected and unscripted ways. But different developers and even different players will point toward different systems, mechanics, and games as "doing emergent gameplay right." Most immersive sims adopt a first-person perspective, but some, like the third-person *Hitman: World of Assassination* trilogy (2016–2021), do not let players see directly through the character's eyes. Instead, *Hitman* maintains a seemingly physical distance between player and character that other immersive sims seek to remove. The *Thief* series (1998–2004, 2014) employs open level designs that encourage stealth-based approaches to tasks, whereas *System Shock* and its sequel (1999) skew toward linear levels and direct combat; *Dishonored* splits the difference by allowing players to choose between the two. Games like *Fallout 3* (2008), *Fallout: New Vegas* (2010), and *The Elder Scrolls V: Skyrim* (2011) have scripted gameplay that pushes them just outside of the bounds of the genre. When we look at the range of immersive sims (and the range of their perspectives and level designs), they are far from a unified and cohesive category, but they all strive to bring players inside the game by weighing real-world moral choices as a core component of gameplay. For our purposes, though, the question becomes how choice matters in a game that does not market itself as an immersive sim and does not stand as a categorial example of the genre at all.

Our baseline for immersive sims is 2K Boston's *Bioshock* (2007). *BioShock* tells the story of the underwater city of Rapture through the eyes of Jack, the sole survivor of a plane crash. Players gradually uncover the cause of the city's collapse and find themselves allied with Atlas, a mysterious folk figure who serves as their guide, against Andrew Ryan, the city founder. They also encounter Little Sisters, genetically modified girls tasked with harvesting ADAM (a genetic substance) from human corpses. Players are given a choice: return the children to normal and save their lives, or siphon the ADAM from them and kill them in the process. *BioShock* consequently leads players to believe that they dictate their own role in the story. By choosing to kill the Little Sisters, they sacrifice life for power but seemingly increase their own chances of survival. By choosing to save them, they appear to hinder their own progression but position themselves as a more benevolent type of hero. The only problem is that the choice is illusory. The game's (in)famous twist reveals that Jack's entire existence and arrival in Rapture was orchestrated by criminal–entrepreneur Frank Fontaine, the true identity of Atlas. Using a trigger phrase ("Would you kindly?"), Fontaine/Atlas guides Jack along a path that begins with his hijacking and crashing the plane and culminates in his murder of Andrew Ryan. The entire story was pre-ordained. Even the decision to save or sacrifice the Little Sisters, which Collin Pointon describes as the only "real free choice" in the game, serves to reinforce this same point: only the "good" ending is considered canonical by the time of *BioShock Infinite* (2013), the third and as-yet final entry in the trilogy.[3] If you harvest ADAM from just one Little Sister, you don't get the good ending no matter how many other Little Sisters you save. To save the Little Sisters is to be right.

To an extent, all games can only give players as much choice as is programmed, but *The Witcher* challenges how we as players make choices rationally during gameplay by forcing us to ask what is rational and what is good. By purposefully designing rational choices to lead to unpredictable or irrational (in the sense of not being logical) choices and consequences, the game's mechanic of choice forces us to reconsider (or maybe consider for the first time) how much choice really matters, if we determine it matters at all. Although we can argue there is a binary moralism created by player choice in *Bioshock*, it becomes much more difficult to make this same argument in *The Witcher*, thereby complicating the boundaries of immersive sims as a genre and presenting a much closer facsimile to the real-world ambiguity of choice.

Irrationality of Freedom in *The Witcher*

The Witcher 3: Wild Hunt is, after all, not an immersive sim. It's a third-person, open-world roleplaying game with a branching narrative—but not a truly emergent world. Players' actions and their outcomes are scripted, not unlike the path that Jack follows in *BioShock*—both the programmed narrative path and the path he is given by Atlas. Even so, actions and outcomes in *Witcher 3* show a measure of depth that far exceeds the limited emergence of some of the most popular immersive sims. Choice in the game is irrational because it refuses to establish a simple opposition between "right" and "wrong," where the right choice leads to the happy ending, yet it is actually for this reason that it comes closer to mirroring the reality of our nondigital world. An immersive sim might give players a freedom of choice, but as we can see in *Bioshock*, that freedom is only to kill or not, and there is only one right answer.

The Witcher 3 wastes little time introducing players to the moral complexity of life on the Continent. Following a gameplay tutorial at Kaer Morhen, the game begins in earnest in White Orchard, an idyllic Temerian village recently conquered by the Nilfgaardian Empire. Here, Geralt begins his search for his adoptive daughter, Ciri, and players receive an extended introduction to the world at large. White Orchard serves as a microcosm of the moral landscape, one that teaches players that Geralt's choices cannot be simply categorized as "good" or bad"—and that even what appears to be the "good" or "right" choice does not lead to predictably good or bad outcomes.

White Orchard offers a handful of low-level, low-stakes secondary quests and treasure hunts, including "On Death's Bed." The quest's premise is simple: a young woman, Lena, has been attacked by the very griffin you've been hunting during the main quest, "Lilac and Gooseberries." The quest log indicates that Geralt might be able to help Tomira, the herbalist trying to heal Lena:

> Once again Geralt had a near impossible choice to make—a choice between a greater and lesser evil. While preparing to hunt the griffin, he had come across one of the beast's victims—a simple peasant woman named Lena. She had been on her way to meet her lover when the griffin attacked. The beast had mortally wounded her. A witcher's potion could save her life ... or cause her to perish in agony.

Players are presented with two options—letting Lena die or trying to help her—but this isn't a choice between good or bad, or the better ending in which she lives and the worse in which she would certainly die. The game calls the quest "a near impossible choice between greater and lesser evil," between certain death or merely possible death, and so gives the lie to the idea that good, rational choices lead to good endings and bad, irrational choices lead to worse outcomes.

Nonetheless, the gameplay seems to strong-arm Geralt into giving her the potion by triggering a fail if the player refuses or does nothing. There's no experience or gold for failing the quest, so choosing inaction has a negative, though minor, impact on gameplay. If you complete the quest, Lena lives but suffers: "Though the wounds on Lena's body healed, the toxins in the witcher's brew had melted her mind. This was not the first time a cure had proven worse than the disease." In hindsight, letting her die might have been the kinder choice. Throughout *The Witcher 3*, choices like this are not meant to funnel the player easily toward the "right" ending but rather to be a realistic representation of making rational choices in a rationally designed irrational system. Players learn here that much like real life, good intentions can still cause suffering or lead to unpredicted outcomes. In "On Death's Bed" there cannot be a wrong choice because there is no correct choice. You can set out to save all the Little Sisters and still get the bad ending.

Questioning the Human

Outside of White Orchard, the player's choices become increasingly burdensome and complex. Quests often revolve around slaying or sparing various enemies, whether monsters or humans or human-like monsters. In "Deadly Delights," something is killing guardsmen in Novigrad, so you accept a contract to find and stop it. This should be simple: witchers trade in killing monsters for gold, and the correct choice should always be to prioritize human lives. In this case, though, you learn that a succubus named Salma is responsible. Unlike many of their monstrous kin, succubi are sentient and capable of rational thought. After talking to Salma, players may choose to kill her or let her go if she promises to leave Novigrad. Both options grant experience and a reward, and both options complete the quest. Although Salma did indeed kill the guardsmen, she insists that she did so out of self-defense after being attacked unprovoked. In this way, "Deadly Delights" functions as yet another lesson that the line between good and bad does not cleanly bisect the categories of monster and human—assuming it even exists at all.[4] Saving human lives is neither always right nor always wrong, because the game rejects a binary moral system like we find in *Bioshock*. Although players are encouraged to weigh the moral implications of their decisions and act accordingly, following a binary moral path becomes almost impossible. A player who spares monsters like Salma may find themselves unexpectedly rewarded for breaking a witcher's traditional code of conduct while the player who follows it rigidly, expecting an easy path to the good ending, may find it harder or impossible to get there at all.

Like "Deadly Delights," the quest "An Elusive Thief" tasks the player with finding a thief, who turns out to be a shape-shifting doppler. Confronting him results in a familiar choice: kill him or spare his life. The contract holder will grant less experience and less coin for failing to provide the doppler's head as a trophy, so we might argue here that choosing to kill is the "correct" option. However, the game again treats this choice as subjective: "In my opinion, his crimes did not match the punishment meted out to him—but, in the end, I am no witcher, and so it is not my place to judge," says the quest log, written as the thoughts of the troubadour Dandelion. Although he would not have killed the doppler, he admits that it was not his choice to make—and thereby left it to the judgment of the player.

As Geralt explores more of the Continent, we begin to see the far-reaching consequences of the player's choices. Decisions made in "Deadly Delights," "An Elusive Thief," and several other quests begin to define Geralt's reputation as a witcher. On Fyresdal in Skellige, for example, Geralt can pick up "Skellige's Most Wanted." The contract starts like most others, but Geralt soon realizes he's been set up and finds himself confronted by a group of monsters: a rock troll, a godling, a doppler, and a werewolf, all of whom hate witchers for killing their friends and families. Based on previous choices, "Skellige's Most Wanted" might allow the player to defend Geralt's reputation as a witcher who does not kill monsters indiscriminately. Dialogue options here are based on the player's track record so far: either the player spared Salma and told her to leave Novigrad, allowed the doppler to escape, and helped the god-lings Johnny (in the quest "Ladies in the Wood") and Sarah (in "Haunted House")—or they didn't. Although the werewolf will attack regardless, fulfilling just two of these quests will pacify the rest of the group. The contract has only one ending, but proving that Geralt doesn't always kill monsters nets you twice the experience and a cool pair of nekker-hide boots.

You can never change the werewolf's mind. This suggests that moral choice in this morally ambiguous, irrational world is complicated because the connection between choices and outcomes is unpredictable and because outcomes do not depend entirely on players' actions. Even if the player earnestly believes in the moment that killing Salma is right, the meaning of "right" is challenged by NPCs who see killing monsters as deeply and unquestionably wrong. They are not obligated (or programmed) to agree with you or understand your choices as part of a broader rational framework about choices and outcomes. Indeed, good does not reliably follow good—in part because the nature of "good" is hardly easy to ascertain.

Trolley Problems and Tower Plagues

To create a realistic world, *The Witcher 3* relies on the player's inability to predict consequences and define "good" in the face of the irrational. An early quest, "A Towerful of Mice," sparks a series of events whose impacts are felt throughout the remainder of the game. Keira Metz, a sorceress and old friend, asks Geralt for help investigating cursed Fyke Isle. At the top of a tower on the island, players meet the ghost of Annabelle, a peasant who was eaten alive by rats and now haunts the island. She asks Geralt to bring her bones to Graham, her lover on the mainland, so that he can bury them and break her curse. Once again, the choice seems clear: grant her request to end her suffering. If you do so, though, your apparent benevolence is quickly brought into question in the quest log:

Sadly, what Geralt took to be the ghost of an innocent woman was in fact death and disease in spirit form—a being known as a pesta, or plague maiden. Having lured Geralt into the open, it killed the unfortunate Graham and then escaped to spread the pox and feed on human suffering. It is possible that this incident caused the local outbreak of Catriona that devastated the kingdom of Kerack and sowed the seeds of the coast city's ultimate downfall.

Poor Graham will die regardless of the player's choice, and so for him there is only the lesser of two unfortunate outcomes. Keeping Annabelle on Fyke Isle, at least, saves Kerack.

Players subsequently return to Fyke Isle to stop Keira in "For the Advancement of Learning." According to the quest log, she "was planning to use the [mage's] notes as a bargaining chip while making a deal with [King] Radovid. His plague research could be her ticket back to life without lice, ticks and omnipresent filth." When confronting her, you have three options: let Keira go to Radovid, kill her, or convince her to go to Kaer Morhen. Each choice has radically different consequences for Geralt and those around him. Convincing Keira to go to Kaer Morhen ensures that she is present for the final battle and saves the witcher Lambert, ultimately surviving to begin a relationship with him. This also helps players earn the "Full Crew" achievement. If you let her go, Radovid executes her, and Keira's death unlocks "A Final Kindness," during which you retrieve her body. Whether you kill Keira yourself or let her go to Radovid, she dies in two of her three endings—this, in turn, may lead to Lambert's death and directly alters his ending cutscene. Put differently, a decision to kill Keira is not simply a decision to end one life but the toppling of an initial domino capable of pushing Lambert over the edge, too. Although the relationship between the two comes largely as a surprise to the player, it reinforces the notion that the lives of individuals in this world are often inextricably—invisibly—linked.

Toward the Endgame

The world of *The Witcher 3* is a world characterized by a certain measure of irrationality, or a disconnect between logical choice and predictable outcomes. From the start, the Continent presents itself as a land of myth and folklore, a home to monsters whose very existence embodies the fantastic and defies conventional reason. Even the once-human witchers now border on the monstrous—mutated by alchemical concoctions, they live their lives on the edges of society in constant contact with darkness. Their actions in defense of humankind should pass as heroic, but they remain outcasts, incapable of ever truly becoming heroes. A neat, happy ending for them is often just another fairytale.

But it's this irrationality that actually makes the world of *The Witcher 3* so recognizable. The quests and contracts and characters and monsters together form a network of interactions that mirrors the structure of choices and outcomes in our own nondigital reality. Lives are never lived in a vacuum, and the effects of actions are rarely immediate or obvious. Morality is consequently nebulous: "Good" and "Bad" are less objective moral categories than they are relative points on a spectrum that the game seems to sometimes pick at random.

The Witcher 3 reaches beyond the simplified moral binary that characterizes some of the most popular immersive sims. In fact, it regularly exceeds their capacity for both freedom and complexity. The choice between silver for monsters and steel for humans is not just a matter of practicality here but a metaphor for the ambiguity, the irrationality, that permeates life in general. To draw your sword is to categorize, to make a deliberate decision to classify the opponent before you. At the same time, to draw is to condemn—and to bear witness to the consequences of your decision. Although the choice may seem simple in the moment, it's only afterward that you can ask yourself, "What if I was wrong?"

Notes

1. "Modern" here means games designed for the seventh (PlayStation 3, Xbox 360) and eighth (PlayStation 4, Xbox One) generations of consoles. *The Witcher 3* was designed for the latter.
2. Chris Baker, "How Warren Spector Created a Genre, and Set Games Free," Glixel (website), June 2, 2017, at https://web.archive.org/web/20170707043400/ http://www.glixel.com/news/how-warren-spector-created-a-genre-and-set-games-free-w485404; Warren Spector, "Postmortem: Ion Storm's Deux Ex," gamedeveloper.com (website), December 6, 2000, at https://www.gamedeveloper.com/design/postmortem-ion-storm-s-i-deus-ex-i-.
3. Collin Pointon, "*BioShock*'s Meta-Narrative: What *BioShock* Teaches the Gamer about Gaming," in Luke Cuddy ed., *BioShock and Philosophy: Irrational Game, Rational Book* (Malden, MA: Wiley Blackwell, 2015), 12.
4. Salma suffers more damage from a steel sword than a silver one despite technically being a monster (related to chorts and fiends), although it is unclear if this is an intentional commentary about an arbitrary line between nonhumans and monsters, or simply a bug.

8

Nothing Is Ever Black and White

Existentialism in *Witcher 3: The Wild Hunt*

Tim Miechels

Rain is pouring down as you enter the village of Blackbough on your trusty horse Roche. The first person you see in the village, a child playing in the streets, yells "freak" at you as you pass. The next villager spits at you as your horse trots along. The environment is hostile, the same as it has been in the other, similarly sad and dreary villages you visited throughout the war-torn region of Velen. The people here are not too keen on outsiders, even when the outsiders are witchers who've come to rid them of their werewolf problem.

In this situation, like many others in the award-winning video game *The Witcher 3: The Wild Hunt*, there are elements of the story you can influence, while other factors lie beyond your control. Examples of these factors are how nonplayer characters react to you based on the way you look or stories they have been told about you. It's up to you, though, how you react to the different kinds of hostility you encounter. Do you answer their pleas for help even in the face of their hostility and distrust? Or do you meet hostility with resentment and refuse to help?

The Witcher 3 constantly places players in situations where they have to make important decisions, though, of course, there are also factors that players are fundamentally unable to control. This makes the game the perfect showcase for the notion of *freedom* in the existentialist philosophy of Martin Heidegger (1889–1976). In particular, we'll focus on the concepts of *thrownness*, *projection*, and *falling*, as he lays them out in his major 1927 book *Being and Time*.

The Witcher and Philosophy: Toss a Coin to Your Philosopher, First Edition.
Edited by Matthew Brake and Kevin S. Decker.
© 2025 John Wiley & Sons, Inc. Published 2025 by John Wiley & Sons, Inc.

Thrown into the Continent

Heidegger coins new philosophical terms in abundance. Speaking his language, we can say that once you start playing *The Witcher* 3, you are *thrown* into the Continent. But what exactly does that mean? By *thrownness*, Heidegger means that a person does not choose to be born, nor do they choose the circumstances that they are born into. In his words, "The expression 'thrownness' is meant to suggest the *facticity of ... being delivered over*."[1] By coming into the world, you're being "delivered over" to existing circumstances, in the sense that you are born in a certain country, to specific parents, at a specific point in time. These factors determine certain cultural factors: which language(s) you learn to speak, which values you hold in high regard, and which laws and social norms you are taught to follow, among others. Furthermore, you're born with certain physical and psychological traits that, to a high degree, will determine how people will react to you based on the other cultural factors at play. All of this is beyond your control.

For example: because I was tall growing up, people always expected me to be good at basketball, but I never surpassed the hand–eye coordination level of a toddler. This means that in each high school year's physical education class, an unfortunate combination of biological traits consistently made me into a disappointment. While this example is trivial, the implications of thrownness can be far-reaching and dire. Think about what it means to be born with a homosexual orientation in contemporary Saudi Arabia, or with a brown skin in the United States before 1865, or with a female body in 1940s Paris.[2] The combination of physical and psychological traits with cultural circumstances that bear on those traits can dramatically influence the degree of approval or hostility you will encounter in your life. Nobody chooses these traits, let alone the circumstances that lead to a particular evaluation of those traits, yet people benefit from—or are burdened by—these factors when it comes to the choices that they can make to shape their own lives and identities. To refer back to one of the examples above: in 1940s Paris, there was an easier and more frictionless path for a man, than for a woman, to obtain a university degree. This means—as we will further explore in the next section—that Heidegger understands human freedom as situated freedom.

With several of its important features, *The Witcher 3* is excellent for illustrating Heidegger's idea of thrownness. Unlike many other role-playing games (RPGs), *The Witcher 3* lacks a character creator—a common feature in many RPGs that lets the player create or customize the character they play with at the outset. Take a game like *Dragon Age: Inquisition*, released by BioWare at the same time as *The Witcher 3*. In *Dragon Age*, the player gets to pick the race, class, sex, and physical appearance of their character before they start playing. The combination of these factors determines how nonplayer characters (NPCs) in the game world react to you, which NPCs are interested in you romantically, what armor you can wear, and what skill sets you can develop. These initial choices influence your interactions with the game world, but most importantly, they are *your* choices.

Contrast this with *The Witcher 3*, in which you *always* play as Geralt of Rivia, who is *always* a witcher (or in some particular instances as Ciri, who is always a princess of Cintra in possession of Elder blood). More specifically, you play a character whose background has already been set by the novels: Geralt was trained to be a witcher by Vesemir in the ancient fortress of Kaer Morhen, and is widely known as the "Butcher of Blaviken" due to the unfortunate series of events that transpired with Renfri and her henchmen in the Redanian town of Blaviken. Of course, you can customize Geralt in-game by finding new gear for him, specializing in different skill sets like combat, use of signs or alchemy, and even by getting a new haircut at the barber. However, unlike the character creator in other RPGs, the level of relatively free choices in the game mimics real life, where you can also develop your skills through practice, choose an education to specialize in a certain field, or even, yes, get a new haircut by going to the barber! Just like in real life, however, there are also aspects of your identity that you don't have any say about that also influence your interactions with the world. This is sometimes underlined by seemingly trivial interactions— such as a little boy yelling "What happened to your mug?" as you enter the village of White Orchard for the first time—and sometimes by more significant interactions—such as a group of thugs who gang up on you and Vesemir just for being witchers.

So just like in real life, you are thrown into a world with certain characteristics and traits that you did not choose. Similarly, you also do not choose the circumstances of the world you are thrown into, which is an experience that *The Witcher 3* simulates by the sense of history that pervades Geralt's world. The mountain of published source material—in the form of the novels and short stories by Andrzej Sapkowski—plays a crucial role in making this world feel grounded and lived in. The Continent in *The Witcher 3* is a place that clearly has existed long before the player arrived and will continue to do so long after they're gone. The player's choices are an important part of the events that unfold over the course of the game, but the player isn't the sole author of these events—and the world does not revolve around the player. When you arrive in the swampy region of Velen, for example, the land has been torn apart by a war with the Nilfgaardian Empire in which Geralt was not involved. However, in the wake of the war with a foreign nation, the villagers are wary of outsiders like a witcher suddenly entering the town, and so this war does influence player interactions.

A final aspect of the game that exemplifies Heidegger's notion of thrownness is the fact that players are thrown into the consequences of interpersonal relations with NPCs that preceded the events of the game. This is of course partly due to the fact that *The Witcher 3* is the third game in a series and most people didn't play the first two parts.³ Granted though, some characters that Geralt has established relationships with, such as Sigismund Dijkstra or Yennefer of Vengerberg, didn't appear in the previous two games. These interpersonal relations help create a feeling of being thrown into a world in which you are tied up in circumstances that are beyond your control, similar to how you do not choose your biological family or the people you grow up with in real life.

Freedom and Projection

The Witcher 3 excels at depicting Heidegger's idea of being thrown into a world with factors beyond your control, but this doesn't mean that you're never in control. You are, of course, playing a video game in which developing Geralt's character through choice and consequence is the core of the experience. How does this relate to the idea of thrownness?

For Heidegger, the world that you are thrown into influences—but does not completely determine—the possibilities you have in life. The reason for this is that "[t]he essence of Dasein lies in its existence."⁴ Dasein is Heidegger's way of referring to human being, and what Heidegger means by the preceding quote is that, unlike the things that exist in the world into which we are thrown, human beings have no pre-given essences that completely determine who we are. Of course, as mentioned earlier, we are born with certain traits that, in combination with the world in which we live, close off or open up certain possibilities. However, we are always free to take up or leave aside specific possibilities; none of them are necessitated by who we are or the world around us. For Heidegger, to be human means that: "In each case Dasein is mine to be in one way or another.... In each case Dasein is its possibility."⁵

This is why Heidegger adds the notion of *projection* to that of thrownness. He writes, "any Dasein has, as Dasein, already projected itself; and as long as it is, it is projecting. As long as it is, Dasein has always understood itself and always will understand itself in terms of possibilities."⁶ Being human means to be open to different possibilities, because it is up to us—despite our thrownness—to form our own projects and plans. This forming of projects and plans is a way of projecting yourself into the future. There are of course certain boundaries to what is possible: we have no say in the amount of adversity we meet or enabling we benefit from, but we do have a say in what we do under such conditions.

In *The Witcher 3*, the player can indeed make impactful decisions and in that sense project a specific version of Geralt into the future, even though the factor of thrownness means you do not make these decisions in a vacuum. Take the lighthearted romantic decision you make in the game, which has divided internet forums for more than ten years: Triss or Yennefer? The player's feelings about these characters is influenced by

Geralt's history with them as portrayed in the game. Making this romantic choice is very much *your* decision, since Geralt's history with Yennefer and Triss does not determine the outcome of the romantic decision. The game doesn't allow you to make *no* decision, though. And trying to romance both Triss and Yennefer at the same time leads them to invite you to a threesome, only to leave you tied to a bed, naked and humiliated, in a Novigrad inn. The player is then locked out of romance options for both of them. Refraining from choosing, or trying to have your cake and eat it too, are very much in line with the existentialist credo that indecision is a form of decision as well. For being human means being open to possibilities, which means that even if you are trying to hide or run away or ignore the fact that *you* have to choose, you are enacting a specific possibility and projecting yourself toward a specific future.

A more serious case of choice and consequence in the face of thrownness and projection is the questline surrounding Philip Strenger, better known as the Bloody Baron. Early in the game, the player is recruited by the baron to look for his missing wife Anna and daughter Tamara in exchange for information on the whereabouts of Geralt's foster daughter Ciri. But the Bloody Baron's wife and daughter are not lost and were not kidnapped by anyone. Rather, they fled due to Strenger's constant drunkenness and abuse, which caused his pregnant wife to miscarry. Confronted with Geralt finding out this information, the baron tells his side of the tale, admitting both the alcoholism and abuse. He explains his addiction as an effect of his inabilities to deal with the horrors of the war he'd been sent off to soon after the birth of their daughter. In his absence, his wife had conducted a long affair with a childhood friend. When the baron found out, he killed his wife's lover and took his wife and daughter back home. His relationship with Anna never recovered from this and turned violent. His alcohol abuse never ceased.

The circumstances are tragic and beyond the player's control. Yet it is still up to you to make a decision about how to proceed: Do you think the baron's circumstances absolve or mitigate the guilt of the baron? Or is he still fully or at least partly to blame for this situation? After his initial attempts at covering up his vices, the baron continues to try to duck full responsibility: "Can't speak for the world you witchers inhabit, but in ours, nothing is ever black and white." Yet, despite his insistence on the fact that he isn't solely to blame, he displays serious signs of being torn apart by feelings of guilt and remorse.

From the existentialist point of view, these feelings are the result of the fact that the baron realized that he did, in fact, always have real choices in how he dealt with his guilt and his family, and is therefore responsible for his choices. His circumstances may have ranged from unfortunate to downright horrible, but he always had the final say in how he chose to act in the face of these circumstances. He could have chosen not to submit to the bottle in the first place, or to quit the army, to spare his wife's lover, to stop drinking, to refrain from hitting his wife. His circumstances were, at least partly, beyond his control. His actions were not.

As a player, you do not control the baron's circumstances nor his actions. But do you respond to his confession of the full story with understanding, or with revulsion, or with apathy? Do you—despite everything that has transpired—continue helping the baron in retrieving his wife from the crones of Crookbag Bog? These decisions are up to you.

Falling into the Optimal Choice

As the romantic choices and the story of the Bloody Baron suggest, *The Witcher 3* gives the player a high degree of freedom in their actions. The outcomes of these decisions often have major influences for the state of the game world and the way the story unfolds. These choices and their outcomes are never black and white, so you as the player have the full freedom to make the decisions you think are the best ones. However, to what extent do you embrace this freedom?

With the notion of *falling*, Heidegger points to the fact that even though we are free to make our own decisions, we usually do not. We typically avoid our freedom in two ways. The first way is by seeking distraction and fleeing into mindless chores. In *The Witcher 3*, instead of moving the story forward and thinking about the consequences of a difficult decision, the player can choose to play another round of Gwent at the local tavern. Or they can try to find that nice set of witcher gear that's supposed to be somewhere in the general area. What about that question mark on the map on the other side of that lake? Maybe you'll find some treasure over there.

Another way people circumvent their freedom and the responsibility for their actions is by doing what they think most people would do, or approve of, rather than actually deliberate about the best action or decision for themselves. We go to our jobs because that's what everybody does, and we mow our lawns because what would the neighbors think if we didn't? Heidegger calls this kind of falling or avoidance "being part of the *they*." In Heidegger's words:

> We take pleasure and enjoy ourselves as *they* take pleasure; we read, see, and judge about literature and art as *they* see and judge; likewise, we shrink back from the "great mass" as *they* shrink back; we find "shocking" what *they* find shocking. The "they," which is nothing definite and which all are, though not as a sum, prescribes the kind of Being of everydayness.[7]

How does the "they" show itself in decision making in *The Witcher 3*? As mentioned in the previous section, the choices the game asks the player to make often involve complicated moral dilemmas for which there is no clear right or wrong answer. Contrast this with another

BioWare game: *Mass Effect*. Moral choices in this science-fiction RPG are governed by a black-and-white morality system called "Paragon vs. Renegade." Any "evil" action moves you toward the renegade side of the scale, while "good" actions increase your paragon level. Players proceed toward a "good" or "evil" ending by having the required number of paragon or renegade points required.

In contrast, in *The Witcher 3*, what seems to be the morally optimal choice might often have unforeseen consequences. For example, in White Orchard Geralt meets a dwarven blacksmith called Willis, whose forge has been burned down in the wake of rising tensions in the area due the Nilfgaardian invasion. Once you find the arsonist, Napp, he will try to bribe you to escape punishment. So you are confronted with a choice: take the bribe or bring Napp to justice. At face value, the morality of the choice seems simple, especially in light of the seemingly racist motifs underlying the culprits' decision to torch Willis's forge.

However, looking at the possible outcomes of the decision, things are not so simple. Turning in Napp gets him sentenced to death by hanging, a sentence carried out without a trial by soldiers from the local Nilfgaardian garrison. Furthermore, tensions between Willis and the locals rise, as one of their own is hung on a tree by Nilfgaardian soldiers. The other option—accepting the bribe—causes less direct harm and bloodshed, but does allow Napp the racist arsonist to walk free.

So what is the best choice here? That is a question that *The Witcher 3* forces players to grapple with, as the game provides no easy, one-size-fits-all answers to these kinds of questions. Unfortunately, there is an easy way to circumvent the stress of decision making: any player can look up an online walkthrough to see what the "optimal decision" is, rather than choosing on their own. Or, in Heideggerian terms: any player can do what the *they* do, instead of thinking through decisions and their consequences. The countless walkthroughs and "optimal decision" videos for RPGs out there speak volumes about our desire to often just do what the *they* think is the right decision, instead of carving out our own path through the game.

Just like in real life, playing *The Witcher 3* means being thrown into a world with certain circumstances that are beyond your control. Both the character you play and the world you play in exhibit characteristics beyond your control, which means you will be confronted with hostility, prejudice, and flawed characters, but also pleasant surprises and intimate friendships. While you cannot control these structures, they do not completely determine your behavior. You still have the freedom to make decisions and the responsibility to live with their consequences. However, walkthroughs and instruction videos allow an easy way out of having to actually think about the consequences of your actions. This is much like times in real life when you take the easy way out by succumbing to societal expectations rather than making the hard choices for yourself. So, just like real life, *The Witcher 3* offers us both great freedom and many ways to avoid it.

Notes

1. Martin Heidegger, *Being and Time*, trans. John Macquarrie and Edward Robinson (New York: Harper & Row 1962), 174.

2. See Simone de Beauvoir, *The Second Sex*, trans. Howard Madison Parshley (London: Lowe & Brydone, 1953), for a thorough existentialist investigation of what it means to live as a woman in 1940s Paris.

3. For comparison, as of April 2022, the original *Witcher* has sold over 1 million copies, *The Witcher 2: Assassins of Kings* has sold 2.2 million copies, while *The Witcher 3: The Wild Hunt* has sold over 40 million copies. Source: https://www.statista.com/statistics/1305779/the-witcher-games-sales-worldwide.

4. Heidegger, *Being and Time*, 67. Note that the term "Dasein" is Heidegger's original German word for what he considers to be the specific way of existence of the human being. The term remains untranslated in most translations of his works.

5. Heidegger, *Being and Time*, 68.

6. Heidegger, *Being and* Time, 185.

7. Heidegger, *Being and Time*, 164.

FEMINISM

9

"This Is the Version of Myself I Have to Be"

Understanding Yennefer's Feminism(s)

Edwardo Pérez

GERALT: It was my honor to fight for the capricious heart of
  Yennefer of Vengerberg.
YENNEFER: And I hope to fight many more battles with you, my dear.
GERALT: With me, or against me?
YENNEFER: Depends on the evening.

"The Art of the Illusion"[1]

Geralt might joke about Yennefer's capriciousness, but the adaptable nature of her character illustrates one of the hallmarks of feminism in philosophy—its diversity of thought. Not all feminisms seek the same goals or see women's lives from the same perspectives. Likewise, not every woman in Netflix's adaptation of Andrzej Sapkowski's *Witcher* series embodies the same mindset. Some, like Yennefer, depict an array of feminist ideas, revealing distinctions and contradictions between various viewpoints. Yennefer is right: the battles she chooses to fight (and who she chooses to fight with or against[2]) depend on many factors (and many feminisms), which can shift from one episode to the next.

What also seems to shift is Yennefer's identity—which is significant, given the fundamental importance of a woman's identity in feminist philosophy.[3] Of course, how we understand Yennefer's identity depends on the feminist perspective we use to examine her. Let's begin with French existentialist philosopher Simone de Beauvoir (1908–1986).

"I envy you, truly. A king's mage. How splendid"

As an existentialist philosopher, Beauvoir argued that our identities are never fixed or complete. Rather, our identities are always being created and modified by the choices we make. Beauvoir famously wrote that, "One is not born, but rather becomes, woman."[4] This is the fundamental dilemma

The Witcher and Philosophy: Toss a Coin to Your Philosopher, First Edition.
Edited by Matthew Brake and Kevin S. Decker.
© 2025 John Wiley & Sons, Inc. Published 2025 by John Wiley & Sons, Inc.

a woman must face.[5] If Beauvoir is correct, then a woman's identity, purpose, role, persona, and femininity (and every other aspect that constitutes a woman) are all defined by society. Yet since identity isn't fixed, it can be changed, and every trait defined by society can be redefined, rejected, or embraced by the individual woman. Thus, a woman must ultimately choose whether to embrace society's construction or create her own.[6] This is certainly what Yennefer experiences throughout *The Witcher*'s first three seasons, as she is constantly (re)defined by the societies she lives in and by the choices she makes. One of the first choices Yennefer makes is to sacrifice her fertility to become a sorceress, which results in her becoming beautiful and powerful. This is perhaps the most significant choice Yennefer makes.[7] But why does she make it?

When we first see Yennefer she is a deformed hunchback who is treated cruelly by society (even Tissaia calls her "piglet"). Becoming beautiful and powerful certainly changes things, and so does giving up her ability to bear children. For Queen Kalis, who bemoans her own fertility, the world doesn't offer women much opportunity beyond motherhood, even for a queen. Kalis confesses to Yennefer that she envies her, not just because Yennefer is a powerful king's mage, but because Yennefer had a choice to define her identity, and because as Kalis sees it, "You made the right choice, giving all that nonsense up" ("Of Banquets, Bastards, and Burials," season 1, episode 4). Yennefer seems to acknowledge this perspective when she mourns Kalis's daughter, telling the dead infant "and let's face it, you're a girl ... we're just vessels ... for them to take and take until we're empty and alone. So count yourself lucky. You've cheated the game and won without even knowing it" ("Of Banquets, Bastards, and Burials," season 1, episode 4).

From this perspective, Yennefer can be seen as embracing Beauvoir's existential feminism by rejecting society's construction so she can create her own identity. Thus, she's Yennefer of Vengerberg by birth *and* by choice.[8] However, as Yennefer remarks to Kalis, she eventually comes to regret her choice. So she makes another choice—to become a mother. Through Beauvoir, we can understand that Yennefer, by rejecting and then embracing motherhood, redefines herself as she (not society) sees fit. Existentially, Yennefer decides who and what she wants to be on her terms. To be fair, her choices could be seen as conforming to society's expectations for a woman: beauty and motherhood. But her resolve seems clear. Either way, whether conforming or rebelling, Yennefer's choices can also be viewed as performances.

"Seen and adored, with everyone watching"

The contemporary philosopher Judith Butler builds on the idea that our roles as women and men are socially constructed by formulating the idea of *gender performativity*. Where Beauvoir saw behaviors as artificial creations of society, Butler sees our actions, our speech, and our behaviors as gendered traits we enact in social situations—not as actors on a stage, but as identities we project every time we're social, repeating our behaviors ritually, because they're not just socially acceptable, they're socially constructed.[9] If Butler is right, gender, which we might normally view as innate, is created by our actions. In other words, we don't just create ourselves as Beauvoir notes, we also *gender ourselves*, and we do this throughout our lives.

Perhaps this is what Tissaia means when she instructs Yennefer to "Imagine the most powerful woman in the world. Her hair, the color of her eyes, yes, but also the strength of her posture. The poise of her entire being. Do you see her? ... She is stunning" ("Betrayer Moon," season 1, episode 3). Indeed, for Yennefer, trading her fertility for beauty and power allows her to perform the gendered role of a beautiful, powerful sorceress. Likewise, in seeking motherhood, Yennefer can perform the gendered role of a mother, not as an actor (she's not pretending to be infertile or maternal), but as socially acceptable (and socially constructed) gendered behaviors. The issue of identity remains, and it remains something that is constructed. The difference for Butler is that it is focused on the performance of gender.

What we see, then, is that Yennefer (re)defines herself through Beauvoir's existential feminism, and then (re)genders herself through Butler's performativity. In making these choices, however, Yennefer gains physical beauty, which is also a (re)definition and (re)gendering. However, if we examine Yennefer's choices through the feminist work of Naomi Wolf we might see Yennefer's beauty differently.[10]

"I want to be powerful"

For Naomi Wolf, society forces women to pursue an unattainable standard of beauty and then punishes women when they fail to meet it. This is what Wolf refers to as "the Beauty Myth."[11] As Wolf explains, "'Beauty' is a currency system like the gold standard. Like any economy, it is determined by politics, and in the modern age in the West it is the last, best belief system that keeps male dominance intact."[12] In Wolf's view, the point of the Beauty Myth isn't just about looks (about women conforming to "a culturally imposed physical standard"[13]), it's about the power men wield over women. Wolf explains, "it is an expression of power relations in which women must unnaturally compete for resources that men have appropriated for themselves."[14] Even more, the Beauty Myth isn't about appearance but about behavior, such as the competition between women.[15]

If we consider Yennefer's fertility sacrifice closely, we see that she was essentially competing with the other girls at Aretuza, especially Fringilla, not for beauty but for power. As she tells Istredd, "I want to be powerful," adding, "It is what I'm owed" ("Betrayer Moon," season 1, episode 3). Yennefer wanted to be the mage of Aedirn, not Nilfgaard, and she was willing to sacrifice her fertility (and endure a great amount of physical pain) to become attractive enough to land King Virfuril. From this perspective, Yennefer can be seen conforming to the Beauty Myth, which for Wolf isn't necessarily a bad thing because it can be empowering for a woman to exercise freedom over her appearance. However, as Wolf notes, this freedom could also be a self-imposed prison, what she calls an Iron Maiden.

In Wolf's conception, women are victimized by beauty, and they are either trapped by society (or they trap themselves) in an Iron Maiden[16] for the sake of conforming. This offers a slightly different interpretation of Yennefer's transformation, one that helps us reconsider Yennefer's choice, illustrating the captive power of beauty. As Tissaia remarks to Yennefer, "there is not a person alive that does not look into the mirror and see some deformity ... except us. We remake ourselves on our own terms. The world has no say in it" ("Betrayer Moon," season 1, episode 3).

Tissaia's words resonate with Wolf's ideas, and so do Yennefer's actions, as she effectively puts herself in her own Iron Maiden, punishing herself for conforming to society's standard of beauty. Likewise, her quest to regain her fertility can also be seen as a form of self-inflicted torture. Either way—whether by choosing the Beauty Myth or by constructing her own Iron Maiden—we can see that Yennefer's transformation wasn't just a choice to define or gender herself, it was a choice to gain power.[17] Indeed, in the third season, Tissaia confesses as much to Yennefer regarding the ritual with Giltine:

> When I came to Aretuza, if a sorceress fell pregnant, she was kicked out. "Divided loyalties," said the men. So I made them take us seriously. The enchantment was never about clearer access to Chaos. It was about getting a seat at the table. And the Brotherhood, they called me bold. I was just desperate. The first of many mistakes. ("The Cost of Chaos," season 3, episode 8)

Tissaia might recognize this as a mistake, and we might forgive her since her choice was born from a feminist desire for equal representation.[18] Yet, through Wolf, we can see that Tissaia essentially chose the Beauty Myth, too, consigning every girl at Aretuza to the fate of an Iron Maiden.

But let's be clear: As the scene with Giltine plays out, it's Yennefer who demands he transform her. It was her choice. Yet, to Geralt, Yennefer claims that Aretuza took her choice, and she wants it back, which leads us to the perspective of maternal feminism—the idea that being a mother is the most natural role for a woman.[19]

"They took my choice, I want it back"

Yennefer wants to reclaim the freedom to choose motherhood, but she doesn't necessarily want to get pregnant. She just wants the option to be a mother. Geralt chides and patronizes her, but as she argues, "They took my choice, I want it back. Not that I'd expect you to understand" ("Rare Species," season 1, episode 6). Later, however, she qualifies this by telling him, "I dreamed of becoming important to someone, someday" ("Rare Species," season 1, episode 6). So it seems her motivation isn't just about having the choice to bear a child. It's about being *needed* by a child, which, arguably, gets at the heart of motherhood as understood by maternal feminism. This is what Sara Ruddick (1935–2011) calls maternal thinking.

As Ruddick explains, being a mother "is to take upon oneself the responsibility of child care, making its work a regular and substantial part of one's working life."[20] For Ruddick, this practice demands that mothers "think out strategies of protection, nurturance, and training"[21] to meet the needs of preservation, growth, and social acceptability for children. In other words, Ruddick's maternal thinking is essentially focused on the constant consideration of survival—physically, emotionally, and socially. Notably, Ruddick observes that "there is nothing foreordained about maternal response."[22] Some mothers neglect and abuse. Accordingly, mothering isn't an identity. It's a vocation that can be performed by men, too. Geralt might not understand this until he starts to care for Ciri, but once he does, he engages in maternal thinking. So does Yennefer. She might desire motherhood, but she doesn't become a mother until she sacrifices herself for Ciri—because it is in this moment that Yennefer engages in maternal thinking, choosing to put Ciri's survival above her own.

This is what Tissaia recognizes when Yennefer returns to Aretuza in the third season and passionately argues that Ciri "deserves control of her destiny" ("Reunion," season 3, episode 3). Consider Tissaia's response:

TISSAIA: After all this time, after all your searching, you actually did it.
YENNEFER: Did what?
TISSAIA: Became a mother. ("Reunion," season 3, episode 3)

What's significant is that Tissaia's observation echoes Ruddick's definition of a mother as someone who engages in maternal thinking and maternal actions[23]—which suggests that even though Tissaia might have been willing to sacrifice fertility for a seat at Aretuza's table, she wasn't willing to give up on motherhood. Neither was Yennefer.

A few episodes later, Yennefer and Ciri acknowledge their mother/daughter relationship, with Ciri urging Yennefer to save Tissaia,[24] telling Yennefer, "I understand what she means to you." So, Tissaia is clearly right, and for Yennefer, her choice to be a mother illustrates another (re)definition of her identity. Of course, while Yennefer's desire for motherhood is informed by maternal feminism, her mother/daughter relationship with Ciri also resonates with the feminism of Adrienne Rich (1929–2012).[25]

"What could you possibly want with a child?"

For Rich, patriarchy often defines the roles of mothers and daughters through antagonism and animosity. As Rich observes, "And it is the mother through whom patriarchy early teaches the small female her proper expectations. The anxious pressure of one female on another to conform to a degrading and dispiriting role can hardly be termed 'mothering,' even if she does this believing it will help her daughter to survive."[26] Thus, as Rich notes, "Many daughters live in rage at their mothers for having accepted, too readily and passively, 'whatever comes,'" adding that "A mother's victimization does not merely humiliate her, it mutilates the daughter who watches her for clues as to what it means to be a woman."[27] In other words, what we think of as traditional mothering is actually a reinforcement of patriarchal dominance, with men controlling not just women's bodies and women's fertility, but also how women are supposed to function as mothers—especially how mothers train daughters to eventually fill the same role. It's an interesting interpretation of motherhood and mothering, one that echoes Beauvoir, Butler, and Wolf. Yet, like these other theorists, Rich's perspective also suggests that women should seek to transcend patriarchy's control, and that seems to be what Yennefer does in her relationship with Ciri.

What's significant for Yennefer and Ciri is that both were raised for a time by mothers who didn't give birth to them—Tissaia and Calanthe. And of course, Yennefer didn't give birth to Ciri, either.[28] To some extent, Tissaia and Calanthe taught Yennefer and Ciri the "proper expectations" as Rich would say. Yet both Tissaia and Calanthe defy the Continent's patriarchy in their mothering, and so does Yennefer, who believes Ciri "deserves to know what [her magic] is capable of" ("Reunion," season 3, episode 3). As Yennefer claims several times, she wants Ciri to make her own choices and control her own destiny. Yennefer pointedly tells Triss: "Do you know when I was most dangerous? When I was desperate, and powerless, and alone. And that will not happen to [Ciri]. Not as long as I'm around" ("The Invitation," season 3, episode 4).

Given how Yennefer sought to sacrifice Ciri to the Deathless Mother in the second season, Yennefer's fierce devotion to Ciri is admirable. What we see is that Yennefer's mothering not only defies patriarchy's prescribed roles, it also empowers Ciri to be able to create her own destiny and define her own life in the ways that Beauvoir, Butler, and even Wolf note. Likewise, as a daughter, Yennefer learns to value Tissaia's mothering, which illustrates another aspect of Yennefer's identity.

"You are our mother"

Tissaia's and Yennefer's relationship is one of the most significant relationships developed in Netflix's adaptation—and it's poignant to see their relationship have a beginning, middle, and end, with Tissaia's death in the third season. Tissaia forges a mother/daughter bond with all the girls she trains at Aretuza. But Yennefer seems special, as we see from Tissaia's actions on several occasions. As Tissaia tells Yennefer when she learns Yennefer has lost her magic, "your pain is my pain"[29] ("What Is Lost," season 2, episode 3). It's a sentiment Yennefer returns, especially in the third season when Yennefer tries to motivate Tissaia after Aretuza has fallen:

> Everything I've done. Everything that's been done to me. I've survived because of your faith. You are the strongest force I've ever known. Remember your strength. You are Tissaia of Vries, you are our mother, and we need you. I need you. ("The Cost of Chaos," season 3, episode 8)

It's tragic that, despite Yennefer's plea, Tissaia takes her own life, feeling intense guilt for Aretuza's destruction and for being fooled by Vilgefortz. Of course, Tissaia's death prompts Yennefer to make another choice that will (re)shape her identity. As she tells the sorceresses who are left: "The most dangerous mage we've ever seen has the most powerful source this Continent has ever known. We need to eliminate Vilgefortz. The old guard is gone. It's up to us. We decide how we move forward" ("The Cost of Chaos," season 3, episode 8).

Given this choice (and given Yennefer's other choices), we can see not only how Yennefer resonates with each theorist we've examined, but we can also see how her choices fit into the perspective of radical feminism.[30]

"To be reborn, you will bear no more"

Seeking to completely change the patriarchal structure of society, radical feminists offered various sweeping solutions for eliminating male dominance. Shulamith Firestone (1945–2012), who called for a feminist revolution, wanted to eliminate distinctions between women and men, writing that "the end goal of feminist revolution must be ... not just the elimination of male *privilege* but of the sex *distinction* itself."[31] For Firestone, feminists must question "not just all of *Western* culture, but the organization of culture itself, and further, even the very organization of nature."[32] For Ti-Grace Atkinson, the oppression of women is global, and it has always existed because women's ability to bear children became a "biologically contingent burden ... thereby modifying these individuals' definition from the human to the functional, or animal."[33]

To some extent, Yennefer, Fringilla, Triss, Sabrina, and all the other female mages mothered by Tissaia at Aretuza function as Atkinson notes—they aren't fertile, but their ability to wield chaos in the service of kings resonates with Firestone's and Atkinson's concerns. As Yennefer confessed to Kalis, she saw herself as nothing more than "A glorified royale arse wiper" ("Of Banquets, Bastards, and Burials," season 1, episode 4).

Given Yennefer's actions against the Brotherhood from season to season, as well as her insistence that Ciri be in control of her own destiny, it seems fair to say that Yennefer embraces the kind of liberation Firestone and Atkinson prescribe. Indeed, from a radical feminist perspective, Yennefer's embrace of beauty and rejection of fertility could be seen as challenging the Continent's society—not just feminine culture, but also notions of motherhood. For example, the removal of Yennefer's ovaries could be seen as a step toward the elimination of the sex distinction Firestone recommends.[34] Yet, her choice to be beautiful (and keep her purple eyes) endows Yennefer with a source of power as potent as her magic. For Yennefer, her deformed appearance was a curse that made her unlovable and "worth only four marks."[35] So she doesn't want beauty for the sake of gaining a man. As she tells Istredd, "that's slow suicide."[36] Rather, Yennefer wants beauty because she wants power. As she says, "It's what I'm owed."[37] And after she gets it, she clearly uses it.

So far, we've examined Yennefer's identity through various feminisms as a woman. But, like most women, Yennefer isn't just a woman. Rather, she's a combination (or composite) of various, overlapping identities. She's an Aedirnian from Vengerberg, who is initially born as a physically deformed quarter-elf, until she sacrifices her fertility to become a beautiful, powerful sorceress. In other words, Yennefer is what Kimberlé Crenshaw refers to as being multiply-burdened, or intersectional.[38]

"'Twas your blood"

For Crenshaw, the gender inequality that traditional feminism focuses upon[39] doesn't account for the intersection of other aspects of a woman's life, such as race, class, and sexuality. For Yennefer, being a woman and being deformed are difficult enough, but when Istredd learns the truth of her elven blood in the first season, her heritage also becomes a problem. Nevertheless, Yennefer overcomes this prejudice by using the tools of the Brotherhood against them. In doing so, Yennefer displays a type of intersectional feminism observed by American feminist Audre Lorde (1934–1992).

As Lorde explains, for women who don't fit into society's definition of "female normalcy," such as women of color (or, in *The Witcher*, elves[40]), survival requires learning how to turn differences into strengths, because "the master's tools will never dismantle the master's house."[41] For Lorde, such tools "may allow us to temporarily beat him at his own game, but they will never enable us to bring about genuine change," adding, "this fact is only threatening to those women who still define the master's house as their only source of support."[42] Yennefer clearly beats the Brotherhood at their own game when she transforms her appearance, shows up to the ball, and steals King Virfuril from Fringilla. Yet as Yennefer eventually admits to Queen Kalis (and as Lorde might have predicted), Yennefer's victory didn't bring about genuine change. If anything, it reinforced the Brotherhood's patriarchy and prejudice, especially Stregobor's (and eventually Vilgefortz's).[43]

Of course, since Yennefer is only quarter-elf and her ears look human, she can pass as a human. So, she doesn't experience the same type of prejudice and racism against elves as, for example, Francesca does.[44] Nevertheless, her identity is one that intersects, even after she's transformed, with various characters continuing to distrust and scheme against her—including the elves!

"Magic wasn't what I was missing"

Ultimately, Yennefer's identity is bound to the family she creates with Geralt and Ciri—an identity forged by one of the most compelling character arcs in contemporary television. Through her choices, she not only creates a family, she illustrates the complexity of feminist theory and a plurality of feminisms. Ciri may shatter monoliths with her screams, but Yennefer shows that feminism isn't monolithic, and that no woman is wedded to one vision or one goal. Whether we view Yennefer as intersectional, radical, maternal, a Beauty Myth, a walking Iron Maiden, (re)gendered, or (re)defined—or whether Yennefer is an elf, a hunchback, a mage, infertile, with powers, or without them—what matters most is that she's able to make her own choices. And regardless of the choices she makes, she is always Yennefer of Vengerberg.

Notes

1. "The Art of the Illusion," season 3, episode 5.
2. As well as who she chooses to love.
3. Along with the issue of equality, the issue of a woman's identity (as a girl, wife, mother, property, and so on) permeates the history of feminist scholarship and activism, especially regarding how a woman is defined, and who gets to define her.
4. A.N. Whitehead, *Process and Reality*, ed. D.R. Griffin and D.W. Sherburne (New York: Free Press, 1978), 39; Simone de Beauvoir, *The Second Sex* (New York: Vintage Books, 2011), 283.

5. One that permeates most feminisms, remaining relevant to contemporary theory.

6. For Beauvoir, women need to recognize the artificial construction and seek to change it, otherwise women might become content and complicit in their own oppression. However, for lasting change to occur, society needs to change, too.

7. Though sacrificing herself for Ciri is just as consequential—not just because Yennefer saves Ciri and regains her magic, but because this act redefines Yennefer.

8. To some extent, Yennefer becomes complicit in society's construction of women. Indeed, her life becomes easier as a beautiful mage. Yet, Yennefer's motivation isn't to conform. As she tells Istredd, her desire is for power, which is a rejection of society, as Kalis recognizes.

9. Like the rituals we see in Aretuza, especially the balls in the first and third seasons.

10. Naomi Wolf's credibility has been criticized over the years, not just in disagreement with her observations but also with her apparent lack of scholarship and rigor—as well as her embracement of conspiracy theories. Nevertheless, her observations are worth exploring, as they offer perspectives that help us understand the social conditioning of women.

11. Naomi Wolf, *The Beauty Myth: How Images of Beauty Are Used Against Women* (New York: Harper Perennial, 2002).

12. Wolf, *The Beauty Myth*, 12.

13. Wolf, *The Beauty Myth*, 12.

14. Wolf, *The Beauty Myth*, 12.

15. Wolf, *The Beauty Myth*, 12.

16. In a metaphorical condition similar to the medieval torture device.

17. Not just chaos power, but also power through beauty.

18. Which, along with a woman's identity, is the most common focus for any type of feminism.

19. And depending on the historical context, the role of motherhood is framed through biology, culture, religion, politics, race, ethics, and nationalism as a responsibility to the past, present, and future of humanity. Yet it can also be seen as a type of antifeminism that supports men's and society's control over women's bodies and fertility.

20. Sara Ruddick, *Maternal Thinking: Toward a Politics of Peace* (Boston: Beacon Press, 1989), 17.

21. Ruddick, *Maternal Thinking*, 23.

22. Ruddick, *Maternal Thinking*, xi.

23. To be fair, Geralt engages in paternal thinking when he begins to take care of Ciri—even to the point that he stops being politically neutral.

24. After Tissaia had summoned Alzur's Thunder as a last resort to save Aretuza.

25. Who was a poet and is often categorized as both a lesbian feminist and radical feminist.

26. Adrienne Rich, *Of Woman Born: Motherhood as Experience and Institution* (New York: W.W. Norton, 1986), 250.

27. Rich, *Of Woman Born*, 250.

28. This isn't necessarily unique, given the historical roles of stepmothers, nannies, and surrogate mothers. Yet it is significant because it defines mothering, as Tissaia did, as a choice that doesn't require giving birth to the child being

mothered, which is notable given the observations made by Beauvoir, Butler, Wolf, and Rich.

29. A mantra that resonates with Ruddick, and one that Tissaia repeats in the third season.

30. All the theorists we've examined thus far (Beauvoir, Butler, Wolf, and Rich) have been labeled radical in their respective feminist ideas. Yet, as a historical and ideological movement, Radical Feminism emerged in the 1960s as an effort to eliminate male supremacy in every social context by radically restructuring society.

31. Shulamith Firestone, *The Dialectic of Sex: The Case for Feminist Revolution* (New York: Farrar, Straus & Giroux, 2003), 11.

32. Firestone, *Dialectic of Sex*, 4.

33. Ti-Grace Atkinson, "Radical Feminism," in Barbara A. Crow ed., *Radical Feminism: A Documentary Reader* (New York: New York University Press, 2000), 85.

34. Calanthe also illustrates this in how she rules Cintra, vowing never "to bow to no law made by men who never bore a child" ("Of Banquets, Bastards, and Burials," season 1, episode 4). Yet, Calanthe balances her radicalism by embracing the role of motherhood, first to Pavetta, and then to Ciri.

35. "Four Marks," season 1, episode 2.

36. "Betrayer Moon," season 1, episode 3.

37. "Betrayer Moon."

38. Kimberlé Crenshaw, "Demarginalizing the Intersection of Race and Sex: A Black Feminist Critique of Antidiscrimination Doctrine, Feminist Theory and Antiracist Politics," *University of Chicago Legal Forum* 1 (1989), 140.

39. By centering on women in a general, perhaps even monolithic, sense.

40. In Netflix's adaptation, which boasts an inclusive cast, racial discrimination has nothing to do with skin color. Elves can be light or dark skinned. What makes them stand out, especially if they're full-blooded, is their pointy ears and elven blood.

41. Audre Lorde, *Sister Outsider: Essays and Speeches* (New York: Penguin, 2020), 102.

42. Lorde, *Sister Outsider*, 102.

43. To be fair, it's significant that Stregobor eventually sacrifices himself in the third season, standing in front of Yennefer to protect her, telling her "Go, I'll buy you some time" ("Everybody Has a Plan 'til They Get Punched in the Face," season 3, episode 6).

44. For a more detailed discussion of racism and passing in *The Witcher*, see my other chapter in this volume.

10

"They Took My Choice, I Want It Back"

Infertility in *The Witcher*

Zoe L. Tongue

Infertility is a recurring theme in the Netflix adaptation of *The Witcher*. Witchers go through mutations at a young age during their training, which leaves them sterile. Geralt of Rivia can't have children but steps into a fatherhood role for Princess Cirilla of Cintra, who's owed to him as a "Child of Surprise." Most sorceresses are also infertile as a consequence of their powerful magic. Yennefer of Vengerberg has her reproductive organs removed in order to acquire beauty and power, a choice she later regrets. But there are clear differences in how Yennefer and Geralt each respond to their infertility and their respective roles toward Ciri. These differences highlight assumptions and stereotypes around pregnancy and parenthood tied to traditional, and often biased, views about gender.

Yennefer's Choice

"Imagine the most powerful woman in the world," Tissaia de Vries tells Yennefer as she looks into the mirror. In the first few Netflix episodes, Yennefer has a twisted spine and misaligned jaw; she is cast out by her own family and believes nobody could ever love her. Tissaia recruits her to the magical academy of Aretuza by purchasing her from her father for four marks—less than the price of a pig. Tissaia abuses her at first, referring to her as "piglet" until Yennefer proves that she can control her emotions. Tissaia tells her to "free the victim in the mirror."

Enamored with this vision of power and beauty, Yennefer won't accept the decision of the Chapter of the Gift and the Art to reassign her to a less influential political seat in the Kingdom of Nilfgaard, rather than to the Kingdom of Aedirn with King Virfuril as she was promised. She finds the enchanter who can make each girl a living work of art, demanding that he remake her completely, leaving only her eyes and her scars untouched.

The Witcher and Philosophy: Toss a Coin to Your Philosopher, First Edition.
Edited by Matthew Brake and Kevin S. Decker.
© 2025 John Wiley & Sons, Inc. Published 2025 by John Wiley & Sons, Inc.

While strapped naked to a chair, the enchanter tells her that "there is a cost to all creation" and that "to be reborn, you will bear no more." Yennefer nods in response; her reproductive organs are removed, set alight, and painted onto her skin to cause a painful transformation. This straightens her spine and jaw. She has to choose between beauty and fertility—sexuality and reproduction, the two characteristics that women are stereotypically valued for according to patriarchal ideals. Once transformed, Yennefer arrives looking powerful and beautiful at the Aretuza ball and wins the seat she desired in Vengerberg, capital of Aedirn, as King Virfuril is drawn to her.

Several decades after these events, the series portrays Yennefer's regret at sacrificing her fertility. Desperate for a child, she blames the Chapter for the loss of her reproductive capacity and unsuccessfully searches for methods of regaining it, even looking into myths about dragon hearts as a cure. She tells Geralt that "they took my choice, I want it back."

Infertility, Loss, and Injustice

In season 1, Yennefer's experience of infertility is one of grief and loss. She can't accept that there is no cure. For women who have had similar losses, this may feel familiar. The desire to carry and give birth to one's own child is visceral, and in modern times, we have assisted reproductive technologies such as IVF (in vitro fertilization) to help people overcome infertility. However, medicine often fails—leaving many in Yennefer's position. Unlike in science fiction and genres set in the present, where infertility can be remedied medically or technological advancements used to "fix" the problem, for Yennefer and other characters in fantasy, no amount of magic can restore what's lost. This representation of the pain felt by the infertile Yennefer is therefore important, as it speaks to the very real experiences of those unable to have genetically related children or to carry a pregnancy.

Research has shown that women who experience infertility often feel moral guilt, inadequacy, and failure: women blame themselves.[1] *The Witcher* does not entirely fall into this trap. Yennefer regrets her choice, and Tissaia implies that Yennefer ruined her own life and should take responsibility for the way things turned out. However, Yennefer places the blame on Aretuza for bringing her into the magical world and making her believe that her transformation was necessary. Yennefer is abused and manipulated, made to believe that she is not worthy of love, that her only redemption would come from ascending to a seat of power. She is already stripped and fastened to the chair when the enchanter tells her of the price she must pay. She denies the herbs needed to relieve the pain because there's no time. She agrees to the price because she believes there's no other choice; in that moment, she has no options left. In one episode, Yennefer speaks of women as "just vessels, for them to take, and take, until we're empty, and alone." Clearly, she believes that Aretuza and the Chapter took everything from her.

In our world, marginalized women have been forcibly sterilized, and coercive sterilization practices continue today—against disabled people, ethnic minorities (particularly Roma), and Indigenous women.[2] Yennefer was treated cruelly for her disability and initially loses the advisory seat to King Virfuril due to her part-elvish blood. In the Netflix series, the elves speak of "The Great Cleansing"—the mass slaughter of elves, including Yennefer's father, following a war with the humans. Some kingdoms retain a hatred of elves. The treatment of Yennefer due to her disability and quarter-elvish status are the catalysts for her agreement to the removal of her reproductive organs, so her consent and "choice" here ought to be viewed as coerced in the context of the broader discriminations she had suffered. Yennefer agrees to sterilization in order to escape this background.

In response to this treatment of marginalized women, the concept of "reproductive justice" emerged as a framework for recognizing the barriers experienced by such women in choosing to have children, as well the obstacles that exist to prevent or end an unwanted pregnancy.[3] Reproductive justice addresses issues such as coercive sterilization and the legality and availability of abortion and contraception. The portrayal of the injustice felt by Yennefer at the hands of Aretuza is directly reflective of the feminist politics of reproductive justice. Her vulnerability to the magical institution and the sorcerer that performs the transformation is akin to the vulnerability experienced by marginalized women in our healthcare institutions in the modern day. Feminism is very much concerned with reproductive freedom, so the denial of Yennefer's reproductive freedom is a significant injustice from a feminist perspective.

Motherhood, Monstrosity, and Representation

While this portrayal of loss and injustice is significant, season 1's characterization of Yennefer is, at times, problematic. Feminist philosophy points to how women are stereotypically defined by the primary reproductive role of being mothers. Women are expected to have an innate maternal instinct; it's viewed as "natural" for women to desire pregnancy, childbirth, and motherhood. Any deviation from this norm is viewed, in a patriarchal society, as a deviation from normal womanhood and reproductive destiny.

As season 1 progresses, Yennefer becomes consumed by the fact of her infertility. Her character development is tied to her desire to fulfill a reproductive role and satisfy her "natural" maternal instincts. Her inability to live up to this norm and have a family of her own leads her to tell Tissaia that her "life has no more to give." The implication here is that Yennefer sees the core purpose of her life as to bear a child, and as she can't do so, her life becomes meaningless. Yennefer views her decision to give up everything for power and magic as a sacrifice not worth making. Her career stagnates and she becomes lost and lonely. The only redemption she can see for herself is to find a way to recover her fertility. Yennefer's character, unfortunately, fits squarely within patriarchal maternal ideals.

Scholars have argued that the portrayals of "abnormal" qualities of infertile women in a number of reality television shows represent *monstrosity*; infertile women become infertile monsters, deviating from the norms of acceptable womanhood.[4] This can also be seen in the fantasy genre, where there's an emerging pattern of infertile women who accrue destructive amounts of power. In the HBO series *Game of Thrones*, for example, Daenerys Targaryen fights for the Iron Throne—but her infertility becomes her downfall and drives her mad. Another example can be seen in the Marvel movie *Doctor Strange in the Multiverse of Madness,* where Wanda Maximoff's grief for her lost family pushes her toward the use of dangerous dark magic to try and get them back. Likewise, Yennefer's experience of infertility makes her increasingly unstable—she's described, at one juncture, as "pure chaos." Where these powerful, infertile women become destructive, they become monstrous. Falling short of one standard of femininity seems to cascade into falling short of others. Women are assumed to be caring, selfless, and nonviolent, but Yennefer's monstrosity is also found in her recklessness and desperate need to fulfill her own desires.

We can also criticize the portrayals of Yennefer's disability and elvish nature. Yennefer is abused for her physical disability, choosing to become conventionally aesthetically attractive, despite the pain the physical transformation causes her and the cost to her reproductive freedom. Disability is therefore presented as a problem to be "cured."[5] Similarly, the elves can be seen as an allegory for Indigenous peoples: the *Witcher*'s elven creation stories and symbolism bear an uncanny familiarity to those of many Indigenous communities, along with the dominant culture's "whitewashing" of Indigenous narratives.[6] It's important to note that Yennefer's disability and elvish-ness symbolize her victimhood early in season 1: the show therefore advances stereotypical negative attitudes about disability and being of Indigenous origin, rather than positive portrayals. As we've already seen, the series uses the very real struggles faced by disabled and Indigenous women in the face of eugenics and sterilization, themes used as tools for Yennefer's character development.

For many feminist philosophers, women must be freed from traditional norms around reproduction and assumptions of maternity.[7] Infertility may complicate this when women have unfulfilled desires to carry and birth a child. Representations of infertility in popular culture feed into this. Yennefer's experience in some ways represents the real experience of infertility and struggles around reproductive choice. However, *The Witcher* also reinforces problematic, patriarchal tropes about women and motherhood and does not say enough about how these struggles affect marginalized people.

Geralt's Surprise, Masculinity, and Single Fatherhood

Geralt is bound to Princess Ciri after claiming the Law of Surprise in repayment for saving her father's life. At first, Geralt refuses to claim his child surprise, but later seeks to find and protect her following the attack on the Kingdom of Cintra. Geralt traces Ciri to the woods, and when they meet for the first time, they embrace as though they were father and daughter. He tells her that "people linked by destiny will always find each other." This fatherhood role strengthens in season 2 as he takes Ciri to Kaer Morhen, a keep for training witchers. He introduces her to his brethren and begins to instruct her in fighting like them. At one point, Geralt even refers to Ciri as "mine"—she is a daughter to him.

Unlike Yennefer, Geralt doesn't experience his infertility as loss. He prefers solitude and believes that the witcher's lifestyle is not suited to having children. Witchers are mutated and trained at a young age (which also raises the issue of a lack of consent from them), but Geralt accepts his infertility as part of being a witcher. Unlike Yennefer, Geralt doesn't desire a child—his infertility is only briefly mentioned and does not feature as a core aspect of his identity or narrative. He's reluctant to claim his child surprise until he discovers the death of her parents, and does not believe, at first, that destiny would tie him to her. In fact, his first reaction to discovering he's owed a child of surprise is to say, "Fuck." This lack of interest in parenting stands in sharp contrast to Yennefer's desperation.

While female infertility ties into social values about womanhood and motherhood, men can similarly experience infertility as stigmatizing, as male virility is often tied to stereotypical masculinity.[8] Portrayals of male infertility as emasculating may risk reinforcing these stereotypes of what it means to be a man. In the HBO series *Game of Thrones*, for example, Theon Greyjoy is castrated while a captive and is subsequently removed from the category of being a "real man."[9] From a confident character of status at the start, once tortured and castrated he becomes a passive servant of his captor, accedes to the name "Reek," and refuses to escape when his sister attempts to rescue him. However, *The Witcher* avoids this. Geralt's infertility is a consequence of his enhanced strength, speed, and other powerful abilities. Witchers are despised for being mutants, and people assume that they are emotionless, but their infertility isn't a reason for their ostracization; in fact, it's largely irrelevant to Geralt's character development.

Moreover, Geralt's relationship with Ciri enables him to step into a positive father role despite his infertility. Geralt becomes the primary figure responsible for Ciri's safety and well-being. There's a shift of core purpose toward becoming a protector that takes priority over everything else. In season 2, Yennefer has lost her magic and kidnaps Ciri, intending to sacrifice her to the Deathless Mother so that she may regain her magic. Though Geralt falls in love with Yennefer, when she threatens Ciri, there's no doubt that Geralt would choose his daughter over the sorceress.

He clearly grows to love and care for Ciri, and she admires and loves him in return. Given the gendered stereotypes which typically position women as children's primary or "natural" caregivers, this positive representation of single fatherhood is one way in which *The Witcher* bucks tradition.

Gender and Nonbiological Family

Feminists have been concerned with the great emphasis that society places on having biological children.[10] Infertility treatments are inspired by the desire to have a child *of one's own*, with adoption or nonbiological family representing an inferior option. Not only does this result in a stigma toward adoptive children, but it also reinforces gendered reproductive roles. These roles suggest that men should "father" children that can carry on their genetic traits. Women should carry, birth, and raise a child that they become maternally attached to from the start of pregnancy. To parent a child that you're not biologically tied to is therefore positioned as a selfless act, perhaps even more so when it comes to men raising "another man's" child.

The Witcher presents a positive view of single, adoptive fatherhood, and the lack of biological link between Geralt and Ciri is unimportant to the story. Biological family doesn't appear to be a priority for Geralt—he briefly mentions his mother, but in many ways, his witcher brethren are his family. Geralt's willingness to protect and care for Ciri isn't limited because he isn't her birth father, or even because he's not the man who raised her. Their link goes beyond the genetic, and they develop similarities as Ciri's powers make her feel like an outcast in the same way that Geralt is. Geralt eventually becomes willing to claim Ciri as his daughter. In *The Witcher*, biology is not destiny—adoption is.

In season 2, Yennefer also comes to have a role in protecting Ciri. While Yennefer first seeks to use Ciri to reclaim her lost magic, she soon develops a bond with her. As their relationship develops, we see a different side to Yennefer, and in the final episode of the season, "Family," Yennefer sacrifices herself to save Ciri. When Yennefer becomes something of a parent figure to Ciri, her focus on overcoming her infertility wanes. Again, this depiction of Yennefer is both good and bad from a feminist perspective. On the one hand, it's important that Yennefer can find what she was looking for in an adoptive parenting role; this helps to overcome biased assumptions about pregnancy, motherhood, and infertility. Following Yennefer's struggle with her inability to have a child in season 1, this change can be viewed as an empowering perspective on infertility. However, there is a marked difference between how Geralt and Yennefer protect Ciri. Yennefer gives up her body in a selfless act to save the child, which feeds into the stereotype that good mothers must make selfless sacrifices for their children. This patriarchal ideal of maternal sacrifice is an expectation that women will always place their needs below those of their children, or accept pain as a routine part of motherhood. The implication of this is that women acting in their own interests are seen as selfish, and as "bad mothers."

Feminist criticisms of the biological family also aim at the idea of the nuclear, heterosexual family as the conventional structure for raising children. In season 2, with both Geralt and Yennefer acting as parent figures to Ciri, the idea of the nuclear family unit is reinforced. Ciri, in effect, takes the place of the child that Geralt and Yennefer could not have biologically. The representation of nonbiological parenthood here is largely a positive one, but it is by no means a radical departure from conventional views about the family.

Netflix's adaptation of *The Witcher* grapples with the complex issues around infertility and adoptive parenthood and should be praised from a feminist perspective on that basis. However, at times Yennefer's portrayal reinforces problematic gender stereotypes about womanhood and the maternal desire to reproduce, and her disability and elvish nature are treated as impulses for character development and subsequently abandoned. So while *The Witcher* raises serious questions about the issues surrounding infertility, it really can't be considered a distinctly feminist portrayal of infertility.

Notes

1. Miriam Ulrich and Ann Weatherall, "Motherhood and Infertility: Viewing Motherhood through the Lens of Infertility," *Feminism & Psychology* 10 (2000), 323–336.
2. Alexandra Minna Stern, "Forced Sterilization Policies in the US Targeted Minorities and Those with Disabilities—and Lasted into the 21st Century," The Conversation (website), August 26, 2020, at https://theconversation.com/forced-sterilization-policies-in-the-us-targeted-minorities-and-those-with-disabilities-and-lasted-into-the-21st-century-143144.
3. For more on reproductive justice, see National Black Women's Reproductive Justice Agenda, "Reproductive Justice," at https://blackrj.org/our-issues/reproductive-justice (accessed February 1, 2024).
4. Marjolein Lotte de Boer, Cristina Archetti, and Kari Nyheim Solbraekke, "In/Fertile Monsters: The Emancipatory Significance of Representations of Women on Infertility Reality TV," *Journal of Medical Humanities* 43 (2022), 11–26.
5. For a short disability justice critique of *The Witcher*, see Kristen Lopez, "What *The Witcher* Gets Wrong (and Right) About Disability Narratives," Gizmodo, December 30, 2019, at https://gizmodo.com/what-the-witcer-gets-wrong-and-right-about-disabilit-1840609870.
6. Jacinda Willeto, "Exploring The Witcher through an Indigenous Lens," A Tribe Called Geek, January 27, 2022, at https://atribecalledgeek.com/exploring-the-witcher-through-an-indigenous-lens.

7. One of the most well-known radical feminist texts on the rejection of reproductive norms is Shulamith Firestone, *The Dialectic of Sex* (first published 1970; London: Verso, 2015), 9–11.

8. For a study on male experiences of infertility treatment, see Liberty Walther Barnes, *Conceiving Masculinity: Male Infertility, Medicine, and Identity* (Philadelphia: Temple University Press, 2014).

9. Shiloh Carroll, "The Emasculation of Theon Greyjoy" in Karl Fugelso ed., *Studies in Medievalism XXX* (Cambridge: Cambridge University Press, 2021), 176.

10. For more critiques on the biological family, see Firestone, *Dialectic of Sex*; Sophie Lewis, *Full Surrogacy Now* (London: Verso, 2018); Sophie Lewis, *Abolish the Family* (London: Verso, 2022).

11

Ciri's Agency and Autonomy
Princess, Sorceress, and Witcher Girl

Emily Vega and Walter Barta

In Andrzej Sapkowski's *The Witcher Saga*, the titular "witcher" is Geralt of Rivia, but Geralt's protégée, Princess Cirilla, better known as Ciri, is the true protagonist. As the Lion Cub of Cintra, then as the first "witcher girl," and later as the most powerful magic-user in existence, saving the Continent (and the spheres) is ultimately *her* destiny, not *his*. Moreover, as the driver of her fellow characters' emotions and motivations, Ciri is the heart of the story. This is true both in the themes and in the world-building, as Ciri's magical powers develop from her trauma and its expression through sorrow, love, and rage. While her power originates from Elder Blood (the blood of elves), it can only be activated by Ciri's emotional state of mind and her control over these emotions. In other words, Ciri's power over both magic and the narrative mainly derives from her discipline in analyzing and overcoming her trauma. What results is her ability to succeed against evil forces and create lasting bonds with those who have been subjected to similar traumas. She shares these experiences with the other two protagonists of the series, Geralt and Yennefer, who become surrogate parents to Ciri and help her achieve her destiny. Whether she's chided and infantilized, or admonished for being aloof and "un-princess-like," Ciri must navigate both her tumultuous past and the social expectations thrust upon her sex ("The End's Beginning," season 1, episode 1). How Ciri copes with—and ultimately overcomes—trauma from these experiences influences the intensity of her power.

The Laugh of the Medusa

Sapkowski and other creators of the *Witcher* universe don't just explore the boundaries of human emotion but also add a distinctively gendered dimension to their characters and themes. Female feelings and their expression, healthy or unhealthy, magical or personal, are elements important to the plot that propel the narrative forward. Sapkowski's story ultimately celebrates female expression and emotional health, while also highlighting the social control of female emotions, including backlash against female expressions of emotion; both are aimed at Ciri and other female characters throughout *The Witcher*'s stories in various media forms. Although a male-authored fantasy, this interest in female issues and characters makes *The Witcher* saga an unlikely but interesting mouthpiece for feminist philosophy.

Western philosophy, like many fields of study, has historically been male dominated in both population and focus; in other words, much of the "groundbreaking" philosophical work to come into common culture has been shaped by men and their experiences. When these philosophical ideas are applied to society as a whole (and when these ideas become ideological movements), they can alienate—if not outright silence—women. In contrast, feminism, as a philosophy, has developed in part as a reaction to male dominance, in order to privilege the experiences of women throughout history, not as an action of supremacy but precisely because women have been "locked out" of historical and cultural conversations. When Western philosophy *has* turned its eye to women, the focus has primarily been about their bodies (and their bodies in relation to men's bodies), tending to relegate women's cultural and historical importance to their roles as mothers or wives rather than as people. The influence of these ideas includes the way women and their social roles have been depicted in popular culture like *The Witcher* saga. Feminist philosophers have hoped to remedy this problematic status within culture and philosophy.

Women's emotion being a source of power, like we see with female characters in *The Witcher*, is a common idea in feminist philosophy, particularly in the works of French feminist Hélène Cixous, who explored the psyche as a space of expression, repression, and oppression. Emotions can be *expressed*, but also internally *repressed* and externally *oppressed*. As a philosopher, she claimed that the freedom of women depended on their overcoming the mental blocks of cultural expectations through personal expression. In one of her most famous essays, "The Laugh of the Medusa," she stresses that women should express their ideas and emotions—particularly those that conflict with male expectation—without hesitation, in both thought and action (which, combined, is the act of writing, according to Cixous). Furthermore, the female body as the site of emotion should be used for female desires, not ones that explicitly benefit men (such as pregnancy/reproduction). As Cixous says, "Censor the body and you censor breath and speech at the same time. Write your self. Your body must be heard. Only then will the immense resources of the unconscious spring forth."[1]

In the eyes of both good and evil characters in *The Witcher*, Ciri is an "immense resource," yet the immense powers with which she was born are dependent upon whether she can discipline her emotions while at the same time finding the strength to express them and anticipate the consequences. In this way, Cixous's feminist philosophies play out in many of the stories of female characters in *The Witcher* saga, especially those about Ciri.

War and Trauma

Ciri's magical power forms, in part, through her bearing personal witness to war, which teaches her tragic lessons in intense, unmitigated ways: when the empire of Nilfgaard invades her kingdom, Cintra, she sees her home burn. The army brutalizes and kills Cintran citizens in front of her very eyes; her entire court is eradicated; her city is razed to the ground. After this, the political structures of the varying nations she travels through restrict her self-expression, leading her to live in isolation; others attempt to kidnap her, kill her, or marry her off as a political and magical brood-mare. Even those who lend an ear and shoulder to cry on have their own agenda: Ciri is treated as a tool to further the destiny of others or as a stand-in daughter for their desires. Furthermore, the complex politics that influence the war in the world of *The Witcher* include the oppression of magical races and national colonization, a campaign which Ciri's family heads. Queen Calanthe's difficult relationships with neighboring nations in part causes the attack on Cintra, leading many Cintran citizens to vocally and harshly criticize the queen. Some even celebrate Calanthe's death within earshot of Ciri. In the aftermath, Ciri must conceal her true identity as princess and sorceress to receive help such as food and shelter. The danger is that she might draw the attention of her would-be captors who would enslave her and use her powers to take over the world. Thus begins Ciri's identity crisis, as an international war ensures that Ciri's family name and legacy is known virtually everywhere on the Continent. With so much against her, Ciri's life and worldview in her formative years are structured by forces beyond her control.

It's in this context that Ciri's powers emerge, but this should come as no surprise since, as Cixous and other feminist philosophers would point out, for women and others who are deprived of power, self-expression usually forms under duress. Experiencing trauma but being unable to express a response to it would affect anyone's emotional and mental health. With this in mind, it's understandable why the controlled expression of Ciri's emotions—along with her Elder Blood power—would be the key to her success. In "The Laugh of the Medusa," Cixous explains that "by writing her self, woman will return to the body which has been more than confiscated from her, which has been turned into the uncanny stranger on display—the ailing or dead figure."[2] In other words, as a powerful sorceress and the "one and only hope" of the *Witcher* world, Ciri's sense of self is "confiscated" by the people around her. Even Geralt and Yennefer guide Ciri's destiny to coincide with their own. Ciri's self-expression, tied to her power, is objectified; she is an "uncanny stranger" to her own desires. But it is this sense of self that Ciri must come to reassert. Could any teenager or young adult, orphaned and traumatized by war, know herself except through extreme trial and error? Being able to make important decisions and learn from mistakes—in other words, being able to have what feminist philosophers would identify as agency (the right to self-govern) and autonomy (the feeling of being in control of one's own actions and their consequences)—and to realize her emotional power in real-world action eventually becomes how Ciri not only succeeds, but how she *survives*.

A Family of Strong Women

Ciri comes from a family of strong women, all of whom excel either in political or magical power, but who also find themselves oppressed by patriarchal power structures. Ciri's magical power debuts when she first expresses her true feelings free from her noble upbringing: by shouting in the bedchambers of her dying grandmother, Queen Calanthe, that she does not want to leave the castle or her grandmother's side. In this, Ciri is like her mother Pavetta, whose power is unveiled when her beloved suitor, Duny, is attacked by Calanthe's guard ("Of Banquets, Bastards, and Burials," season 1, episode 4). Both Ciri's and Pavetta's powers surface in stressful emotional situations, specifically when their autonomy and agency—already controlled throughout their lives by being nobles—is threatened. In fact, for both women, the "magic word" that affirms and represents their true emotional power is "NO!" ("The End's Beginning," season 1, episode 1). As feminist philosophers would point out, this is a particularly powerful shout for fictional females and their real-life readers given the importance of that word as signifying consent, especially when female autonomy and agency is up for debate. The Lion Cub of Cintra's first roar expresses raw emotions of rage and fear, newly formed from the trauma of war and witness to death. Subsequently, Ciri uses her newfound magical power against Nilfgaardian soldiers who try to capture her during their siege of Cintra. Her magical expression is directed and used against the forces that would oppress her.

This raw female utterance of autonomy and agency in *The Witcher* is reminiscent of the feminist idea of *écriture féminine*, coined by Cixous in "The Laugh of the Medusa."[3] With this phrase Cixous refers to the expression of women (especially through language and writing) that both prioritizes female experiences and challenges the patriarchal systems that dominate creation of meaning and systems of power.

Queen Calanthe most clearly embodies the *écriture féminine*, particularly when she addresses her soldiers and her court. Consider Calanthe's displeasure with the Law of Surprise during her daughter Pavetta's betrothing ball. Faced with her daughter marrying someone of the less-than-noble class (who also happens to be a cursed monster), while also having to concede to her deceased husband's decisions (in which she had no part) regarding their daughter's future, Calanthe expresses disgust, framing her criticism in two especially powerful feminist declarations. First, after Geralt steps in between two arrogant, competing lords, Calanthe rolls her eyes and, loudly in a tone of bored irritation, says, "All this because male tradition demands it." Second, later that same evening, after Pavetta and Duny's secret betrothal is revealed, Calanthe roars in rage that she "bow[s] to no law made by men who never bore a child" ("Of Banquets, Bastards, and Burials," season 1, episode 4). This is *The Witcher's* purest expression of feminist philosophy in general and Cixous's *écriture féminine* in particular. Calanthe boldly declares her resistance against patriarchal standards. She then roots her rebellion in the material reality of female biology: it's *her sex* that carries, grows, and births children, and thus continues humanity. She reasons that it's the cunning of males that develops oppressive systems of power meant to control the means of reproduction, something of which they contribute a relatively minor part.

However, Calanthe's words largely fall flat, too radical for her male subjects and not radical enough for her female subjects. As queen, she will not be subjected to patriarchal systems of power, but she *will* subject her daughter and granddaughter to those systems because it serves her agenda as queen. So, both Pavetta and Ciri are expected to passively sit through their respective banquets, which ultimately serve as political auctions where these coming-of-age princesses are meant to be sold off to the worthiest (wealthiest) bidder. Though Calanthe denigrates patriarchal laws that would treat her female heirs as pawns, she also perpetuates these laws, all while lamenting her loss of control. This makes Pavetta's and Ciri's powerful debuts into the world of magic all the more significant, as their chosen word of power stems from their raw (female) feelings and breaks with the patriarchal control that the court, and Calanthe complicitly, exerts over them.

The Witcher's Other Women

Ciri's and Geralt's adventures bring them into contact with other powerful women who serve as role models and foils for Ciri's emotional development. Many of these women are monsters that Geralt ends up slaying, either because they can't control their own powers or because patriarchal standards have dubbed them "monstrous." Other women are accepted in their powerful roles, but only when they've learned to control that power according to the will of the male-dominated political institutions of the Continent and because their power benefits the men around them. In the philosophical framing of Cixous, these are the "Medusas," the powerful women who the patriarchy has sought to quell. The emotional qualities of these strong women usually contrast with the personality of Geralt, who, with his witcher brothers, is a paragon of the idealized masculine qualities of self-discipline, stoicism, and calm professionalism. Witchers are said sometimes to feel no human emotions at all, a "virtue" that requires emotional reserve and restraint, if not outright repression, unlike the unrestrained (often feminine) monsters that they slay.

Nivellen's bruxa is an example of a female of uncontrolled power. Geralt's friend, Nivellen, is a former rapist, punished by a magical priestess with a curse that makes him take the form of a hideous beast. Nivellen's lover, Vereena, is a bruxa, a monster in the form of a young girl, who has vampiric powers and bloodlust. They live together in a remote manor and appear to be a truly loving couple ("A Grain of Truth," season 2, episode 1). Unfortunately, Vereena has man-eating tendencies and overwhelming powers. Vereena tries to control herself for Nivellen, who attempts to help her, but she is ultimately unable to stop herself from going on a rampage of mass murder. Her lack of control over her emotions and powers leaves Geralt (and Nivellen) to take up the paternalist role of protecting the community, and so they kill her. Vereena's tragedy, that of a truly out-of-control woman inadequately assisted and eventually disposed of by her male counterparts, contrasts with Ciri's success, as Ciri struggles with but eventually masters her powers, expressing them for personal and social benefits.

On the other hand, Princess Renfri, "Shrike," is an example of a female dubbed too powerful by the male authorities. According to the master sorcerer Stregobor, Renfri is a monster (like Vereena), born under a bad moon, cursed by black magic to do evil deeds ("The End's Beginning," season 1, episode 1). Stregobor's account seems convincing at first: Renfri has gathered an entourage of men to do her bidding and murder Stregobor, and, at one point, she even seduces Geralt himself. However, Renfri tells a different story in an equally convincing manner: Stregobor has falsely accused her of villainy, and she's merely defending herself against the sorcerer's prejudiced witch hunt. Geralt's perception of Renfri is strongly influenced by Stregobor's account of her—an example of the transmission of patriarchal fear of women with power. Unfortunately, Renfri struggles to tell her own side of the story, or even defend herself against Stregobor's violence, without herself falling into the role of "seductress" and "villainess." But, as feminist philosophers have observed, these are the very roles that Stregobor's patriarchal narrative has cast her in. Without being able to, in Cixous's terms, tell her own story, Renfri becomes a villain in and victim of the stories men tell about her. Geralt kills Renfri reluctantly, eventually realizing that he's been a pawn in Stregobor's scheme. Renfri's tragic story is a cautionary tale of what might happen to a powerful princess like Ciri who cannot speak in a patriarchal world that seeks to control and oppress her.

Falling somewhere between Renfri and Vereena is Princess Adda, daughter of King Foltest of Temeria. Cursed by her father's incest into becoming a striga, a man-eating monster, Princess Adda terrorizes her father's land ("Betrayer Moon," season 1, episode 3). Like the bruxa's power, Adda's striga power is completely uncontrollable, consuming her entire life and transforming her appearance monstrously. However, like Renfri, Adda is still a human girl on the inside. Instead of hunting and killing Adda, Geralt goes out of his way to break her curse and rescue her. This incident, and Geralt's willingness to go out of his way to help powerful young women, foreshadows the witcher's surrogate fatherhood of Ciri.

In contrast to these powerful women who are deemed "monstrous," sorceresses are women who've subordinated their powers to the standards of the Brotherhood of Sorcerers and the Kingdoms of the Continent. These women are permitted use of their powers only within the constraints of these patriarchal institutions. As an example of this balance between power and constraint, sorceresses are transformed into forever-young, if traditionally beautiful, icons of femininity, but they also have their uteruses removed, depriving them of reproductive abilities even as they gain their magical abilities. In this dual act, sorceresses satisfy their society's standards of femininity but are also stopped from passing on their powers to future generations. Despite this, Yennefer of Vengerberg and Triss Merigold both serve as female role models and parental surrogates for Ciri.[4] Triss identifies Ciri's powers and Yennefer hones them. Yennefer also comes to see Ciri as the child she never had, compensating for her own regrets about her inability to have children ("Bottled Appetites," season 1, episode 5). In fact, Yennefer eventually comes to call Ciri her "daughter."[5]

Incentives for preserving patriarchal power infect even the female sorceresses as they rise in authority. When they set up their own Lodge of Sorceresses, what one might expect to be a feminist institution, these powerful women end up replicating many of the power structures of the Brotherhood of Sorcerers, eventually intending to control the world using Ciri's magic in their service. The Lodge intends to control Ciri's reproduction, crossbreeding her genetics to start a magical bloodline for themselves, just as the patriarchs of the Nilfgaardian Empire had planned.[6] However, when they finally have Ciri unwillingly in their custody, the Lodge ends up voting to release Ciri. They let her leave to visit Geralt to "think the matter over" and return to them with an answer, even though they strongly suspect (and Ciri strongly implies) that she will probably never come back. Arch-Sorceress Philippa Eilhart casts the deciding vote to release Ciri and explains the decision by appealing to a balance of masculine traits with more feminine traits, "sentimentality, which is not always naïve ... gentleness and trust ... and heart," and the emotion of "hope" as her most important deciding factors.[7]

Cixous, and other feminist philosophers, would approve. This vote at the Lodge is a moment of female cooperation and collaboration based on women's shared experiences, especially contrasted against the contentious and violent masculine forms of expression in the world, like war. Cixous would call this:

> *Woman for women.* There always remains in woman that force which produces/is produced by the other—in particular, the other woman.... Everything will be changed once woman gives woman to the other woman.... It is necessary and sufficient that the best of herself be given to woman by another woman for her to be able to love herself and return in love the body that was "born" to her.[8]

In other words, in a world controlled by men, it's crucial for women to support other women and to encourage other women to express themselves in ways that aren't framed in masculine terms, or in ways that reproduce masculinist power structures. Ciri is "given woman"—that is, given the encouragement and opportunity to embrace her femaleness and stand independent in her own expression and sense of self as an emotional, powerful woman—and thus becomes the woman she was always meant to be, the Lady of the Lake, the Lady of Space and Time, or ... simply Cirilla.

A Triumph of Feminine Expression

As *The Witcher* saga progresses and Ciri develops her powers, she becomes the most powerful being in the universe—maybe in the multiverse—capable of dimension-hopping via magic. In her last adventures, it is revealed that Ciri is actually the "Lady of the Lake" of Arthurian legend, the powerful demi-goddess that gives King Arthur his sword Excalibur. Her power transcends even the bounds of the world of the *Witcher* and allows her to enter other narrative worlds (even, it's implied, our *real* world).

However, in the climactic moment of the series, it is not Ciri's magical power but her emotional power that triumphs. The emperor Emhyr var Emreis of Nilfgaard captures Ciri, Geralt, and Yennefer, sentences the latter two to death, and plans to marry and impregnate Ciri, in spite of this being incest—the emperor is Ciri's biological father, unbeknownst to her. The plan is heavily paternalistic in that the emperor intends to birth a magical dynasty to rule the Continent and protect it from prophesized catastrophe, but this ultimately ends up being a somewhat contrived rationalization to abuse a female body for the self-serving perpetuation of patriarchy. However, Ciri manages to persuade the emperor, her father, to have a change of heart. Although trained as a "witcher girl," Ciri does not use her training to escape or resist or retaliate; instead, she goes against Geralt's advice, presents herself before the emperor, and simply *cries*.[9] This emotional appeal softens the emperor's heart and, realizing that he cannot bring himself to harm his once beloved daughter, the emperor releases Ciri and spares the lives of her surrogate father and mother, Geralt and Yennefer. In the end, Ciri's true power seems inseparable from this expression of emotion, and even the rationalizations of the patriarchal empire itself cannot withstand her.

Thus, even though the titular character of *The Witcher* saga may be the embodiment of masculine emotionless reserve, the narrative arc of the saga bends toward the power of expressive emotion, especially in its uniquely female forms. Like Ciri's own dimension-hopping, ideas can dimension-hop as well. Perhaps in our own world, the movement toward empathy and understanding will become a more important trend, especially with the ascendance of feminist philosophies into mainstream culture, as we increasingly see feeling and femininity achieving greater and greater power.

Notes

1. Hélène Cixous, "The Laugh of the Medusa," trans. Keith Cohen and Paula Cohen, *Signs* 1 (1976), 875–893.
2. Cixous, "The Laugh of the Medusa," 880.
3. Cixous, "The Laugh of the Medusa," 880.
4. Andrzej Sapkowski, *Blood of Elves*, trans. Danusia Stok (New York: Orbit Books, 2008), 34–35.
5. Andrzej Sapkowski, *The Lady of the Lake*, trans. David French (New York: Gollancz, 2017), 492.
6. Andrzej Sapkowski, *Baptism of Fire*, trans. David French (New York: Orbit Books, 2022), 36–40.
7. Sapkowski, *The Lady of the Lake*, 492.
8. Cixous, "The Laugh of the Medusa," 881.
9. Sapkowski, *The Lady of the Lake*, 399–400.

RACE AND CULTURE

12

Race and Racism in the World of *The Witcher*

Gerald Browning

The feudal world of Geralt of Rivia has very clear social dividing lines. Because of the system of castes and classes, knights and lords, kings and queens, a person's lineage is important and conveys information about them to others. The role of the stoic warrior Geralt is to stalk the land, dispatching monsters for pay. But humans may be the worst monsters on the Continent. Why? Because, as the Netflix series shows, humans are routinely guilty of prejudice, racism, and discrimination.

Witchers Are a Minority

Communities on the Continent often call on witchers to help them slay beasts rampaging in their lands and destroying their homes. Witchers are paid well, but there is a price to pay for being a witcher. The elixir that endows Geralt with superhuman strength, speed, and powers also alters his complexion, giving him an inhuman, even monstrous appearance. Because of this visible change, humans view him as something less than human. The first episode of the Netflix series begins with Geralt entering the town of Blaviken after doing battle with a kikimore. He goes into a bar where he's insulted for being different, and several men try to pick a fight with him. Geralt, though, chooses not to take their bait.

Many times in the series, the same thing occurs: Geralt is targeted for abuse by those who judge him for his appearance or for his job. Humans willingly use the talents of witchers, but they do not trust them. A witcher uses magic, and magical beings are usually shunned outright. Geralt, of course, uses magic—witcher signs like quen which projects a shield, or, in the video games, a glowing sword—in order to protect people or dispatch a creature.

Unlike Geralt, humans are quick to execute the creatures they encounter. We see this when Geralt is hired to go on a dragon hunt with the enigmatic Borch Three Jackdaws ("Rare Species," season 1, episode 6). While on this

The Witcher and Philosophy: Toss a Coin to Your Philosopher, First Edition.
Edited by Matthew Brake and Kevin S. Decker.

hunt, he is met by other dragon hunters, including Sir Eyck of Denesle. The inept Sir Eyck seems to be the embodiment of a human who has yet to learn how to coexist with nonhumans. Upon seeing a hungry-but-not-dangerous hirikka stumbling from a bush, he is quick to kill the animal. Sir Eyck is proud of his achievement, even though it's painfully obvious that no one else shares that pride. Eyck is an ineffective hunter, but he is an effective example of what many people are like in the kingdoms of the Continent. His ignorance is a clear reflection of the bigotry prevalent in many episodes of the series. He seems to have a view about how the world works that excludes unfamiliar beings from importance.

One very powerful point to note about this episode is that though it presents no discussion about race and culture, the flaws and errors of the Eyck character were focused on power and status. In "Sociology of Racism," Matthew Clair and Jeffrey S. Denis define racism as "processes and structures that are implicated in the reproduction of racial inequality."[1] They also mention that bias may occur due to beliefs and that the actions that stem from this can be seen as expressions of power. White privilege, according to Frances E. Kendall, is when white people "[have] greater access to power and resources than people of color [in the same situation] do."[2] White privilege has little to do with race, but everything to do with social access and status. Ignorance is a direct result of a lack of experiences of racial injustice, and we see this privilege embodied in Eyck. After Eyck kills the forest creature, and heaps praise upon himself for killing the "beast," Geralt proceeds to tell him that the creature was no threat. Being a member of the aristocracy, Eyck is obviously in a very privileged group and Eyck refuses to listen to Geralt.

The Anger of the Elves

The first season of *The Witcher* highlights the prejudices people have against Geralt and other witchers. In season 2, we see the storyline shifting to discrimination against elves. The historical backdrop for this is a past war that took place between humans, elves, and other nonhuman species. (Some nonhumans now form an antihuman guerilla force, the Scoia'tael.) The humans conquered the land, meaning that elves, gnomes, halflings, and dwarves were dispersed to find homes for themselves. The elves, for example, are now found in wooded areas and excluded from the major human towns and villages like Oxenfurt, Redania, or Nilfgaard.

In Sapkowski's world, racism isn't based on skin color. This parallels the rejection of the idea that race is a "fixed category" in Critical Race Theory. As the sociologists Michael Omi and Howard Winant argue, race is "unstable and decentered" and is primarily defined and transformed by "political struggle."[3] In the Northern Kingdoms, it appears that this "political struggle" came in the form of epic war. In "Four Marks" (season 1, episode 2), Geralt and Jaskier are captured by elves who are quite resentful of humans. Filavandrel, leader of the elves, painfully mentions the tense history that the humans had with elves: "My elders worked with humans, but the humans betrayed the elves. When they fought back, they were slaughtered. Humans called this ... the Great Cleansing." Notably, Filavandrel mentions "a mass grave." Filavandrel's words echo the words used to describe the Holocaust, the systematic extermination of European Jews during Adolf Hitler's reign of tyranny. Filavandrel addresses both Jaskier and Geralt as humans, but Geralt is quick to reply, "Don't call me human." His understated tone belies the anger that we know he feels toward humans for ostracizing him. If Geralt ever felt connected to humanity before, he doesn't now. This simple line may seem innocuous, but Geralt distances himself from humanity more and more.

In *The Witcher*, racial lines aren't drawn by skin color or even by geography, but by species. The elixir that Geralt drinks turns his skin pale and his eyes black. These are obvious signs that he is not quite human. Nonetheless Geralt moves among humans and nonhumans with some ease: he's not human enough to be protected by humanity, but also not nonhuman enough to be considered an obvious threat. In lands where there is much disdain for his profession, Geralt is treated as a necessary evil.

The Political Power of Elven Identity

Yennefer of Vengerberg, with her elven identity, is another character who enjoys power over humans, yet who is also feared by them. In season 2, Yennefer is captured and interrogated by elves. She tries to tell her inquisitors that she has some elf blood in her, but the elves are resistant to accepting her. This should not surprise us. In season 1, we found out that Yennefer is part elf, but nonetheless she was rebuked by the elf ruler Francesca Findabair: "Do you sing our songs? Do you honor our elders? Have you ever shed a tear for anything elven? You are no elf." In both Geralt and Jaskier's capture as well as Yennefer and Fringilla's capture, their elven captors show pride in their own culture. It's important to note that both Francesca and Filavandrel make a connection between elven identity and a shared culture and history. This kind of effort at "self-naming" is a move to recapture political power in the real world.[4] In the Northern Kingdoms, it's a way for the elves to reclaim their identity and their pride. As season 2 opens, Yennefer becomes sympathetic to the plight of the elves and seeks to help them.

But season 2 also ramps up the tension between the species. In "Redanian Intelligence" (season 2, episode 4), a human has scrawled the words "a good elf is a dead elf" on the wall of a town populated by humans. Graffiti drawings of pigs with elf ears are peppered around the town as well. The dehumanization of people through racist drawings is nothing new. Just consider the caricatures of Jewish or African people with exaggerated noses, lips, or teeth. It's not just words and pictures. Elves tied together in rope and chains are led away by the local government. One of the elves needs to relieve himself, and the guard humiliates him by making him uri-nate in his pants. The elf has a look of utter pain written on his face. This seems to be a common event, since many of the human citizens either treat the elves with scorn or ignore the scene altogether, choosing to look away. The imagery of chained elves being led in a single-file line parallels old rep-resentations of enslaved African people being brought to the new world in shackles. They, too, were subjugated to intense horrors and humiliations.

Race seems to be the reason for the discrimination against elves, but it is also tied to power. In the series, we frequently see kings and queens wrestling to retain power and control of their kingdoms, and with this comes the subjugation of others. Consider how the settlements of elves seem to be relegated to small, hidden, forested spaces on the outskirts of human areas. The tension between the elves and the humans builds until we see emotions erupt in revolt and chaos near the end of season 2. Juxtaposed with the slowly building tension between classes and races, we see the political intrigue of the humans and sorcerers. With the living envi-ronments of the classes and the dividing lines of battle between the humans and the elves, social and political power dynamics erupt into a full-scale war. Even from the beginning of the first season (where we see the training of the witches and mages), the political dividing lines are being drawn.

Yennefer's Dilemma

Yennefer of Vengerberg had humble beginnings. She was born with physical deformities and as a result was abused by her family. After she displayed magical prowess as a young woman, she was sold to Tissaia de Vries, a rector at Aretuza. According to Tissaia, Yennefer had "an aptitude for channeling chaos." Some of her prowess came from being a quarter-elf. (Her mother was half-elf.) In the Netflix series, Yennefer constantly finds a need to move between the elven and human worlds, all the while realizing that she does not really belong in either. She states the philosophy that helps her to do this: "The most important thing they teach you at Aretuza isn't magic! It's to make people in power believe anything you want them to. Do anything you want them to!" ("Redanian Intelligence," season 2, episode 4). However, controlling magic and powerful people comes at quite a cost for her.

Many of Yennefer's interactions with humans and elves feature attempts to manipulate them in some way. Not surprisingly, her powers as a sor-ceress make her feel ostracized from humanity. Ruing the loss of her womb as part of the cost of her magic, Yennefer is always desperately searching for a way to have children. Much like Geralt, her self-isolation seems to aim at protecting her from getting too close to anyone. Of course, this is part of what attracts these two characters to one another.

In a world where lineage and "pure blood" history is very important to personal identity, Yennefer is pushed away from both groups. According to the philosopher Naomi Zack, mixed-race identities can act as a "breakdown" in social order, or serve as a viable threat, inciting acts of racism.[5] In a society that includes racial distinctions such as blackness and whiteness, a spectrum of "others" can act to reject these designations. As a person who easily moves within both races, Yennefer seems to represent such a threat, and indeed, she seems intent on destabilizing the power of the ruling class. The fact that this represents a social power dynamic again suggests that racism in *The Witcher* is a social construct that has less to do with bloodlines and cultural identity than it does with creating rifts and divisions in classes, which can (and often does) cause power struggles.

Parallels

Subjugation, prejudice, power, and inequity are all too real in our world. However, when we see these same notions through the lens of a fantasy world, we can look at these sobering topics a little differently. Geralt, Jaskier, Yennefer, and others can cause us to be more reflective when we see the faults of our societies reflected in the lives of these characters. Yes, it is true that Geralt has encountered dragons, strigas, and demons, but the humans of Nilfgaard are not immune to dark temptations—they are not exempt from being called "monsters." The parallels between the world of *The Witcher* and our world show how racism, classism, and other prejudices can be based more on power and society than on physical characteristics of certain groups. The American Association of Biological Anthropologists agree with the premises of Critical Race Theory, noting that "race" and "racism" are social constructs. Race, they say, "was invented to assign some groups to perpetual low status, while others were permitted access to privilege, power, and wealth."[6]

In the real world, prejudiced and racist groups preach racial purity and the evils of racial mixing, but in *The Witcher* we see how inessential "pure blood" is to being strong and noble. Yennefer is a powerful character who is ostracized due to her bloodline, but as we've seen, Naomi Zack's idea of how mixed-race identities can destabilize the current notion of race suggests that the mere presence of a person who can live between the different races (and in essence two different worlds) can promote a different kind of perception in all of us. Such people create a blurred line between the races, and Yennefer demonstrates that her lineage is strength and not weakness time and again.

Stories in the fantasy genre operate in worlds whose rules are quite easy for us to feel disconnected from. However, when we connect with characters we feel some attachment to them. Many of us appreciate Geralt's ability to disconnect from his own emotions: those who have been discriminated against might feel this as well. In fact, Ciri mentions that she wants to be a witcher for that very reason. The plain fact is that characters like Geralt and Yennefer embody the best and worst in us. The Witcherverse is not so unlike our world. How its people deal with prejudice and hatred may be different, but they help to create a world that we can connect to. Their fears become our own, but their aspirations can become ours as well. And this is what makes the world of *The Witcher* such a compelling one.

Notes

1. Matthew Clair and Jeffrey S. Denis, "Sociology of Racism," in James D. Wright ed., *The International Encyclopedia of the Social and Behavioral Sciences*, 2nd ed. (Amsterdam: Elsevier, 2015), 857–863.
2. Cory Collins, "What Is White Privilege, Really?," Southern Poverty Law Center: Learning for Justice 60, Fall 2018, at https://www.learningforjustice.org/magazine/fall-2018/what-is-white-privilege-really.
3. Michael Omi and Howard Winant, *Racial Formation in the United States*, 3rd ed. (New York: Routledge, 2015), 110.
4. M. Keith Claybrook, "Black Identity and the Power of Self-Naming," Black Perspectives, September 10, 2021, at https://www.aaihs.org/black-identity-and-the-power-of-self-naming.
5. Naomi Zack, *Race and Mixed Race* (Philadelphia: Temple University Press, 1993), 6.
6. American Association of Biological Anthropologists, "AABA Statement on Race & Racism," AABA, 2023, at https://bioanth.org/about/position-statements/aapa-statement-race-and-racism-2019.

13

Disadvantage, Demeaning, and Power
Is Geralt of Rivia Being Discriminated Against?

Wulf Loh

As a professional monster hunter, Geralt of Rivia often meets with fear and contempt. Indeed, the fear of villagers and peasants (but also local militia or even warlords and members of organized crime syndicates) is often palpable. For example, at the beginning of *The Witcher 3: Wild Hunt*, Geralt encounters a gang of the Baron's men-at-arms at the Inn at the Crossroads. They interrogate him, and if the player chooses the answer, "I'm a witcher," their leader responds, "Don't touch him. Don't even look at him. Worse than lepers, that lot." In much the same way in the short story collection "The Sword of Destiny," Geralt responds to a dinner invitation, "There are those who prefer the company of lepers to that of a witcher."[1]

The mistreatment Geralt experiences—the hostility, taunts, and insults, the ridicule and denigrations—are an everyday fact of his life. But does that actually make him a victim of discrimination? Is he really an outcast, an underdog in the societies of *The Witcher* franchise, marginalized and oppressed by a powerful majority within those societies?

Why should we even bother asking whether Geralt is discriminated against? The answer has to do with the success of the franchise. The video games have sold more than 75 million copies, and the Netflix series broke several viewing records, with the second season gathering more than 142 million views in just a few days, while the third season had about 30 million views in the first two weeks. This means that a lot of people have been exposed to *The Witcher* on a global scale, internalizing many messages from the franchise. The worry is that the "public pedagogy" of *The Witcher* might encourage a distorted view of how discrimination occurs in real life.[2]

The Witcher and Philosophy: Toss a Coin to Your Philosopher, First Edition.
Edited by Matthew Brake and Kevin S. Decker.
© 2025 John Wiley & Sons, Inc. Published 2025 by John Wiley & Sons, Inc.

Mistreating Geralt of Rivia

As a group of professional monster hunters in a fantasy world similar to the European Middle Ages, witchers hunt down deadly monsters for money. To match the powerful, often supernatural abilities of these monsters, witchers are trained rigorously and ruthlessly from an early age and must undergo the "Trial of the Grasses" in their early teens. During this process, they're given a series of magical potions with such severe side effects that a majority of the children don't survive. For this reason, witchers are mostly recruited from orphans or children sold by their financially desperate parents to the witcher schools.

Over the course of several weeks of severe intoxication, the survivors of the potions experience physical mutations that ultimately give them superhuman abilities. These include faster reflexes, greater muscular strength, endurance, and speed, enhanced sensory perception, especially smell and hearing, night vision, resistance to enchantment, hypnosis, disease, and poisons, faster wound healing, a slowed aging process, and the ability to cast basic combat spells. In turn, their eyes become visibly cat-like, and there are changes to their bone marrow and hormones.

So witchers fall between being heroes endowed with superhuman abilities, on the one hand, and trained professionals, on the other. In important aspects they are akin to modern-day superheroes. For one, the status of "witcher" is not entirely a self-chosen role, not a profession that could, in principle, be changed or abandoned. Rather, to be a witcher is a social status defined by features that witchers themselves have very little influence over. Witchers can't hide the physical telltale signs (especially the cat's eyes, but also, for some witchers, the white hair) under a superhero costume or mask. A secret "day" identity different from their heroic "night" identity is not possible for witchers. As a (high) fantasy kind of superhero, Geralt faces the same fate in many respects: "The superhero is necessarily an outsider, unlike ordinary mortals: super is, by definition, marginal."[3]

For Geralt of Rivia, many of his social interactions earn him a mixture of fear and contempt. He describes his professional interactions: "I did my job. I quickly learned how. I'd ride up to village enclosures or town pickets and wait. If they spat, cursed and threw stones I rode away. If someone came out to give me a commission, I'd carry it out."[4]

Geralt has every reason to be wary. Throughout his adventures, villagers, soldiers, and others often react with hostility or even disgust. Geralt experiences this mistreatment particularly from the poorer and less educated part of the population. But are these taunts and hostilities really instances of discrimination? After all, there's such a stark power asymmetry between witchers and the general population that the term "discrimination" doesn't seem to truly apply.

This is even more so, since people of power all over the Continent tend not to hold many of the common folks' prejudices against Geralt. Even if witchers' interactions with mages, kings, warlords, and others are mostly based on a service relationship, it would be an exaggeration to call Geralt a true outsider in circles of wealth, education, and power.

Discrimination

Clearly, people "discriminate between" Geralt and non-witcher residents of the Continent, but that is not the issue here. We need to be concerned with whether people "discriminate against" Geralt, as this is morally wrong.[5] In this wrongful sense, discrimination means treating people worse because of their membership in one social group rather than another, if this treatment is unjustified.[6] For example, it would be unjustified (and unjustifiable) to put all women in jail just because of their gender-based group membership. This would clearly be an injustice. What makes this injustice a form of *discrimination* is that the kind of group membership in question can't be justified as deserving such treatment.[7]

You could define a group based on a single shared characteristic of its members (the group of car owners) or a bundle of characteristics (the group of criminals), but the groups that suffer discrimination are somehow different. The difference is that they are "socially salient" groups.[8] A group is socially salient "if perceived membership of it is important to the structure of social interactions across a wide range of social contexts."[9] In other words, a socially salient group plays significant roles in many social practices. For example, the group "women" is socially salient in this sense, because it comes with many role expectations that are widespread throughout the practices of society. On the other hand, being a member of the group "car owners" makes important differences in a few aspects of society, but it lacks significance in many others.

To sum up, discrimination is: (i) treating someone worse than others; (ii) this treatment is unjustified; and (iii) based on the membership in a socially salient group.

Let's use this framework to determine whether Geralt has been discriminated against. Most of the mistreatment Geralt and witchers in general receive is based on a mixture of xenophobia, or suspicion of outsiders, and fear of their supernatural abilities. Let's use the groups "stranger" and "witcher" for our consideration and ask: Are both of these socially salient?

Concerning the group of "strangers," the difficulty lies in the question of who precisely *belongs* to this group. After all, everyone is a stranger somewhere. But if Geralt is a stranger in some contexts, but not in others, can this group category even be attributed to him? Even though the group "stranger" may be socially salient, each member is only a temporary member in very few contexts.

Against this, one could say two things: First, Geralt and the other witchers travel most of the time and so they are strangers in most contexts they encounter. Second, the definition of "socially salient group" doesn't require that each member has to be taken as a member in *all* contexts. Granted, this is the case for many of the paradigmatic socially salient groups that are typically subjects of discrimination, such as those based on race, gender, religious affiliation, sexual orientation, and so on. However, this doesn't have to be the case, and Geralt could very well be discriminated against in his role as "stranger."

In the case of the group "witcher," the question is not whether Geralt belongs to this group, but rather whether it is a *socially salient* group at all. To count, it would have to be "important to the structure of social interactions across a wide range of social contexts,"[10] as we've seen before. For this to be the case, most inhabitants of the *Witcher* world must have either interacted with witchers, or at least heard about them. One or the other is necessary in order to form "reactive attitudes," attitudes toward witchers that will determine how others react toward them.[11] And this seems to be the case, since most inhabitants of the Continent have an idea what a witcher is. Witchers are often desperately sought after to get local monster infestations under control; therefore, they are a necessary fact of life for most people, although many may have only heard fairy tales or scary stories about them.

But are those reactive attitudes also formed "across a wide range of social contexts"? After all, most people in Geralt's world almost never encounter a witcher. Their everyday lives are structured around very different problems and social practices. Here, we have two options: social salience depends either on the range of contexts, or on "the importance in the contexts it actually structures."[12] So it could be the case that the group category "witcher" does not play an important part in most people's daily lives, but they are very important in some people's lives. After all, monster infestations are still a very real and existential threat to most people, especially in small villages without the military infrastructure to get rid of them. Also, treating Geralt as a witcher will create expectations for future interactions with him, however infrequent they may be. Kasper Lippert-Rasmussen acknowledges this perspective when he writes: "Being constantly reminded of membership in a certain group increases the significance to social interactions of perceived membership of this group."[13]

If this is true, both the categories "stranger" and "witcher" are socially salient groups, and this means that Geralt could be discriminated against as a member of both of them.

Blame Geralt?

But before we ask whether Geralt has suffered discrimination, let's see whether others' negative attitudes toward Geralt could be somehow justified. If so, the treatment he receives would not be discriminating. Do villagers simply offer reactions to witchers' hostile, arrogant, unlawful, or even violent actions? If they did, or if witchers typically acted in an adversarial manner, others might be justified to respond in kind.

Geralt is often grumpy, taciturn, and not very sympathetic, but his interactions are seldom, if ever, enough to incite the hostile or denigrating reactions he often faces. But what about generalizations about members of the groups "stranger" or "witcher"? Could they not justify him being treated in this way as a typical representative of these groups? Many philosophers argue against using such stereotypes and statistical generalizations as a fair assessment of an individual. They claim that these kinds of generalizations fail to respect individuals in a morally adequate way.[14] Such a statistic only tells us something about a possible *correlation* between a certain behavior and membership in a certain group, and not about the causes of the behavior.[15] It might be the case that group membership is not the cause for the behavior. In this case, members of such a group would be punished for a characteristic that's not the locus for their behavior. Therefore, a risk assessment in the form "member of the group of strangers/ witchers is more likely to interact in a hostile or denigrating way" is morally objectionable.

What's more, most "risk assessments" of Geralt as a witcher or a stranger are based either on hearsay or anecdotal evidence. They're far from statistically sound, but rather are mere prejudice. Villagers don't seem to weigh the probability that Geralt will start hostile actions nor the potential amount of harm his actions might cause against the resulting disadvantage for Geralt *in each individual case*. This suggests villagers and soldiers don't treat Geralt as an individual in a morally adequate way. And even if it was true that the average encounter with witchers or strangers was more dangerous than other encounters, it would be morally wrong to mistreat Geralt based on the sparse evidence and without proper risk assessment for each single interaction.

Discrimination as Demeaning

So far, we've ticked off all the boxes that are required in order to say that Geralt is discriminated against: he is a member of at least two socially salient groups, he is being mistreated *as* a member of these groups, and this mistreatment is unjustified. But does this mistreatment really disadvantage him? After all, despite being an outsider, Geralt occupies a comparatively prominent social position in his world. Not only does he have many acquaintances and friendships among the wealthy and powerful, but he also performs a service that is desperately needed—to get rid of monsters. Also, his superhuman abilities further privilege him in a world dominated by physical violence.

Given all these advantages, it seems clear that the taunts, insults, hostilities, and denigrations do not disadvantage him in terms of money or status.

But what other kinds of disadvantages does he face? Potentially, the mistreatments could cause psychological injuries, such as damage to his self-esteem.[16] Axel Honneth claims that we as human beings need different forms of recognition—a kind of social validation—in order to develop and sustain a "positive relation-to-self."[17] One could argue that, by frequently mistreating Geralt, others withhold this kind of recognition. On the other hand, Geralt seems mostly unfazed by the taunts and petty insults, knowing that they are the result of ignorance and fear. Of course, his withdrawn demeanor could be a result of a long-term psychological scarring caused by these mistreatments, but nothing he says or does leads us to that conclusion.

If Geralt is not affected by the mistreatment, then it seems that there is no wrong done to him, and therefore he is not discriminated against. But this doesn't have to be the case. At this point, it's worth taking a look at Deborah Hellman's concept of "demeaning," which focuses on the discriminatory act itself, rather than the consequences of such discrimination in terms of disadvantage: "Rather than emphasize the effect (psychological or social) produced by classification, I claim that sometimes it is wrong to classify because of what one expresses—regardless of whether the person or people affected feel demeaned, stigmatized, or degraded."[18]

According to Hellman, what counts as "demeaning" depends on whether a particular behavior has a "loaded meaning" in a society.[19] "Loaded meaning" here indicates that the insulting, denigrating, or hostile nature of that behavior is known within that society, particularly if there is a long-standing history of discrimination with respect to that behavior. (Think about use of the N-word, for example.) In order to demean, a behavior has to be widely understood as denying the demeaned "equal moral worth."[20] Thus, even if there was no long history of discrimination against witchers, spitting at them, throwing stones, and refusing to serve Geralt would still demean him insofar as those actions are culturally used and understood as demeaning in the world of *The Witcher*.

This kind of demeaning behavior *expresses* a denial of equal moral worth, rather than having a disadvantaging psychological effect on its target. So even if Geralt is not harmed in his sense of self-respect by the mistreatments he faces, as an act of demeaning they effectively reduce him to a person of lesser moral worth—and this marks a significant disadvantage.

Hellman insists, though, that any discrimination in the form of demeaning must be based on an *asymmetry of power*: "To demean, rather than merely to insult, requires a certain degree of power."[21] It is the difference in power or status between the demeaning and the demeaned that establishes a form of subordination that's necessary for discrimination: "To demean thus requires not only that one express disrespect for the equal humanity of the other but also that one be in a position such that *this expression can subordinate the other*."[22]

Geralt, though, is in no way powerless, at least not with respect to those who typically mistreat him. On the contrary, he is far more physically capable and knowledgable, and typically has a lot higher social status. Due to his almost complete self-sufficiency, he is hardly affected physically by the social exclusion he sometimes experiences. On the contrary, the people who mistreat him are dependent on him to fight the monsters that haunt their communities. And so, perhaps surprisingly given all we've said so far in favor of Geralt as a victim of discrimination, his taunters and oppressors have no position of power or status to demean him and, according to Hellman, cannot be discriminating against him.

Imbalance of Power

In conclusion, it seems that Geralt's interactions with others lack the power asymmetry we'd need to see in order to say that he is really discriminated against. On the contrary, Geralt is much more powerful than the odd village dweller or soldier. To be sure, these mistreatments are unjust and morally wrong. However, they don't amount to the particularly severe and problematic form of injustice that we call *discrimination*.

In the real world, victims of discriminations are typically already marginalized, subjected to power asymmetries, and therefore often face multiple oppressions (intersectionality) that they in many cases have no means to counter, avoid, or defend against. In this sense, discrimination is a particularly severe form of injustice. Portraying a superhero-like individual such as Geralt as a victim of discrimination potentially obscures these realities and makes discrimination in our world seem less severe or dangerous. This worry has been raised before about narratives of racial prejudice against superheros, such as in Marvel's *X-Men*.[23]

Superheroes are not the canonical victims of discrimination, they typically have much more agency. This is particularly true for Geralt, as he is a fantasy genre superhero in a world with comparatively little centralization of power and relatively sparse law enforcement. For this reason, it's important to carefully evaluate fictions that feature apparent discrimination against superhumans and point out the similarities and differences to real, everyday cases of discrimination. Ultimately, it also involves making clear when discrimination doesn't occur, even if we think we've seen it. As a matter of justice, this is not only about treating like cases alike and unlike cases unlike, but also about overuse of the word "discrimination" that can eventually diminish its moral edge.

Notes

1. Andrzej Sapkowski, *Sword of Destiny*, trans. David French (London: Gollancz, 2015), 8–9.
2. Brian D. Schultz, Jennifer A. Sandlin, and Jake Burdick, eds., *Handbook of Public Pedagogy: Education and Learning beyond Schooling* (New York: Routledge, 2010).

3. Helene Shugart, "Supermarginal," *Communication and Critical/Cultural Studies* 6, no. 1 (2009), 98–102.
4. Andrzej Sapkowski, *The Last Wish*, trans. Danusia Stok (London: Gollancz, 2010), 118.
5. Contrary to Lippert-Rasmussen, I reject a purely descriptive (in his words "generic") definition of discrimination. Kasper Lippert-Rasmussen, *Born Free and Equal? A Philosophical Inquiry into the Nature of Discrimination* (New York: Oxford University Press, 2013), 15–16. In my view, "discrimination" is a term that has descriptive and evaluative parts. Cf. Bernard Williams, *Ethics and the Limits of Philosophy* (Cambridge, MA: Harvard University Press, 1985).
6. See Kasper Lippert-Rasmussen, *Born Free and Equal?* and Andrew Altman, "Discrimination," in *The Stanford Encyclopedia of Philosophy* at https://plato.stanford.edu/archives/win2020/entries/discrimination.
7. There are other ways to think about discrimination; for a different approach, see Deborah Hellman, *When Is Discrimination Wrong?* (Cambridge, MA: Harvard University Press, 2008).
8. Lippert-Rasmussen, *Born Free and Equal?*, 30.
9. Benjamin Eidelson argues against the concept of social salience in *Discrimination and Disrespect* (Oxford: Oxford University Press, 2015), 30.
10. Lippert-Rasmussen, *Born Free and Equal?*, 30.
11. Peter Strawson, *Freedom and Resentment and Other Essays* (London: Routledge, 1962), 66.
12. Lippert-Rasmussen, *Born Free and Equal?*, 31.
13. Lippert-Rasmussen, *Born Free and Equal?*, 31.
14. See David Edmonds, *Caste Wars: A Philosophy of Discrimination* (New York: Routledge, 2014), and Benjamin Eidelson, "Treating People as Individuals," in Deborah Hellman and Sophia Moreau eds., *Philosophical Foundations of Discrimination Law* (Oxford: Oxford University Press, 2013), 203–227.
15. See Laurence Thomas, "Statistical Badness," *Journal of Social Philosophy* 23, no. 1 (1992), 30–41.
16. See Larry Alexander, "What Makes Wrongful Discrimination Wrong?," *University of Pennsylvania Law Review* 141 (1992), 149–219, 195–197.
17. Axel Honneth, *The Struggle for Recognition: The Moral Grammar of Social Conflicts* (Cambridge, MA: MIT Press, 1996), 118. Benjamin Eidelson calls this an "interest-regarding concept" of discrimination that takes discrimination to be dependent on "the interests of the discriminatees in being treated one way or another." See Eidelson, *Discrimination and Disrespect*, 34.
18. Hellman, *When Is Discrimination Wrong?*, 27.
19. Hellman, *When Is Discrimination Wrong?*, 32.
20. Hellman, *When Is Discrimination Wrong?*, 29.
21. Hellman, *When Is Discrimination Wrong?*, 36.
22. Hellman, *When Is Discrimination Wrong?*, 35; emphasis added.
23. Demby, Gene, "Who Gets to Be a Superhero? Race and Identity in Comics," Code Switch, January 11, 2014, https://www.npr.org/sections/codeswitch/2014/01/11/261449394/who-gets-to-be-a-superhero-race-and-identity-in-comics.

14

"I'm Part Elf, I'm Part Human"
Understanding Racism in *The Witcher*

Edwardo Pérez

CIRI: If I can offer something different, a way forward that doesn't divide, but unites. I'm part elf, I'm part human. I understand both because I am both and that is my strength.
"Shaerrawedd" (season 3, episode 1)

In Netflix's adaptation of Andrzej Sapkowski's *Witcher* series (including the prequel series *Blood Origin*), the issue of racism emerges through a humans-versus-elves dynamic.[1] In the show's mythology, humans are the initial aggressors, arriving on the Continent after the Conjunction of the Spheres and assuming dominance over the elves. However, as *Blood Origin* depicts, elves weren't entirely peaceful and innocent when they had the Continent to themselves. They were tribal and prejudiced long before the arrival of humans. And in *The Witcher*, elves are hateful toward humans as much as humans are toward elves.

It's significant that both humans and elves practice and experience racism. It's also significant that Netflix's adaptation includes a diverse cast in the portrayal of both humans and elves. This could be seen as masking racism or as an attempt to equate both sides—with humans and elves being racially diverse and sharing the blame of racism. Certainly, racism isn't always black and white. However, if we consider Ibram X. Kendi's observation that racism is rooted in power—not just individual power but also systemic power—we see that racism on *The Witcher* exists through the choices characters make to either maintain power or thwart it. In other words, racism in *The Witcher* isn't about assigning blame. Rather, it's about understanding how power is wielded oppressively over others. Considering Kendi's observations, it's also about understanding that racism isn't inevitable; it can be changed through antiracism.[2] From this perspective, *The Witcher* becomes a cautionary tale, illustrating how racism can infect those who choose to embrace it. At the same time, *The Witcher* offers the possibility of the change Kendi

The Witcher and Philosophy: Toss a Coin to Your Philosopher, First Edition.
Edited by Matthew Brake and Kevin S. Decker.

calls for, especially through the character Ciri, who seeks a different way forward for elves and humans.

Of course, being racist or antiracist isn't simple. As *The Witcher* also illustrates, those fighting to keep power often have armies. And whether you're a witcher, a mage, a bard, an elf queen, or a hybrid princess, fighting against those in power requires more than just elixirs, spells, catchy songs, and prophecies. To better understand this, let's begin with the issue of *colorism*.

"You don't deserve the air you breathe"

Racism is easiest to see and understand in terms of skin color, the most obvious physical trait distinguishing groups of people. As Kendi explains, "Colorism is a collection of racist policies that cause inequities between Light people and Dark people, and these inequities are sustained by racist ideas about Light and Dark people."[3] For Kendi, "Colorism is a form of racism. To recognize colorism, we must first recognize that Light people and Dark people are two distinct racialized groups shaped by their own histories."[4] Yet, as Kendi notes, humans didn't group one another into color-based groups until the fifteenth century. Nevertheless, as Kimberly Jade Norwood and Violeta Solonova Foreman observe, *colorism* is a global practice based on the "coalescence of needs, beliefs, justifications, and practices" that produces the practice of colorism and the stratified social structure that emerges.[5]

This stratification happens because we often place ourselves into groups based on how we look. We might generally do this through color, but there are many physical traits we use to justify our sometimes-prejudicial treatment of one another. In *The Witcher*, the key physical trait is pointy ears: if you have them, you're an elf. If you don't, you're human. Or you're a mixed-race elf like Yennefer and Ciri, who can pass as human. Of course, Yennefer and Ciri might not have pointy ears, but they do have another distinguishing trait—elven blood.[6]

In *The Witcher* (and *Blood Origin*) the lore surrounding elven blood builds tension in the story, especially in the feud between humans and elves.[7] It's what drives Stregobor to prevent Yennefer from being assigned to Aedirn. It's what prompts Yennefer to hide her elven heritage when she seeks a post at Aedirn—and then to claim elven heritage when she's captured by elves, though Francesca doesn't show Yennefer any sympathy. Blood is also what makes Ciri so powerful and special.

Perhaps most disturbingly, the significance of Ciri's blood drives Vilgefortz to kidnap girls like Ciri from Aretuza and experiment on them in an abandoned castle.[8] And this is where the tale gets cautionary. It's one thing to classify people based on their lineage, or even to reject or embrace one's lineage. But it's an entirely different thing to experiment on people because of their lineage. Yet, as Kendi notes, blood itself is significant when it comes to prejudice and racism—for all sides:

> White people have historically employed the one-drop rule—that even one drop of Black blood makes you Black—to bar Light people from pure Whiteness. Dark people employ the two-drop rule, as I call it—two drops of White blood makes you less Black—to bar Light people from pure Blackness. Light people employ the three-drop rule, as I call it—three drops of Black blood means you're too Dark—to bar Dark people from pure Lightness.[9]

As Kendi explains, these so-called "'drop' rules of racial purity were mirages, just like the races themselves and the idea of racial blood. No racial group was pure."[10] Still, Kendi's observation is noteworthy because it doesn't just resonate with how drop rules implicitly operate in *The Witcher*, especially with a character like Yennefer, but also how these types of practices inform another aspect of racism—*dehumanization*.

"Go to hell, fucking mongrels"

In each of *The Witcher*'s three seasons, humans treat elves not just as different, but as beings unworthy of autonomy or respect. This is also how Filavandrel treats Geralt, and it's how Francesca (and especially the Scoia'tael) treats most humans. For Kendi, the *very idea of race* is dehumanizing.[11] And this is where the cautionary tale is reiterated. Because dehumanization isn't just about removing any sense of humanity from a person; it's about the brutality such an act seems to sanction. Humans and elves show horrible disregard for one another. Indeed, with events like the Great Cleansing, it's easy to understand why Geralt doesn't want to be considered human, and why Jaskier (who speaks and sings in elvish!) eventually becomes the Sandpiper.

As Yennefer recounts the tale, when humans arrived on the Continent, elves considered them nothing more than "a nuisance, like a plague of locusts or a drought."[12] Similarly, characters like Stregobor refer to elves as "fucking mongrels."[13] Indeed, many nonhuman characters are treated this way, including witchers. And given the way elves and humans slaughter and betray one another, there isn't much thought given to being civilized and humane. As Francesca vows, "We tried sharing the Continent for centuries. If there is to be another genocide, this time, it'll be the humans." ("Shaerrawedd," season 3, episode 1).

Perhaps the battle at Aretuza near the end of the third Netflix season offers the clearest example of dehumanization, with both sides fighting brutally against one another. But it's not just that both sides are guilty of dehumanizing one another. What we see is that both sides are also guilty of dehumanizing themselves, highlighting the cautionary tale. To be clear, this isn't meant to suggest equivalence between both sides—on the Continent, humans have always been the aggressor.[14] Rather, this illustrates what happens when anger turns to vengeance. And what we see is that dehumanization leads us to another concept related to the practice of racism—*dignity*.

"I'm only worth four marks"

Dignity is a complex concept, and philosophy offers several approaches to understanding how we define dignity. One of the clearest expressions is found in the moral theory of Immanuel Kant (1724–1804) and its categorical imperative (fundamental principle) regarding humanity. As Kant states, "So act that you use humanity, in your own person as well as in the person of any other, always at the same time as an end, never merely as a means."[15] In other words, racist practices such as slavery and dehumanization treat people as means to ends—such as forced labor—and deny the humanity and dignity Kant says every rational being has.

Again, we see this occurring on both sides in *The Witcher*. For example, when Nilfgaard offers a haven to the elves in the second season, Filavandrel remains suspicious, telling Francesca, "I've never known a human to give out of the kindness of his heart" ("What Is Lost," season 2, episode 3). Kant might say that Filavandrel distrusts humans because he assumes that humans are using the elves as a means to an end. He would be right. But couldn't the same be said of Francesca? In asking Fringilla for a home for her people and for the future of the elves, isn't she using humans as a means to an end as much as humans are using elves? Later, in the third season, aren't Francesca, Fringilla, and Emhyr all using each other to achieve their goals? Isn't this what most characters do? Of course, as Yennefer remarks to Cahir, "It's funny how quickly people forget about you when you're no longer of use to them, isn't it?" ("Redanian Intelligence," season 2, episode 4). What's significant is that characters' choices such as these illustrate how anyone can make racist choices, and view such choices as justifiable means.

For Kant, the decisions we make should comply with a universal moral law. This means that our actions are only moral if anyone would be able to act in the same way under the same circumstances. Dehumanization and enslavement are actions that could never pass the test of Kant's categorical imperative—they could never be moral. Further, according to Kant we have inherent worth as humans, and so we shouldn't treat others as means to our own ends. If we do, then we fail at our moral duty, betraying our own dignity and violating the dignity of others—which is what happens at the battle of Aretuza. It's one thing to fight in defense, or to reclaim territory, but it's another thing to resort to savagery. That's the cautionary tale.

Perhaps dignity—how we uphold it, use it, diminish it, or seek to destroy it—requires more than just an imperative telling us how to treat one another. Indeed, for Suzy Killmister, Kant's conception of dignity falls short because "dignity is taken to be a universal feature that does not admit of degrees."[16] In other words, dignity isn't as black and white as Kant sees it. Let's examine this further.

"You elf scum!"

Killmister's concept of dignity is a tapestry of three interwoven strands: personal dignity, social dignity, and human dignity. Killmister also suggests that a theory of dignity must satisfy three needs:

> It should be able to explain why all human beings are owed respect, and what kind of respect we are owed; it should be able to explain how acts such as torture damage dignity, and what kinds of harms this brings about; and finally, it should be able to explain why dignity is held to a higher degree by certain individuals.[17]

Importantly for Killmister, Kantian dignity can't fulfill these needs. So she suggests that dignity be "subject to normative standards" of a community.[18] For Killmister, an individual possesses personal dignity and social dignity. And as Killmister explains: "What matters is the extent to which [an individual] upholds, respectively, [their] own standards and the standards of the communities of which [the individual is] a member."[19]

This is what makes Geralt's neutrality so interesting. By his own standards he doesn't want to get involved in the Continent's politics. And by society's standards, he upholds laws such as the Law of Surprise, because, as he tells Calanthe, "a promise made must be honored, as true for a commoner as it is for a queen" ("Of Banquets, Bastards, and Burials," season 1, episode 4). These standards cause Geralt to refrain from killing Duny when Calanthe orders it. They also cause him to eventually uphold his own commitment to Ciri, who became his child of surprise. In both instances, by Killmister's definition, Geralt upholds his dignity and the dignity of others.

For Killmister, damages to dignity matter morally because these damages harm a person's sense of agency, and damages to social dignity inflict a social cost. For example, Yennefer and Calanthe both choose to hide their elven heritage, because being outed would inflict a social cost on them. Of course, Yennefer is outed, and she initially pays a cost when she's assigned to Nilfgaard instead of Aedirn. While Yennefer overcomes this obstacle, the price she pays (losing her fertility) exacts a greater cost, one that haunts her. Calanthe, who denies her elven lineage, also pays a price, one that eventually costs the life of her daughter, Pavetta, the loss of Ciri, and of her own life and kingdom when Nilfgaard attacks Cintra. It's significant that Yennefer and Calanthe both damage their *own* senses of dignity. While Calanthe, who eventually jumps to her own death, isn't able to restore her dignity (at least in Killmister's way of thinking), Yennefer makes several attempts, eventually finding a sense of dignity when she becomes a mother to Ciri.[20]

We also see this with Jaskier, who as the Sandpiper in season 2 smuggles elves to safety. Jaskier is human, and he never displays any hatred toward elves. Yet he seems ashamed of how humans treat elves, which he witnessed at the raid of Bleobheris. As he tells Yennefer, he wants to "make this right" ("Redanian Intelligence," season 2, episode 4). So, though his actions might not be performed as a way of restoring his individual dignity, his willingness to help rescue elves could be seen as a way of restoring the dignity of humans, while also honoring the dignity of elves. And it's notable that Jaskier even speaks and sings in the elven language, suggesting something more than sympathy.

Even villainous characters like Cahir and Stregobor (who seem to have no dignity at times) work to restore their individual dignities at the end of the third season—with Cahir kneeling before Ciri and offering his life to her, and Stregobor actually sacrificing himself to save Yennefer and the other mages. Thus, restoring dignity (or at least upholding it) is also part of the cautionary tale. Of course, just prior to their heroic actions, both Cahir and Stregobor were engaged in something related to racism—*othering*.

"I'm also an elf"

Viewing people as others is a process that focuses on differences rather than similarities. It's also a process that is inherently negative, as those deemed to be others are often excluded, shunned, oppressed, or subordinated.[21] As Jaskier notes to Yennefer, anyone can be othered: "They come for the elves, Yennefer. They'll come for the dwarves. And sooner or later, they will come for everyone. Anyone that they deem the 'other,' so eventually, no artist is safe" ("Redanian Intelligence," season 2, episode 4). To some extent, Yennefer experienced this firsthand when she was captured by the elves. It didn't matter that Yennefer was a quarter elf. Francesca considered Yennefer to be an outsider, reasoning: "Do you sing our songs? Do you honor our elders? Have you shed a tear over anything elven? You are no elf" ("Kaer Morhen," season 2, episode 2).

It's an interesting turn for Yennefer, who sought to hide her elven status from the Brotherhood in the first season. Because Francesca is right. Yennefer doesn't live an elven life, and even if her biological father was a half-elf, Yennefer's claim is weak. To be fair, Yennefer does seem emboldened after seeing so many elves hiding in the forest, which suggests that she feels, on some level, a sort of kinship as if she were among her own people. When she becomes a mother to Ciri, Yennefer certainly views Ciri's elven blood as a connection they share.

The philosopher Jean-Paul Sartre (1905–1980) is notable for exploring the concept of "the other." For Sartre, when we perceive someone else—an "Other-as-object"—we experience an inner conflict as we struggle to understand the reality of ourselves in relation to someone else.[22] To Stregobor, but not to Francesca, Yennefer is an elf. Throughout the narrative, Yennefer's identity fluctuates, not just as a human or an elf, but also as a hunchback, a woman, and a mage. Put another way, we construct our notion of others in relation (often in opposition) to how we see ourselves, and others do the same to us. Yennefer is othered in many situations. Accordingly, nearly every character operates not as a being-for-others, but as being-for-themself, which often leads to strife. As Julie Van der Wielen notes, this is why our perception of others is always a conflict. She explains, "The Other constitutes me in my being by making me into an object of which I cannot deny that it is me, although I am not an object."[23] And as Van der Wielen notes, as a subject we must face a fact of human reality: "there are other free human subjects like me, and like me they can perceive other persons as objects."[24]

But as Van der Wielen further notes, being-for-others is what "makes it possible for us to see another person as another for-itself, and not as an object."[25] If our perception and understanding of others is inherently a conflict of two realities vying to coexist, then we can see not only why we tend to reduce the conflict to "myself as a subject" versus "the other as object," but also why we might choose to exist, like Yennefer, on one side or the other of the duality whenever it suits us.

Of course, regardless of which side you identify with, you're defined by another or by your relation to another (even if you're the one doing the defining). Thus, like in the case of colorism, dehumanization, and dignity, any one of us can other or be othered. Most characters on *The Witcher* experience this, and depending on whether they're doing the othering or they're being othered, they face the conflict Van der Wielen notes. Dara is a good example of this.

"If I keep carrying this hatred, it'll kill me"

After saving Ciri's life several times, Dara eventually chooses to leave Ciri because of his hatred for Calanthe and his fear that Ciri is just like her grandmother. With Jaskier's help, Dara escapes to Xin'trea where he finds other elves and eventually fights alongside the Scoia'tael. But this doesn't last long, and Dara leaves again, finding refuge in Brokilon forest. As he confesses to Jaskier:

DARA: After my family was killed, I was alone for a long time. And when I found my own people, I thought I'd recovered what I'd lost. Purpose, hope, family, peace. But they agreed to help the White Flame start a war. And I couldn't do it. So I ran.

JASKIER: It's alright to be scared.
DARA: I'm not scared, I'm just tired of running. If I keep carrying this hatred, it'll kill me.

("The Cost of Chaos," season 3, episode 8)

In a sense, Dara has always been an other—in relation to humans, in relation to Ciri, and in relation to other elves like those in the Scoia'tael. Constantly being an other likely contributed to his growing hatred, and it's significant that he recognizes the danger of continuing to harbor hate. This is where the cautionary tale turns prescriptive, suggesting that hatred doesn't kill the ones we hate, and implying that activism starts with the individual. Or, to paraphrase Kendi: in the end, hating elves becomes hating humans, and hating humans becomes hating elves.[26] Thus, the hatred needs to stop, even if it means laying down arms and walking away, as Dara does.

Ciri recognizes this, too, especially when she learns the story of Aelirenn and equates Aelirenn with Calanthe. As Ciri surmises: "They lived centuries apart but burned with the exact same mission: wipe the other species off the Continent" ("Shaerrawedd," season 3, episode 1). Initially, Ciri sees herself as the solution, suggesting that being part elf and part human allows her to forge a different way forward. As she argues to Geralt and Yennefer:

> Nenneke said I have the power to change the cycle of hatred. And I want to. To be the balance between kings and mages, and to align the Continent instead of constantly pitting parts against each other. Because I am sick and tired of destruction and loss! ("Shaerrawedd," season 3, episode 1)

Given Ciri's power (she can destroy monoliths with a single scream!) and her training, we might assume she'd use her abilities to unite the continent in some epic battle. Instead, we see Ciri choose to relinquish her powers after encountering a vision of Falka in the Korath desert. And after killing Skomlik in a sword fight (her first intentional kill of a person) she also relinquishes her name, telling Mistle to "call me Falka." It's a bold choice, one that resonates with Kendi's observation on power and with Dara's conclusion on hate, emphasizing the tale's prescriptive message.

"What has been, need not always be"

Ciri's blood endows her with power, and most of the continent wants to use Ciri for her power. Only Geralt, Yennefer, and Jaskier love her unselfishly. And it's Ciri's love for them that compels her to relinquish her power. Falka wants Ciri to use her power for revenge, but Ciri doesn't want to continue the cycle of hatred and lose her humanity. In making her first kill, she also realizes the weight of taking a life, even if Mistle doesn't. It's a decision Ciri almost made when she faced Cahir, who offered his life to

Ciri. While she hesitates with Cahir, she doesn't hesitate with Skomlik. Yet, as the scene plays out, we see Ciri (who is clearly a superior fighter) defeat Skomlik not with joy but with sadness, as if each blow she deals is a blow to herself. And it's with tears in her eyes that she assumes the alias of Falka.

Given Ciri's goal, this choice could be seen as an attempt to change the cycle of hatred and offer something different than Calanthe and Aelirenn. By giving up her power and her identity, Ciri can walk away, as Dara did. Because, as Kendi notes, racist and antiracist identities are not fixed. As he suggests, "What we say about race, what we do about race, in each moment, determines what—not who—we are."[27] In choosing to be called Falka, Ciri isn't necessarily choosing Falka's identity (or Falka's history). Rather, she's choosing to not be Ciri—not because the identity of Ciri is racist, but because the identity of Ciri has become a means for the racist ends humans and elves seek.

Thus, to Kendi's observation, it's not about who Ciri is, it's about what she is. She's part elf, part human, and she's antiracist—even if it means she needs to be Falka and forgo her power as Ciri. Because as the elvish saying goes, "what has been, need not always be."

Notes

1. We also see elves versus elves, especially elf clan versus elf clan in *Blood Origin*.
2. Which requires activism that seeks changes in power and policy.
3. Ibram X. Kendi, *How to Be Antiracist* (New York: One World, 2019), 110.
4. Kendi, *How to Be Antiracist*, 109.
5. Kimberly Jade Norwood and Violeta Solonova Foreman, "The Ubiquitousness of Colorism: Then and Now," in *Color Matters: Skin Tone Bias and the Myth of a Postracial America* (New York: Routledge, 2014), 9, 15.
6. And Ciri has Elder blood, referencing her lineage to Lara Dorren.
7. Especially stories about Ithlinne's Prophecy, Lara Dorren, Aelirenn, and Falka.
8. Where he creates a fake Ciri (a girl named Teryn) and a grotesque flesh monster.
9. Kendi, *How to Be Antiracist*, 113.
10. Kendi, *How to Be Antiracist*, 113.
11. Kendi, *How to Be Antiracist*, 40–41.
12. "Shaerrawedd," season 3, episode 1.
13. "Everybody Has a Plan 'til They Get Punched in the Face," season 3, episode 6.
14. This doesn't render the elves completely innocent, nor does it give them license to dehumanize.
15. Immanuel Kant, *Groundwork for the Metaphysics of Morals*, trans. Mary Gregor and Jens Timmermann (New York: Cambridge University Press, 2012), 41. It should be noted that Kant has been criticized for being sexist (believing men were superior to women) and racist (believing whites were the superior race). Nevertheless, Kant's formulation regarding humanity and its implications, I contend, transcend his personal beliefs and actions.

16. Suzy Killmister, "Dignity: Personal, Social, Human," *Philosophical Studies* 174 (2017), 2066.
17. Killmister, "Dignity: Personal, Social, Human," 2063.
18. Killmister, "Dignity: Personal, Social, Human," 2079.
19. Killmister, "Dignity: Personal, Social, Human," 2079.
20. For a more detailed discussion on this, see my chapter "Understanding Yennefer's Feminism(s)" in this volume.
21. Even from within one's own people, which is what happens to Fjall in *Blood Origin* when he's banished.
22. Jean-Paul Sartre, *Being and Nothingness: An Essay on Phenomenological Ontology*, trans. H.E. Barnes (New York: Routledge, 2003), 320.
23. Julie Van Der Wielen, "The Magic of the Other: Sartre on Our Relation with Others in Ontology and Experience," *Sartre Studies International* 20 (2014), 60.
24. Van Der Wielen, "The Magic of the Other," 60.
25. Van Der Wielen, "The Magic of the Other," 60.
26. Kendi, *How to Be Antiracist*, 131. The exact quote reads: "In the end, hating White people becomes hating Black people. In the end, hating Black people becomes hating White people."
27. Kendi, *How to Be Antiracist*, 10.

MAGIC

15

Magic and the Elder Speech in *The Witcher*

Andriy Ivanchenko

In the *Witcher* saga, the Elder Speech functions as the medium for magic. But how? The anthropologist Bronisław Malinowski (1884–1942) found that, in our world, ritual and magic are special modes of communication. This means that it matters what words are spoken, by whom, and in what context. To understand this magical and "performative" power of language we'll look to the speech act theory of the British philosopher J.L. Austin (1911–1960), who explained how the world can be changed in various ways by *declaring* it so changed.

Spell-Casting: The Force, the Medium, the Addressees

What happens when a spell is cast in the *Witcher* books? According to Yennefer's explanation in *Blood of Elves,* a controlled issue of force powered by one of the four elements occurs. Yenn speaks dismissively of the witchers' signs (the psychokinetic Aard in particular), calling them "primitive," while proclaiming her own version of psychokinesis as the only one worth learning. She points out that the witchers obviously didn't have the magical formulae to start with and so had to rely on brute force, "thrusting energy in the required direction."[1] For each spell, there seems to be a formula and a gesture that need to be precisely reproduced for the spell to work as intended. The spoken formula of the spell is invariably given in the Elder Speech, the Elvish tongue.[2] Sapkowski's method of creating the Elder Speech relies on reference to Celtic languages, plus some Romance and Germanic influences. As Sapkowski himself has said, a conversation in the Elder Speech should feel alien but also be reasonably understandable to the reader without translation or footnotes.[3] Incidentally, the Elves themselves do not need to heed the gesture + formula rules, as demonstrated to Geralt

The Witcher and Philosophy: Toss a Coin to Your Philosopher, First Edition.
Edited by Matthew Brake and Kevin S. Decker.

by the Elvish sage Avallac'h, whose silent spell-casting is done in "the elven fashion."[4]

The human way of spell-casting in the Witcherverse conforms pretty closely to the views of Emile Durkheim (1858–1917) on "primitive" ritualism: "since the formula to be pronounced and the movements to be made contain within themselves the source of their efficacy, they would lose it if they did not conform absolutely to the type consecrated by success."[5] The need for a magic ritual to remain the same over time was reiterated by Bronisław Malinowski, who defined the spell as "a sequence of words, more or less mysterious, handed down from immemorial times and always taught by an accredited magician to his successors, received by the first human wielder of the magic from some supernatural agency."[6] (In the Witcherverse, of course, this reception is naturally traceable to the elves, from whom the human magic is supposed to be descended along with its medium, the Elder Speech.) Malinowski, though, objected to Durkheim's view that "the substance of magic, that is *mana* or magical force, is nothing but society personified," saying that it "explains one mystical attitude by inviting us to assume another."[7]

What is meant by *mana* is "magical force," and Yenn refers to the Witcherverse version as simply "the force." Malinowski says that the magical force resides with the magician; magic passed down through tradition affirms "a human power of creating desired ends."[8] Each rite is the "production" or "generation" of a force and "the conveyance of it, directly or indirectly, to a certain given object." Mages in the Witcherverse generate spell force by drawing energy from "intersections" (of ley lines, presumably). In contrast, Mother Nenneke refers to the priestly belief in gods as personified Nature and thus treats *mana* as divinely granted (while also demonstrating her own awareness—and tolerance—of Yenn's alternative viewpoint).[9] We should also consider the idea that while *mana* "essentially belongs to personal beings [that is, spirits] to originate it," it may also "act through the medium of water, or a stone" and "can be conveyed in almost anything."[10] This recalls Yennefer's musings in *Blood of Elves* on the relative convenience of drawing the magical force from water veins (the easiest), earth and air (much more difficult), and fire (forbidden to Ciri without any explanation at that point).[11] Based on this classical combination, the resulting kind of magic might perhaps be regarded as elemental, but one should keep in mind that it is the actual physical substance (in the form of various natural bodies of water, for instance) that is tapped for the spell-powering "force"—no elemental spirits per se are involved.

The magician's "breath," or speaking voice, according to Malinowski, is the medium carrying the magical force: it is "the voice of the accredited and fully instructed magician" correctly uttering the words of "an absolutely authentic spell" that generates the power of the magic.[12] "Correctly uttering the words" echoes the Witcherverse requirement that the magician faithfully reproduce the "frequently complicated intonations" associated with the spell formulae. But for Malinowski, the most difficult problem with magical formulae is linguistic: What role or function does a magical utterance serve in language? A magical formula is "neither a piece of conversation, nor yet a prayer, nor a statement or communication." "What is it?" Malinowski wonders about the Trobriand magician saying, "I am striking thee, O soil!" while striking the soil of the garden; "what sort of co-operative act, if any, is involved?"[13] Malinowski believes that the ritual is regarded by the believers as "a verbal communion between the magician and the object addressed," including spirits, animals, plants, and soil. The magician's words are meant "for things that have no ears." These words, however, also "fall upon ears they are not meant for": tribe members may potentially overhear the incantations and believe that "the recital is a cause and condition of all that happens afterwards."[14]

Malinowski was never satisfied concerning the question of what supernatural entity was addressed to do the magician's bidding.[15] Locating this entity is more complicated in the case of healing spells that are overheard by the patient—who is not, in fact, the intended recipient of the message.[16] It's been suggested that without the "other-worldly listener," the charm loses its essential feature, its communicative element.[17] The charm's "power" therefore depends on the attentions of "diffuse, yet ever present, supernatural forces."[18] The magician's articulate speech is aimed at a recipient who won't respond verbally. Rather, the otherworldly power is expected to respond by healing the patient. Malinowski, however, stops short of defining the nature of the supernatural agents of healing spells. For his purposes, it sufficed to describe the act as aimed at achieving a certain effect of conveying a certain power or force.

Spells as Speech Acts

Malinowski's attention to the use of "magical" words which "invoke, state, or command the desired aim" prompted others to compare his ideas to the speech act theory of J.L. Austin.[19] Austin argued that some *social acts* are performed by speaking certain words and phrases like, "I hereby declare you husband and wife." This must be done by a clergyman or an official during a ceremony to be legally binding (or, as Austin writes, for the speech act to be felicitous or "happy"—that is, to actually perform its function). Similarly, for healing to occur through a magical ritual, the person uttering the incantation must be a qualified magician and the spell formula must be a proper one. Malinowski quotes healing formulae from Trobriand magic that he believes are based on "exactly the principles" of the Nancy (France) school's idea of psycho-therapeutic "direct suggestion." He regards this school's hypnosis-centered method as "the best example of modern magical use of words":

> It passes, it passes,
> The breaking pain in thy bones passes,
> The ulceration of thy skin passes,
> The big black evil of thy abdomen passes,
> It passes, it passes ...[20]

Strictly speaking, a *performative* utterance should be in the first person, present tense, indicative mood, active voice, and it should describe its speaker as performing a speech act.[21] And surely enough, there are plenty of first-person spell formulae found in Trobriand magic:

> I smooth out, I improve, I whiten.
> Thy head I smooth out, I improve, I whiten.
> Thy cheeks I smooth out, I improve, I whiten.
> Thy nose I smooth out, I improve, I whiten ...[22]

Trobriand spell formulae describe physical rather than speech acts (though in a much more long-winded fashion, being of ritualistic nature and thus not "immediately effective," unlike the ones in the Witcherverse). They may also vary grammatically. What they share is the belief by all parties involved that the repetitive statement of certain words will produce the reality stated.

This fits with Stanley J. Tambiah's idea of how performative statements might be applied to magic: "Magical acts, usually compounded of verbal utterance and object manipulation, constitute 'performative' acts by which a property is imperatively transferred to a recipient object or person on an analogical basis."[23] According to Tambiah, ritual acts, like performative speech acts, have consequences that should be understood in terms of a specific society's conventions and as solutions to its existential problems. Various other kinds of speech acts are thought to exist apart from performatives, with a number of classifications proposed over the years, starting with Austin's own. The speech acts named "declaratives" by Austin's best-known follower and critic John Searle, are words that change the world, in effect, by declaring it changed. This category includes all cases where "saying so" can somehow change the world by making people "married," "guilty," or "cursed." As Searle says, declaratives "make their propositional content true"—just like magical spells![24]

In effect, Searle's declaratives enact what they describe.[25] This is relevant to Malinowski's view that Trobriand magical spells don't command supernatural agents to execute their propositions; instead, the magician supposedly effects the spell through *mana* manipulation—by the power vested in him (to borrow our civil servants' wording). This allowed Malinowski to dismiss (or at least circumvent) the role of supernatural agents in Trobriand spells.[26]

Changing the World

It's plain to see that the Witcherverse magical formulae name their effects (such as light or fire) in the briefest possible way. Consider the formulae with known translations (occurring in the text nearby, along with some kind of comment on the spell effect):

1. *Aine verseos!* = "A tiny light," which produces the same.
2. *Aen'drean va, eveigh Aine!* = "Arrive, eternal Light!"
3. *Aenye!* = "Fire!" produces enough fire to light up a small pile of wood, and
4. *Hael, Aenye!* = "Hail, Fire!" in combination with a hand gesture producing much stronger fire which doesn't require physical fuel to burn (so "hail" may here refer to wishing someone "health" or "strength").[27]

The world is changed by the mage simply "saying so" in the precise wording that descends from the language's ultimate source. These are the right words uttered by a person with the authority to declare the world changed in these particular ways. The spells are thus performative in Tambiah's sense, if not in Austin's. As Malinowski himself put it, "it is the use of words which invoke, state, or command the desired aim."[28] The change in the world is powered by the elemental force, the Witcherverse equivalent of *mana*. No "critical magical agents" are named in the course of this spell-casting because the Witcherverse mages don't believe in personal deities and don't address them in spell-casting.

Verbal Magic and Making Truth

Whether spoken out loud in public or "secretly mumbled" by the sorcerer while alone in his hut, words are used to access or guide magical power. Tambiah points out that in most ritual systems there is a reciprocal relation between the word and the deed. He argues that the connection between language and magic is due to a belief in the inherent ability of words to influence the universe.[29] According to Malinowski, this belief is an extension of humans' basic use of language to describe their surroundings, in which "the knowledge of the right words, appropriate phrases and the more highly developed forms of speech" gives humans a power over and above their own "limited field of personal action."[30] The essence of verbal magic, Malinowski concludes, consists in "a statement which is untrue, which stands in direct opposition to the context of reality." But it is the belief in magic that inspires humans with the conviction that this untrue statement *must* become true.[31] This belief is the basis of real-life magical practices, as well as the fictional ones—which makes sense in the *Witcher* world where magic is observably real. Malinowski's idea about the magician as the generator and operator of magical force (as opposed to being the conduit for divinely granted *mana*), is realized in the Witcherverse quite literally.[32] Witcherverse mages draw magical force from nature at their own discretion: unlike the classical *mana*, its supply doesn't depend on rites or observances. As long as the genuine Elder Speech spell formula is uttered in the prescribed manner (along with any requisite hand gestures) and sufficient magical force is applied, one should expect the spell to take effect. At several points in the saga, spells fail or misfire when some of these conditions aren't met: when Ciri was learning the basics under Yenn's guidance, having trouble with hand gestures at first; when Ciri tried casting spells in the desert but couldn't draw sufficient force; and when Triss accidentally created the spell later named Merigold's Destructive Hailstorm while trying to invoke a different one, by speaking indistinctly because her mouth had been cut (or perhaps because of her tongue "faltering from fear").[33]

Even though the Witcherverse magic may appear somewhat mechanical due to the need to observe these conditions, it should be clear that the "essence of verbal magic" described by Malinowski applies to it as much as it does to any real-world magical practices—with the Elder Speech as its medium, "gushing out" with the mage's speaking voice and ultimately affirming one's own "power of creating desired ends."[34]

Notes

1. Andrzej Sapkowski, *Blood of Elves,* trans. Danusia Stok (London: Gollancz, 2021), 309.
2. The idea of a separate or dedicated "magical" language is hardly a new one. As Aleister Crowley (a.k.a. Master Therion) famously said, "the most potent conjurations are those in an ancient and perhaps forgotten language." Aleister Crowley, *Magick in Theory and Practice* (Paris: Lecram Press, 1929), 68.
3. Andrzej Sapkowski and Stanisław Bereś, *Historia i fantastyka* (Warsaw: SuperNOWA, 2005). For Elder Speech glossaries, see https://witcher.fandom.com/wiki/Elder_Speech (accessed February 1, 2024).
4. Andrzej Sapkowski, *The Tower of the Swallow*, trans. David French (London: Gollancz, 2016), 240.
5. Emile Durkheim, *The Elementary Forms of the Religious Life,* trans. J.W. Swain (New York: Free Press, [1912] 1965), 50.
6. Bronisław Malinowski, *Coral Gardens and Their Magic: A Study of the Methods of Tilling the Soil and of Agricultural Rites in the Trobriand Islands,* vol. 2: *The Language of Magic and Gardening* (New York: Routledge, 1935), 217.

7. Malinowski, *Coral Gardens and Their Magic*, 240.
8. Bronisław Malinowski, *Magic, Science and Religion and Other Essays* (London: Souvenir Press, 1974).
9. Andrzej Sapkowski, *The Last Wish*, trans. Danusia Stok (London: Gollancz, 2007), 37.
10. Friedrich Max Müller, *Lectures on the Origin and Growth of Religion as Illustrated by the Religions of India: The Hibbert Lectures, Delivered in the Chapter House, Westminster Abbey, in April, May and June, 1878* (London: Longmans, Green, & Co., 1878), 54.
11. Sapkowski, *Blood of Elves*, 301.
12. Malinowski, *Coral Gardens and Their Magic*, 216; Sapkowski, *Blood of Elves*, 297.
13. Malinowski, *Coral Gardens and Their Magic*, 214–215.
14. Malinowski, *Coral Gardens and Their Magic*, 240–241, 257.
15. Malinowski, *Coral Gardens and Their Magic*, 229.
16. Henni Ilomäki, "Oral Charms, Literal Notes," in Éva Pócs ed., *Charms and Charming: Studies on Magic in Everyday Life* (Ljubljana: Scientific Research Centre of the Slovenian Academy of Sciences and Arts, 2019), 202.
17. Anna-Leena Siikala, "Variation in the Incantation and Mythical Thinking: The Scope of Comparative Research," *Journal of the Folklore Research* 23 (1986), 200.
18. Michelle Z. Rosaldo "The Things We Do with Words: Ilongot Speech Acts and Speech Act Theory in Philosophy," *Language in Society* 11 (1982), 221.
19. Stanley J. Tambiah, *Culture, Thought, and Social Action: An Anthropological Perspective* (Cambridge, MA: Harvard University Press, 1985), 60, 78. Also, J.L. Austin, *How to Do Things with Words* (Oxford: Clarendon Press, 1962).
20. Malinowski, *Coral Gardens and Their Magic*, 236.
21. Mitchell Green, "Speech Acts," in *The Stanford Encyclopedia of Philosophy* at https://plato.stanford.edu/archives/fall2021/entries/speech-acts.
22. Malinowski, *Coral Gardens and Their Magic*, 238.
23. Stanley J. Tambiah, "Form and Meaning of Magical Acts: A Point of View," in Robin Horton and Ruth Finnegan eds., *Modes of Thought: Essays on Thinking in Western and Non-Western Societies* (London: Faber & Faber, 1973), reprinted in *Hau: Journal of Ethnographic Theory* 7 (2017), 451.
24. John R. Searle, "How Performatives Work," *Linguistics and Philosophy* 12 (1989), 553.
25. John R. Searle and Daniel Vanderveken, *Foundations of Illocutionary Logic* (Cambridge: Cambridge University Press, 1981), 53.
26. Later research found that ancestral spirits were "critical magical agents" in Trobriand magic, which is at odds with Malinowski's view. But his version of magic—where "saying so" changes the world—should still work for the reasons discussed above. It certainly does in the *Witcher* saga. See Mark S. Mosko, "Malinowski's Magical Puzzles: Toward a New Theory of Magic and Procreation in Trobriand Society," *Hau: Journal of Ethnographic Theory* 4 (2014), 1–47.
27. Spell 1 comes from Sapkowski, *Blood of Elves*, 306–308; spells 2–4 from Andrzej Sapkowski, *Time of Contempt*, trans. David French (London: Gollancz, 2020), 262, 280.
28. Malinowski, *Magic, Science and Religion and Other Essays*, 74.

29. Stanley J. Tambiah, "The Magical Power of Words," *Man, New Series* 3, no. 2 (1968), 175–176.
30. Malinowski, *Coral Gardens and Their Magic*, 235.
31. Malinowski, *Coral Gardens and Their Magic*, 239.
32. To be fair, this was suggested long before Malinowski by the esotericist Eliphas Levi saying that "Magical Power exists only in the trained Will of the operator." See Eliphaz Levi, *The Magical Ritual of the Sanctum Regnum*, trans. W. Wynn Westcott (London: George Redway, 1896), 19.
33. Sapkowski, *Blood of Elves*, 306–308; Sapkowski, *Time of Contempt*, 262–280; Andrzej Sapkowski, *The Lady of the Lake*, trans. David French (London: Gollancz, 2017), 496–530.
34. Malinowski, *Magic, Science and Religion and Other Essays*.

16

Worlds within Words
Names and Naming in *The Witcher*

Fiona Tomkinson

What's in a name? What can be said about the significance of a single word—a proper or common noun, in itself? A word like "fire," or a given name such as "Geralt," or "Temeria"? Does it have its own magic, its own intrinsic value? And if so, how should we explain it? Simply in terms of its definition, its semantic meaning or etymology, or in terms of an actual *reference* to something beyond the person or object that it designates? What happens if the reference indicates something that cannot easily be pointed out with a finger?

Proper names have often been considered magical and to have a secondary reference beyond the individual to whom they are given. Names such as "Rose" or "Faith" are not arbitrary identifiers, but words intended to express the essential qualities of the person named or perhaps the qualities which those naming them wish them to develop. This also seems to be the case in the Witcherverse: for example, the Elvish form of Ciri's name, Zireael—which she later gives to her sword—means "swallow," and so connects her with her ultimate destiny in the Tower of the Swallow.

Names also link their bearers to ancestors or heroic figures, as when Ciri in defiant celebration of her Elder Blood takes "Falka" as her *nom de guerre* among the Rats, a sign that she's embracing the path of violence. The reader may also be aware of something that Ciri isn't. "Falk," a character in a short story by Joseph Conrad, is a man forced by desperate circumstances to commit murder and cannibalism; "Falka," a feminine form of this name, makes the analogy with Ciri's situation clear.

Philosophy of language prompts us to ask questions like these about names: When "Falka" is spoken, does it simply refer to the person who is being mentioned, or does it also refer to all or some of its previous bearers? And does the name "Zireael" refer not only to a particular person and a sword, but to the idealized essence of "swallow"?

What terms in a language refer to—"linguistic reference"—is already complex in the real world; it becomes even more complicated within a work of fiction. Sometimes we may get so involved in a fiction like *The*

The Witcher and Philosophy: Toss a Coin to Your Philosopher, First Edition.
Edited by Matthew Brake and Kevin S. Decker.

Witcher that it seems to exist like the real world! But when we stop suspending our disbelief, do invented languages and proper names (magical or otherwise) within a fantasy universe refer to, or designate, anything at all?

In what follows, we'll explore the relationship between word and world in the *Witcher* novels, showing some of the ways in which naming words carry traces of other worlds—mythical and literary worlds, and the past world of human history. We'll finally consider how this complexity might be understood in terms of the philosophy of language, taking as a point of departure the thinking of Gottlob Frege (1848–1925) and his famous distinction between the "sense" of a word and its "reference."

Fantasy Forebears

Andrzej Sapkowski's creation of a fantasy language—Elvish or Elder Speech—based on elements of existing languages creates relationships between *The Witcher* and the real world and suggests analogies with reality— even if, as Ciri points out to Jarre, analogies are not always to be trusted. For example, the Celtic sound of Elvish words might well lead us to compare the political situation of the elves with that of "Celtic" peoples in Britain, who have been seen as displaced by "Anglo-Saxon" invaders in the same way that the elves of the Continent were displaced by humans. The main protagonist is also inserted into this tradition: "Geralt" is Irish for "farmer" (perhaps an ironic allusion to the peaceful rural life that he sometimes dreams of). But matters are complicated by the fact that, in this use of real-world languages, Sapkowski is also following in the footsteps of his predecessors in the creation of realms of high fantasy and linking the Continent of the Witcherverse with other fantasy worlds.

The most obvious influence on Sapkowski's name-creation is J.R.R. Tolkien's *glossopoeia*—Tolkien's own word for language invention. Sapkowski's use of Celtic and Nordic elements in the Elder Speech has parallels with Tolkien's use of European languages—primarily Finnish, but also Celtic languages, Latin, and Greek—in constructing the Elvish languages, Quenya and Sindarin. Tolkien also understood his "translation" of the language of Rohan—Rohirric—to stand in the same relation to the Common Speech of Middle Earth as the Mercian dialect of Old English does to modern English.

Tolkien's *glossopoeia* sometimes even gives us words with double or triple etymologies. For example, *mathom*, used by hobbits to mean "antique," "heirloom," or "anything that Hobbits had no immediate use for but were unwilling to throw away" comes from *māþum*, the Old English word for "precious thing" or "treasure," and the Proto-Germanic *maiþmaz*, meaning "gift, present."[1] Likewise, Saruman's tower of Orthanc means "Mount Fang" in Sindarin and "Cunning Mind" in Rohirric, which is close to "cunning device," the word's meaning in Old English.[2] The relationship with real-world languages is not arbitrary and may reveal deeply held beliefs, as in the devout Catholic Tolkien's use of "marië" to signify "happiness" in Quenya, which almost certainly alludes to the Virgin Mary.

Similar techniques were adopted by Tolkien's contemporaries and successors. C.S. Lewis used Turkish nouns such as *aslan* ("lion") and *taş* ("stone") in *The Chronicles of Narnia*, and Ursula Le Guin occasionally used Japanese lexical items, for example "the Lord Segoy" from the Japanese word すごい ("sugoy," "great") to refer to the deity or force of nature worshipped in Earthsea. Le Guin also referenced previous fantasy worlds: for example, her use of the word *tolk* for "stone" in the "Old Speech" almost certainly conceals a tribute to Tolkien himself.[3]

Sapkowski makes the same kind of puns and also takes a number of words from Tolkien and Le Guin: for example, Myrkvid (Mirkwood) Forest and Riverdell (Rivendell).[4] Ori Reuven probably owes his name to Tolkien's dwarf Óri in *The Hobbit*, and the names Ettariel and Toruviel echo Tolkien's Elvish names, such as Tinúviel.[5] The name of the legendary dwarf ancestor Rhundurin is obviously derived from Tolkien's Durin, the ancestor of the race of dwarves, and from Rhûn (meaning "east" in Sindarin), which references the Sea of Rhûn associated with the first awakening of the elves. The name therefore combines the origin myths of two of Tolkien's races. Likewise, Duny, the discarded child-name of Ged or Sparrowhawk in Le Guin's *The Wizard of Earthsea* is recycled as the discarded name of the Emperor Emhyr in the *Witcher* novels.

But there's more to all this than just literary name-dropping. The echoing of "old names" from previous fantasy realms creates the sense of a shared world where some of the same rules may apply.

Schools of Magic and the Mystical Power of the Word

It's not surprising, then, that Sapkowski's use of names in incantations and talk about magic also has a link with other fantasy worlds. When he gives us a detailed account of Ciri's instruction in magical language by Yennefer, he's also continuing a tradition harking back to Le Guin's school of wizardry and its study of naming in the Old Speech or True Speech overseen by the Master Namer of Roke—a vital practice in a fantasy world where power over persons or entities is gained by learning their true names.[6] Ciri's gradual mastery of the Elder Speech also recalls passages in Tolkien when a non-native speaker of Elvish rises to the occasion by breaking into the High Speech in moments of encounter, crisis, or triumph. Examples include Frodo's words of greeting to the elves that he meets in the Shire, Sam's invocation of Elbereth in the fight against Shelob, and Aragorn's echoing of the words of Elendil at his coronation.

The connection between the *Witcher* novels and other fantasy literature through invented language also invites us to compare the word's
relation to the world in terms of magical invocations across this tradition. In Tolkien's work, words have a power transcending the world,
based upon the belief in a divine Word which brought the world into
being. Though Tolkien is adamant that only the One can truly create and
anything else is a case of sub-creation, we are (perhaps paradoxically)
given hints that Elvish magic and the music of the angel-like Ainur can
call things into being (as in Galadriel's "I sang of leaves, of leaves of gold/
And leaves of gold there grew ..."), which seems to be a *speech
performance* in the way that Stanley Tambiah understands it.[7] In Le
Guin's writing, the power of the word in magic can summon or change
things or create illusions, but cannot create things themselves *ex nihilo*
(out of nothing); nevertheless, as previously mentioned, knowledge of the
true name of a person or object confers immense power over it, so there
is a sense in which the word still dominates the world. Despite her
declared preference for a nature-focused Taoism over a mystical
Christianity, Le Guin's fantasy world is still dominated by the power of
words.[8] According to the Master Namer of the world of Earthsea, true
magic can only be worked by those who speak the Hardic tongue of
Earthsea and the Old Speech from which it grew, which is "the language
Segoy spoke who made the islands of the World."[9]

In Sapkowski's fantasy world, the transcendent power of the word is not
as great, since magic is the channeling of the energies of nature, and words
may sometimes be entirely dispensed with. Yet to name in the Witcherverse
is often to command the presence of that which is named. Also, despite the
avowed atheism of Sapkowski himself and many of the witchers and wizards in the narrative, it's hard to detach naming as invocation from the
mystical, especially in the invocation of eternal light (*eveigh Aine*). Aine is
also the Irish goddess of the summer, and knowing this opens up another
world within the word. This could be taken as part of a materialistic
account of how religion arose from natural magic, but might equally be
seen as indicating a sacred source of the invoked light.

Echoes and Intertexts

"Didn't you go to Oxenfurt?" Yenn asks Geralt in the third season of
Netflix's *Witcher*, when he claims to have difficulty in taking in the names
of all those present at the magical-academic cocktail party at Aretuza. Few
will have difficulty in translating this into "real-world" terms as "Didn't
you go to Oxford?" Locations and other proper names in *The Witcher*
novels echo twentieth-century fantasy fiction, but they also point toward
our contemporary reality, as well as to its inherited myths, history, folktales, and literature.

There are numerous echoes of Arthurian legend: the forest of Broklilon references the enchanted forest of Brocéliande; the name "Yennefer" can be taken as a form of the name of Arthur's wife "Guinevere" (whose infidelity and childlessness Sapkowski's Yennefer shares); the mortally wounded Geralt and Yennefer are taken to an Isle of Apples which may be the same as the Arthurian "Avalon" or "Ynys Afallach" (which is also referenced in the Elvish name "Avallac'h").[10] Sometimes names taken from northern mythologies are retained intact, as when the statue of the goddess in the temple on Skellige is given the name of Freya's necklace Brisingamen.[11]

Then there are the nods to the classics and the Western literary canon of the Renaissance, sometimes made for comic effect, as when the chivalric Chequered Knight rides a horse with the same name as that of Alexander the Great ("Bucephalus") and references *Don Quixote* by meeting his end in the "Cervantes pass."[12] Likewise, Hotspurn, the dashing young horseman dying of his wounds before he can take Ciri's virginity in *The Tower of the Swallow*, obviously owes his name to Shakespeare's Hotspur in *Henry IV: Part I*, whose rash character and untimely end he has inherited. Aretuza certainly owes its name to the Fountain of Arethuse in Sicily and the Nereid Arethusa, much referenced in English poetry, notably by John Milton.[13] The "back-story" of Arethuse as a virgin nymph in flight from Alpheus obviously resonates with the nature of Aretuza as a seat of female magic.

Proper names like these form a network situating the Witcherverse within the wider world of literature and myth. They are present in the earliest stories in *The Last Wish*, which references the myth of Adam's first wife Lilith ("Lilit"). They coexist with other intertextual references made through stories rather than names, often because the name is so obvious that it needn't be mentioned, as in the reworking of fairytales such as "Beauty and the Beast" and "Cinderella." Such allusions persist in the last pages of the final novel, the prequel *Season of Storms*, where the shapeshifting vixens of Japanese *kitsūne* myth make an appearance as *aguaras* and Dandelion references twentieth-century legend by giving us a version of the song "As Time Goes By" from the film *Casablanca*.[14] In recognizing these allusions, the reader straddles two worlds, the Witcherverse and the original folktale, myth, or movie.

Political Applicability in Disguise

Literary and cultural references in the *Witcher* novels are complemented by the use of proper names from the "real world" which, though they might appear arbitrary, often allude to political events.

Sometimes it's not entirely clear whether a proper name appears primarily for its historical resonance or as a reference to fantasy fiction. Does the name of the swordsmith Esterhazy reference the Hungarian noble family, or Avram Davidson's *Doctor Eszterhazy* fantasy stories set in a fictional version of a crumbling Balkan empire, or both?[15]

Elsewhere, analogies with the real world are more obvious, though Sapkowski uses what Tolkien, in his introduction to *The Lord of the Rings*, called "applicability" as distinct from simple allegory, or a story with hidden meaning.[16] Cintra's buffer-state status between the expansionist Nilfgaardian empire and the Northern kingdoms obviously resembles the predicament of Sapkowski's native Poland, its tragic history of partitions and its predicament in the twentieth century, caught between the powerful and aggressive states of the Soviet Union and Nazi Germany. The name "Cintra" itself references the 1808 "Convention of Cintra," a notorious failure of British statecraft against the expansionist ambitions of Napoleonic France. This suggests an analogy with the failure of the Allied powers to protect Poland against the threat of Soviet expansion and domination in the postwar period, resulting in its incorporation into the Eastern Bloc as a satellite state of Russia during the era of the Warsaw Pact. The connection is made all the more explicit by the negotiations, concluded by the Peace of Cintra, which end the war between the Nordlings and Nilfgaard. This is a peace which various flash-forwards show will end in the domination of the Continent by Nilfgaard. The implication is that Nilfgaard is what the Napoleonic Empire might have been had Napoleon not been defeated at Waterloo, and that it is also what the Soviet Union and its successor, the Russian Federation, has since aspired to be.

Untranslatable Puns ... or Conjunctions of the Spheres?

Sapkowski's allusions to Eastern European politics coexist with multiple references to East European folklore. When the vampire Regis names the mule stolen from the Lyrian army "Dracul," claiming it is "an untranslatable pun," the allusion to Count Dracula hardly needs to be spelled out, even to non-native speakers of Romanian.[17] However, Regis's comment leads us to a linguistic question. We can understand the puns and allusions of the Witcherverse in two ways. They could be seen as the author giving a sort of wink to the reader, cracking a joke, hiding an "Easter egg," airing his knowledge of history, myth, and literature, and playing intertextual games. But we could also provide a meaningful explanation from *within the Witcher narrative itself* of this "stuff from outside," if we speculate that proper names derived from human history entered the Continent along with humans at the time of the Conjunction of the Spheres. When we see Ciri in her role as lady of time and space passing through portals and jumping from one dimension to another, inadvertently spreading bubonic plague and finally ending up with an amorous Sir Galahad on the way to

Arthur's court at Camelot, mythical and historical worlds that we might have thought of as being outside the Witcherverse become part of the plot and world of the novels. According to the Alder King's theory, time is like the ancient snake Ouroboros—and every moment holds past, present, and future—"Eternity is hidden in every moment."[18] Maybe Sapkowski is asking us to take his words seriously and imagine a universe—at least within his fictional world—in which travel to any moment in time and space is possible. His narrative is thus open-ended and we can imagine that other portals or conjunctions might yield passage to an infinity of worlds—who knows, perhaps it is even possible to portal from the Continent to Middle Earth, Earthsea, or Narnia! According to this second perspective, there is no "stuff from outside," because *nothing* is outside.

So there are two ways to understand the significance of Sapkowski's names: on the one hand, the allusive qualities of names are only there in the text, pointing away from the fantasy world toward our own; in the second they are there as *part* of the world of *The Witcher*.

Venus or Evening Star?

We can clarify the difference between the two views by using Gottlob Frege's famous distinction between the "sense" (*Sinn*) and the "reference" (*Bedeutung*) of a word.[19] According to Frege, if we speak of the planet Venus as "the evening star" and "the morning star," we have two different *senses* of the name "Venus," but only a single object of reference; the phrases "the evening star" and "the morning star" both refer to the second planet in our solar system. The reference is to a physical object in the example given, but it's more of a problem to decide which non-physical objects (like ideas, geometrical figures, deceased persons, future discoveries) could be considered objects of reference. Frege himself wasn't sure whether the word "Odysseus" could be said to refer to anything, but philosophers who contested his theory tended to reject the possibility of fictive or mythical entities as referring to anything at all. Bertrand Russell (1872–1970) speaks of "non-entities" such as "Hamlet" and "Apollo" as "denoting terms which do not denote anything."[20] Even if we decide that epic and mythical heroes *can* be objects of reference, then we have to decide whether we are dealing with the same object of reference in, say, the many different versions of the Odysseus or Apollo story. The same question could easily be posed of "the Witcher." It seems clear that "Geralt," "the Witcher," and "the White Wolf" all refer to the same person. But is the Witcher of the novels the same object of reference as that of the Netflix series, the film, and the games? Does the Witcher-as-played-by-Henry-Cavill have the same referent as the Witcher-as-played-by-Liam-Hemsworth?

Let's imagine that the names of fictive and mythical persons do indeed have a referent and that the above problem can be solved by allowing for sub-referents ("the-Witcher-as-played-by-Henry-Cavill" being a sub-referent of "the Witcher"). If this is the case, then "the mule of Regis" and "Draakul" would, according to Frege's theory, each have a different sense but one reference, the beast itself. But how shall we explain that the name "Draakul" also points to another fictional thing, Count Dracula?

If we wish to stick with Frege's distinction between sense and reference, modifying his theory somewhat to cover reference as allusion, we could return to the distinction between the imagined world of the Continent and other locations in the fictional realm created by Sapkowski and the larger pool of information the author points to in his choices of names. We could say that within the Witcherverse the name "Draakul" refers to a mule belonging to Regis and that, since there is no Count Dracula in the Witcherverse, there is an additional *sense* (but not an added reference) to the name. However, we could see the world of the *Witcher* novels as being wider than that of the Witcherverse of the Continent and to include the objects alluded to from our world's history and myth: so in the *Witcher*verse, as distinct from the Witcherverse, we might well have two referents: the mule and the vampire count.

However, things get really complicated when we think of the implications of Ciri traveling through portals to enter the world of Arthurian romance and the historical world. We might then, alternatively, see the Witcherverse (as opposed to the *Witcher*verse) as extended, through the possibility of open portals, to include Transylvania in the time of the legendary Count. In this case, we might say that, in both the Witcherverse and the *Witcher*verse, "Draakul" has two referents, to the mule and to Dracula. The same could be said of any of the examples of "punning" given above. Perhaps ultimately, the consideration of fictive entities might also lead us to abandon Frege's *Sinn/Bedeutung* distinction in favor of a view in which "evening star" and "morning star" both refer to something perceived, but do not refer to exactly the same thing.

Whichever view we take, we are confronted within the *Witcher* novels with a rich realm of meaning and reference in which a single word opens portals and pathways into other worlds, or, to use a different metaphor, creates its own conjunction of the spheres.

Notes

1. J.R.R. Tolkien, *The Lord of the Rings* (Boston: Houghton Mifflin Company, 1993), 18.
2. See https://tolkiengateway.net/wiki/Orthanc#:~.
3. Ursula Le Guin, *The Earthsea Quartet* (London: Penguin, 1993), 47–48.
4. Andrzej Sapkowski, *The Tower of the Swallow*, trans. David French (London: Gollancz, 2020), 265.

5. Andrzej Sapkowski, *The Time of Contempt*, trans. David French (London: Gollancz, 2020), 208–210, 212. "Etariel" also resembles "Estarriol," the true name of Vetch in Le Guin's *A Wizard of Earthsea*, in *The Earthsea Quartet*, 70; Andrzej Sapkowski, *Baptism of Fire*, trans. David French (London: Gollancz, 2020), 30.
6. Le Guin, *The Earthsea Quartet*, 50–52.
7. Tolkien (1993), 392; Stanley J. Tambiah, "Form and Meaning of Magical Acts: A Point of View," in Robin Horton and Ruth Finnegan eds., *Modes of Thought: Essays on Thinking in Western and Non-Western Societies* (London: Faber & Faber, 1973). For a more detailed discussion of Tambiah, cf. Ivanchenko, chapter 15 in this volume.
8. Lao Tzu, *Tao Te Ching, A Book about the Way and the Power of the Way: A New English Version by Ursula K. Le Guin* (London and Boston: Shambhala, 1998), Introduction, ix–x.
9. Le Guin, *The Earthsea Quartet*, 50.
10. Afallach, a legendary Welsh figure, member of a divine triad, is associated with Avalon by Geoffrey of Monmouth. For the etymology of the name, also associated with apples, see https://en.wikipedia.org/wiki/Afallach.
11. Sapkowski, *The Tower of the Swallow*, 314–316.
12. Sapkowski, *The Tower of the Swallow*, 254.
13. John Milton, *Lycidas*, l. 85, in *Complete Shorter Poems*, ed. John Carey (Harlow: Longman, 1997), 249.
14. Andrzej Sapkowski, *The Season of Storms*, trans. David French (London: Gollancz, 2020), 349–350.
15. Sapkowski, *The Tower of the Swallow*, 132.
16. Tolkien, *The Lord of the Rings*, 11.
17. Sapkowski, *The Tower of the Swallow*, 79.
18. Sapkowski, *The Lady of the Lake*, 176.
19. Gottlob Frege, "On Sense and Reference," *Zeitschrift für Philosophie und philosophische Kritik* 100 (1892), 25–50. Reprinted in A.W. Moore ed., *Meaning and Reference* (Oxford: Oxford University Press, 1993), 23–42.
20. Bertrand Russell, "On Denoting," *Mind* 14 (1905), 491.

Between Two Camps in the Swamps of Velen

Platonism and Naturalism in the Worlds of *The Witcher*

Steven Kammerer

> Show me, if you can, this invisible chain, stretching from the spiritual world to the one that we perceive, this hidden order, made up of so many diverse beings, which Alexander Pope, following Plato, thought that he could see.
>
> Voltaire[1]

"Metaphysics grounds an age," Martin Heidegger (1889–1976) famously declared in his essay *The Question Concerning Technology*.[2] Applied to the world of *The Witcher*, what Heidegger is saying is that the worldviews that ground social practices (like magic and alchemy) and give meaning to material culture (such as the seals and signs that summon djinn) embody an implicit understanding of what it is to be a human being (or an elf, witcher, monster, or djinn). Or, to express Heidegger's idea more simply, our everyday practices, material culture, and technologies are ultimately grounded by our relation to the whole nature and structure of reality.[3]

For fantasy creators, the historical depth and detail of world-building, offering a sense that a different metaphysical reality is at play, are what makes characters and story arcs feel grounded in reality. Their work can throw into stark relief the interplay of worldviews within our own universe, as well as create carnival mirrors (often only slightly distorted) out of fantasy creations like the *Witcher* world.

The Witcherverse is renowned for pushing the envelope of gritty realism, for its subversion of fantasy genre clichés, its use of horror elements, as well as cutting-edge social and political commentary. These are all characteristics of a "new wave" of dark fantasy world-building, of which *The Witcher* became a flagship.[4] *The Witcher* continues to expand, drawing on a range of Germanic, Slavic, Arabic, Persian, and Japanese folklore.[5] Yet it also rests on the authenticity of magic lore and practices drawn from the

The Witcher and Philosophy: Toss a Coin to Your Philosopher, First Edition.
Edited by Matthew Brake and Kevin S. Decker.
© 2025 John Wiley & Sons, Inc. Published 2025 by John Wiley & Sons, Inc.

storehouse of *Western esotericism*. This includes talismanic magic, alchemy, and astrology that not long ago were relegated to the fringe category of "occultism" (and long banished from serious academic scholarship), but which have taken on increasingly prominent roles in both fantasy world-building as well as academic study today.[6]

These practices of Western esotericism—magic, alchemy, and astrology—are dependent on a mostly discarded worldview that has only recently come into sharp scholarly focus.[7] Francis Yates (1899–1981) called this worldview the "Hermetic tradition," but this name may be too narrowly conceived.[8] In fact, most of the Renaissance mages that Yates studied understood themselves to be followers of Plato (427–347 BCE), and they followed a primordial wisdom tradition—a continuous lineage of prophets and sages to which Plato was a relative latecomer. For these Platonists, the three most ancient sources of wisdom in religion, magic, and science were the Egyptian prophet Hermes Trismegistus, the Persian prophet Zoroaster, and the Hebrew prophet Moses. Lloyd Gerson calls this tradition "big tent Platonism," a continuous, 2300-year story unfolding from the original Platonic Academy (founded in 387 BCE) to the present. For Gerson, Platonism is characterized by a metaphysics of top-down cause-and-effect (in which higher levels of any kind of system exert causal influence over lower levels). An opposing worldview, modern *naturalism*, is essentially characterized by bottom-up causality—like the operations of a machine.[9] Wouter Hanegraaff emphasizes the cosmic "monism" of the Platonic-Hermetic worldview: reality is a continuum stretching from the highest divine source to the coarsest matter, and beings up and down that continuum differ only in the degree of refinement of the elements out of which they are composed.[10]

The world of *The Witcher*—with its peculiar mix of gritty realism, folkloric beings, and magic elements—is a rich environment to track the fault lines between Platonism and naturalism, which play out their conflict in an uncanny mirror-reflection of our own world. The very existence of magic, in particular the practice of talismanic magic that depends upon the correspondence between a sign or image and a celestial intelligence, disrupts naturalism's fundamental distinction between nature and the supernatural.

Where's That Magic to Come From?

Let's take a closer look at those magic witcher swords. Mid-way through *Season of Storms*, Geralt and Dandelion are riding in search of Geralt's stolen swords.[11] The two get to chatting about the legendary magical properties of their quarry, particularly the silver (magic-enhanced) swords required for fighting monsters. Dandelion wants to establish a clear distinction between *natural phenomena*, such as falling meteorites, and *magic*, *or supernatural phenomena.* Dandelion says there's a belief that the magical power of witcher weaponry resides in the steel, in the very ores found in meteorites. But we know that meteorites aren't magical. After all, "They're a natural phenomenon, accounted for by science." So, Dandelion asks: "Where's that magic to come from?"[12]

Geralt challenges Dandelion to recollect his classes in astronomy at the Academy of Oxenfurt with Professor Lindenbrog, known as "Fiddle-Faddle." As it turns out, both Dandelion and Geralt had attended Lindenbrog's astronomy class, though at different times. Geralt walks Dandelion through the structure of the cosmos as taught by Fiddle-Faddle: meteorites break off from the firmament and fall through the elemental planes, which are imbued with powerful energy—the source of all magic and supernatural force—and the meteorite absorbs and retains that energy. "The entire sword is magical," Geralt baits Dandelion, before saying: "Poppycock. Fabrication. You don't find meteorites under every bush. More than half the swords used by witchers were made from steel from magnetic ores." Such swords are "as good as the ones that fell from the sky when it comes to the siderites penetrating the elements."[13]

At first glance, Geralt seems to be pouring his usual cold water onto the notion that witcher swords are magical, and this is certainly how Dandelion takes it: another myth busted by the caustic and level-headed Geralt! But note that Geralt did not in fact reject Fiddle-Faddle's description of the elemental planes as the "sources of all magic," he merely said that witchers use magnetic ore, rather than meteorites, to forge their swords more than half the time. As far as Geralt is concerned, the siderites that penetrate magnetic ore are just as potent as those emanating from the higher spheres, those "sources of all magic and supernatural force."

Rather than myth-busting, he has slyly confirmed the magical status of witcher swords. This is typical for Geralt, and one of many instances where cold water is seemingly thrown onto some supernatural notion, only for the notion to slip away from conversation, quite un-deflated. Sapkowski is once again playing with the idea of magic as merely an augmented type of science. The answer to Dandelion's question, "Ok, but where does the magic *really* come from?" is left open.

What Makes Magic Go?

The exchange between Geralt and Dandelion, along with many other scenes, suggests that the uneasy coexistence of multiple realities is baked into the very structure of *The Witcher*'s cosmology. In it, the great cataclysm called the "Conjunction of the Spheres" tore fissures between universes, allowing humans, monsters, and "chaos magic" to emerge onto a Continent already inhabited by elder races. These races brought their own source of magic from a previous universe, and so differing views on how magic works are at the heart of much of the conflict on the Continent. We see book burnings, witch burnings, alchemy as both summoning divine power and as practical medicine, the synthesis and separation of magic and science, and the warfare of cult-gangs in the streets. All this could be a description of fourth-century Alexandria, Egypt, center of the Platonic School during the rapid rise of Christianity.

It's also descriptive of the Free City of Novigrad in the 1270s, the time of the video game *The Witcher 3: Wild Hunt*. Built on Elvish foundations during the First Arrival, Novigrad hosted the signing of a nonaggression pact in the eighth century by mages, priests, and druids. Ultimately, the union split over differences regarding the concept of magic. Four hundred years later, Novigrad has become the center of a racist and anti-magic pogrom led by the cult of the Eternal Flame as part of their inquisition against elves, mages, sorceresses, and any humans who would harbor them. Unfortunately, any way out of these dark times can only be through an understanding of the complexity of these many differences. And that starts with metaphysics—from the ground of reality on up.

In our world, Heidegger thought that for 2300 years only one metaphysical worldview dominated the West, what he called "western philosophy since Plato," or "the tradition of metaphysics," or "the forgetfulness of being."[14] According to Heidegger, all of Western thinking since Plato tended to divide reality into dead matter and transcendent Forms—which both produce and make intelligible what we call "nature," tilting civilization inexorably toward the eventual triumph of thinking-as-calculation and technology.[15]

However, there's been a broad consensus that Heidegger was a bad reader of Plato—such criticisms had already been leveled at Heidegger by his own students.[16] They pointed to later Platonic dialogues, such as the *Timaeus*, which present the cosmos as just the kind of dynamic "presencing of being"—in which the mental and physical realms are deeply enmeshed rather than divided off from one another—that Heidegger sought.[17] It was through commentaries on Plato's *Timaeus* that later Platonists elaborated the structure of the cosmos as anything but static and dualistic. Instead, it was interpreted as a "great chain of being," with what's contained in the ultimate source separated out with increasing admixtures and dilutions.[18] Spheres embedded within spheres like a Russian doll or a telescoped antenna, it was this cosmic structure that made magic "go" in "big tent Platonism."

Court mages and street magicians are all about instrumentalizing magic and manipulating celestial beings like djinn (we're looking at you, Yennefer of Vengerberg!). But nature as seen in the Platonist picture ultimately resists being "enframed," as Heidegger put it, as mere "standing reserve"—raw materials—to be exploited. Yennefer often frames her view of magic in terms of technology, for instance in her lessons to Ciri at the Temple of Melitele: "Magic extends its hand towards you from behind the closed door, towards you, a tiny grain of sand in the workings of the Clock of Fate. Chaos extends its talons towards you, still uncertain if you will be a tool or an obstacle in its design!"[19] In other lessons to Ciri, she harnesses different viewpoints: "those who believe magic is an art are also correct."[20] And in "The Last Wish" quest in *The Witcher 3* video game, she summons a djinn—not to harness its power for her own ends, but to negotiate a deal whereby the djinn, in exchange for its freedom, dissolves the bonds of Fate that had tied her and Geralt together since *The Last Wish*. It's a great tie-in from book to game, showing that Yennefer has learned greater respect for the power and autonomy of djinn, while she's also intent on resolving issues of consent and free will in her relationship with Geralt.

A Cosmic Waterfall

Heidegger saw our age of technology as the necessary outcome of Platonic metaphysics, but in *From Plato to Platonism*, Lloyd Gerson presents the opposite view. He argues that the core of the philosophies and traditions under "big tent Platonism" can best be understood in negative terms, a conjunction of "antis," such as *anti-materialism, anti-mechanism,* and *anti-nominalism* (nominalism being the view that reality is ultimately comprised of discrete, individual entities), all of which together make up the view *anti-naturalism*. For Gerson, any analysis in, for example, the life sciences or philosophy of mind that invokes top-down cause-and-effect pulls toward the Platonist camp, while bottom-up or "moving billiard ball" explanations of physical processes pull toward the naturalist camp.

The term "supernatural," most often used to distinguish established science from mysterious, possibly science-like magic, might seem to be helpful here, but it's actually quite slippery. When characters like Yennefer use signs and seals to summon djinn, the place of such supernatural creatures in a Platonic cosmos is not made clear. In the "big tent Platonist" universe, a continuous cycle of causation is always flowing out from a Source and returning to it—it's not a one-time event. Reality gushes like a waterfall from the source in the One, gradually mixing with ever coarser elements as it flows down through the celestial spheres while generating a literal *pan-demonium* of beings and intelligences (djinn and daemons, angels and demons, and legions of celestial intelligences organized by the eight celestial spheres) until, flowing out into the sublunary sphere down at the hard material end of things, it finally tatters off into nothingness, like the raggedy edge of your worn pair of bell-bottom jeans.[21]

We see something like this alluded to in *Season of Storms*, when Geralt describes to Dandelion how meteors gather magic power as they descend through elemental planes. The Aristotelian–Ptolemaic model of nested cosmic spheres that Sapkowski draws on for this passage presupposes the emanation structure just discussed.[22] A hierarchy of nested spheres that are interlocked—and increasingly more magically potent as you ascend—derive their being, step-wise, from the sphere above and ultimately from the source at the top of this hierarchy.

Every level in this hierarchy is subject to the workings of magic and can affect it. It is the burden of the magician to understand the intricate interrelationships that exist between the various objects and powers on the chain of being before embarking on their operations. Performing magic within a reality structured according to this worldview is no easy thing. From a foundation of knowledge of the vast and intricate structure of the cosmos, the magician learns the hidden correspondences between the plants, animals, and minerals of the lower world and the spiritual forces of the heavenly bodies in the upper world. The Neoplatonist philosopher Plotinus (c. 204/5–270 CE) argues in *The Enneads* that true magic is not merely a technology because spell-binding is "dependent on no interfering machination; the true magic is internal to the All."[23] For this reason, "even the Celestials, the Daimones" are not immune from the effects of magical operations, since each level within an emanationist cosmos is bound internally to each other by true magic.[24]

How to *Really* Summon a Djinn

Modern fantasy tends to divide magic into two types: natural magic (*magia naturalis*) is sharply distinguished from necromancy and *goetia* (or calling upon demons). In our world, this distinction fully hardened under the intense pressure of the early modern witch-hunts and the anti-Platonic, anti-magic movements of the Reformation and Counter-Reformation.[25] The anonymous author of the thirteenth-century *Speculum astronomiae* (*Mirror of the Science of the Stars*) coined the term "astrological images" (*imagines astronomicae*)—talismans whose power was supposed to come only from the natural influence of the stars, and thus not from the "demons." A long-lasting debate about natural magic versus *goetia* subsequently arose between supporters such as Albert the Great and opponents like Albert's student, Thomas Aquinas.

Yennefer, in her description of the magic and religions of the Continent written for Dandelion's compendium *The World of the Witcher*, also sharply distinguishes natural magic from necromancy and *goetia*. For the sorceress of Vengerberg, necromantic practices are concerned with "acquiring simple information from the recently departed" whereas *goetia* is, "plainly speaking, demonology."[26] Both are banned under the edicts of the Old Conclave, although special dispensations are granted to study them. Yennefer says there's a sound, self-preservative rationale for the banning of *goetia*: because of the ferocity and power of most demons, "a successful summoning usually results in the would-be goet's death."[27] In the Witcherverse, summoning a demon doesn't require great ability or knowledge, but merely access to the appropriate magical formula. Thus, the temptation to conjure is strong among novices.

Let's take a closer look at the magic formulae of *goetic* practice. Many of the signs, sigils, and runes of *The Witcher*, like those in medieval grimoires of our world, have their origin in the hundreds of magic signs and a mysterious celestial alphabet known to scholars as the *charaktêres* found in the Greek Magical Papyri. Scholars of magic are only now beginning to fully catalogue and categorize these *charaktêres* in an attempt to crack the code.[28] But the positioning and function of the *charaktêres* within the hundreds of formulae indicates that the mysterious signs both summon celestial intelligences and hold power in reserve within themselves. This system of mysterious writing to address celestial beings forms the original blueprint for the magic signs of the medieval grimoires, from the formulae of the twelfth-century *Picatrix*, to Agrippa's *Three Books of Occult Philosophy* to the famous grimoire published in Calvinist Switzerland, the *Arbatel*—as well as to the eight-point star of Yennefer's medallion and the nine-point star over a pentagram that she draws on the floor to summon her first djinn in *The Last Wish*.[29]

This corresponds with the apparent properties of the seal in the "The Last Wish" quest: Yennefer and Geralt must piece together the shards of a broken seal that is imprinted with the sign of a moline cross surrounded by pentagrams. Those images are the direct calling card of a particular djinn, and, in combination with Yennefer's incantation, the djinn has no choice but to attend to its summoning.

The *Witcher* world here is combining talismanic image-magic with the folklore of the three-wish-granting djinn. This particular synchronizing of disparate sources in fact winds up providing a more accurate reflection of djinn-lore within our world than do some of the tales of our *1001 Nights*. It was Antoine Galland, the French translator of the *Nights*, who adopted the three-wishes or "foolish-wishes" motif from central European folklore and indeed appears to have invented the Aladdin story to add to his French *1001 Nights* translation.[30]

Djinn-summoning by way of talismanic magic organized around the central image of the pentagram has a long tradition in the East in our own world. This lore reaches back through medieval Islamic culture to the second-century-CE *Testament of Solomon*, in which the archangel Michael first gifts King Solomon a ring imprinted with a "pentalpha" (literally meaning "five A's," more commonly known as a pentagram) in order to summon "daimons" to help build the Temple in Jerusalem. Thus, djinn are well accustomed to responding to the call of the pentagram and other magic signs and *charaktêres*.[31]

Forward in All Directions! (By Way of the Grimoires of the Platonic Tradition)

This indeterminacy, I've been arguing, opens a space for "inter-worldview" dialogue. The *Witcher* world's post-conjunction Continent is a mess of humanity, elves, monsters, and magic lore thrown together from out of a multitude of incommensurable universes. It's an ideal place to deepen our awareness of how worldviews coexist and compete to ground our practices and define our relation to others. My hope is that fantasy world-builders will further enrich their creations by grounding distinct worldviews with more sharply defined metaphysics, as well as with a more comprehensive exploration of the grimoires of the "Platonic-Hermetic" tradition. This would lend greater coherence to their magic practices and intermediary beings such as djinn. Whether we're immersed in the *Witcher* world or going about the day in our world, we too are being continually pulled between the opposing "big tent" camps of Platonism and Naturalism, even those of us just trying to remain neutral and roam the swampy No-Man's land of Velen, hunting monsters for coin.

Notes

1. Voltaire, "Discours en vers sur l'homme," in *Oeuvres* completes, vol. 9 (Paris: L. Moland, 1877–1883), 415.
2. Martin Heidegger, *The Question Concerning Technology* (New York: Harper & Row, 1977), 115.
3. For an excellent example of a comparative worldview approach as applied to *The Game of Thrones*, see Nathan Fredrickson, "Comparative Worldview Studies and *A Song of Ice and Fire*: World Religions, Comparison, and Fictional Worlds," in Matthew Brake ed., *Theology and Game of Thrones* (Lanham, MD: Lexington Books, 2021), 314–379.
4. "New wave" dark fantasy is often characterized by its mix of social-political critique with gothic-horror elements. See Mark Lawrence's *The Broken Empire Trilogy* or the *Castlevania* franchise. A prime example of "old wave" dark fantasy would be Michael Moorcock's *Elric* series. Elric indeed had a direct influence on the look and character of Geralt. The invention of the fantasy antihero in a world rife with racism and complex political intrigue was one of the many innovations of the *Elric* series.
5. The most recent Dark Horse comic sees Geralt hunt the mysterious beings known as yōkai within a Japanese-inspired secondary world. See Rafal Jaki (story) and Hataya (art), *The Witcher: Ronin* (Milwaukie, OR: Dark Horse Books, 2022).
6. See Wouter Hanegraaff, *Esotericism and the Academy: Rejected Knowledge in Western Culture* (New York: Cambridge University Press, 2012).

7. For much of the twentieth century, Western Esotericism was still part of the "wastebasket category of rejected knowledge," as Hanegraaff calls it in *Esotericism and the Academy*, 230. There are many indications that medieval magic is no longer regarded as a marginal topic: see Penn State University Press's outstanding Magic in History series in particular!

8. See Francis Yates, *Giordano Bruno and the Hermetic Tradition* (Chicago: Chicago University Press, 1964).

9. See Lloyd Gerson, *From Plato to Platonism* (Ithaca, NY: Cornell University Press, 2013). The term "Platonism" is often used by Anglo-American philosophers to refer to the idea that there are abstract objects, such as Platonic "Forms" and mathematical objects, that exist in a realm distinct from either the material world or mind. But Gerson argues this is much too narrow a way of using the term: it isn't what the Church Fathers mean when they talk about Platonism, nor any of the Middle or "Neoplatonists," nor any of the Renaissance or Cambridge Platonists.

10. For a description of Platonic-Hermeticism as a kind of monism see, in particular, "Infinite Fire Webinar IV—Wouter J. Hanegraaff on Platonic Orientalism," YouTube video, March 10, 2013, at https://www.youtube.com/watch?v=s2HCOuY-EiE.

11. Andrzej Sapkowski, *Season of Storms* (New York: Orbit Books, 2022), 129.

12. Sapkowski, *Season of Storms*, 130.

13. Sapkowski, *Season of Storms*, 131.

14. See S.L. Bartky, "*Seinsverlassenheit* in the Later Philosophy of Heidegger," *Inquiry* 10 (1967), 74–88.

15. Martin Heidegger, *Basic Writings*, ed. David Ferrell Krell (New York: Harper, 1977), 177.

16. See Hans-Georg Gadamer, "Plato," in John W. Stanley trans., *Heidegger's Ways* (Albany: State University of New York Press, 1994), 81–93.

17. For Heidegger's most sustained meditation on "presencing" – how subjective experience is enmeshed with the rest of reality – see Martin Heidegger, *What Is Called Thinking?* (New York: Harper & Row, 1968).

18. It was the forgotten figure Eudoxus of Cnidus (c. 408–355 BCE), student of Plato and a teacher of Aristotle, who was the first to formalize the basic cosmic model of concentric celestial spheres revolving around the earth. He gained his astronomical knowledge studying in Heliopolis, Egypt.

19. Andrzej Sapkowski, *Baptism of Fire* (New York: Orbit Books, 2022), 132.

20. Sapkowski, *Baptism of Fire*, 140.

21. I'm indebted to Justin Sledge for this evocative metaphor. See his "Esoterica" channel on YouTube, where he covers a wide variety of topics in Western esotericism.

22. Sapkowski, *Season of Storms*, 131.

23. Plotinus, *The Enneads* (New York: Penguin, 1991), 327.

24. Plotinus, *The Enneads,* 330.

25. See for example Giovanni Battista Crespo's massive volume "On Reading Plato Carefully" (1598), which, despite its gentle title, condemns Platonism in bellicose terms. Crespo frames Plato as "the very source of heresy as such" (quoted in Hanegraaff, *Esotericism and the Academy,* 94).

26. Marcin Batylda, *The World of The Witcher: Video Game Compendium* (Milwaukie, OR: Dark Horse Books, 2015), 88.
27. Batylda, *The World of The Witcher*, 88.
28. See Kristen Dzwiza, "Insight into the Transmission of Ancient Magical Signs," *MHNH: International Journal of Research on Ancient Magic and Astrology* 15 (2015), 31–56. For more on Dzwiza's classification system, see "Ancient Magical Artefacts Explained: 'Solomon's Seal Has Annihilated You'—A Unique Bronze Amulet," in *The Archeology of Ancient Magic and Ritual Practice*, educational video, January 10, 2023, at https://www.youtube.com/watch?v=poJCkknCVQo.
29. Andrzej Sapkowski, *The Last Wish* (New York: Orbit Books, 2022), 271.
30. The Aladdin tale is not in any original Arabic or Persian manuscripts. See Marina Warner, *Stranger Magic: Charmed States & the* Arabian Nights (London: Chatto & Windus, 2011), 16.
31. See Pablo A. Torijano, *Solomon the Esoteric King: From King to Magus, Development of a Tradition* (Leiden: Brill, 2002).

18

"Witch Hunts Will Never Be About Witches"
Scapegoating and Stereotypes of Persecution

Ryan Smock

The Northern Kingdoms are ravaged by war, poverty, lawlessness, and terror. Nilfgaard invades Temeria and Redania from the south while the Scoia'tael—a ragtag army of elves, dwarves, and halflings—wages guerilla warfare from within. Soldiers from all sides sweep through villages, plundering everything of value. Bloodthirsty brigands prowl highroads and alleyways because local authorities are too harried to keep order. Worse still, ghouls, nekkers, drowners, wargs, and all sorts of monstrous baddies stalk the wilderness. What's a villager to do in such grim times? Especially when a white-haired, magic-wielding mutant shows up demanding coin for his "protection." Who's to blame for all the suffering and death?

"It's the non-humans and mages," says the Church of the Eternal Fire, "the creatures twisted and defiled by the Conjunction of the Spheres. It's those who meddle with unholy forces, lusting for power and wealth. They're the reason for our misfortune and only by eradicating them can we have peace and order."

It's easy to think the Church's perspective villainous since it targets *all* nonhumans and mages, including those not associated with war or crime, and therefore blames innocent people for societal problems and failures. Further, we like to think this kind of scapegoating is willful and deliberate, something only wicked people do to avoid responsibility. Sadly, though, René Girard (1923–2015) suggests this is something we all do unconsciously, and more often than we'd like to admit.

"This is open incitement to bloodshed"

To understand how scapegoating works, we must first understand some of Girard's foundational ideas: *mimetic desire*, which may grow into *mimetic rivalry* and then escalate into a *mimetic crisis*. To help with this, let's look

The Witcher and Philosophy: Toss a Coin to Your Philosopher, First Edition.
Edited by Matthew Brake and Kevin S. Decker.

at a central myth of *The Witcher* that links together the short stories, novels, Netflix series, and games. Queen Calanthe throws a birthday ball for Princess Pavetta and dozens of noble suitors attend to compete for her hand.[1] By having the nobles openly contend against each other, Calanthe wants to maximize Pavetta's prestige and, through her marriage, secure an alliance with Crach an Craite of Skellige. There's a hitch, though: Pavetta is betrothed to a cursed knight named Duny. So Calanthe hires Geralt, a witcher, to kill Duny when he appears and prevent the betrothal from being fulfilled.

Almost like clockwork, Pavetta enters the ballroom, the suitors begin their wooing, and Duny appears to announce the betrothal. When Calanthe tricks him into removing his helmet, Duny's curse is revealed. Although human by night, by day he is a beastly creature with prickled fur, a long muzzle, and sharp fangs. Exactly the kind of monster witchers kill, Calanthe thinks. Yet Geralt hesitates, takes Duny's side, and tries to reason with Calanthe and the suitors. It doesn't work. Talk soon erupts into battle, with everyone attacking everyone else.

In *Deceit, Desire, and the Novel*, Girard introduces us to imitative or "mimetic" desire; the idea that, rather than arising spontaneously from within ourselves, desires are copied from others.[2] Whenever we desire, he says, there is a triangular relationship between three elements: the *subject* who desires something, the *mediator* or *model* who points out what should be desired, and the desired *object*.

For now, let's assume Crach is the subject, Calanthe is the mediator, and Pavetta is the object. In this situation, Calanthe shows Crach that Pavetta is desirable, like when one friend says to another, "Hey, check her (or him) out." This is the reason for the ball and why Pavetta is dolled up and paraded. Before Pavetta even enters the room, Crach has internalized Calanthe's modeling and mistakenly thinks his desire for Pavetta arises when he sees her. The truth is, he only imitates what Calanthe first suggests.

Crach isn't alone, though. Dozens of suitors intend to marry Pavetta, so we have several triangular relationships, all of which overlap and interrupt each other. This means Calanthe is not the only mediator. Since the suitors also look to each other, they all become both subjects *and* mediators. Each one stokes the others' desire and this in turn redoubles their own. The problem is that, rather than simply modeling desire, they stand in each other's way as obstacles or *rivals* who must be eliminated. There's only one Pavetta, after all. Eist Tuirseach, Calanthe's romantic partner, warns her that it's only a matter of time before everyone starts fighting. "This is open incitement to bloodshed," he says, "you're simply setting them against each other."[3]

Now let's suppose a suitor other than Crach, like Duny, attracts Pavetta's attention. This introduces still more triangles with Calanthe and the suitors as desiring subjects, Duny as the mediator or obstacle, and

Pavetta as the desired object. When Geralt refuses to kill Duny, things explode. Calanthe shouts for her guards, forcing Geralt and Duny to defend themselves, and the sight of violence spurs the suitors into combat. The conflict is so infectious, with everyone now imitating everyone else, that even Calanthe and Pavetta are drawn into the fray. "As antagonism and violence erupt," states Girard, "they both spread in the same mimetic way, by cumulative resentment and vengeance, producing a state of ... all against all."[4]

The state of "all against all" is called a *mimetic crisis* because the antagonists imitate each other so intensely that they become indistinguishable. Girard writes, "[T]o the extent that their antagonism becomes embittered, a paradox occurs: the antagonists resemble one another more and more. They confront one another all the more implacably because their conflict dissolves the real differences that formerly separated them."[5] At the beginning of the birthday ball, there are real social differences and a code of behavior everyone respects. Calanthe is queen of Cintra, her guests are lesser nobility from various lands, and Geralt is there to provide a service. Everyone acts with respect and honor. As events transpire, however, hierarchy and etiquette collapse. Calanthe is reduced to being a competitor like the rest, Geralt becomes a significant obstacle, and all senses of honor and respect erode. Eventually, it no longer matters what ranks they hold or why they are there: they're all equally engaged in violence, and they're all equally vulnerable. This is where scapegoating begins.

"Novigrad at this time was not the city Geralt knew from his earlier travels"

So far we've focused on a single event, but Girard's concepts also help explain larger cultural events in the world of *The Witcher* as well as in real-life situations. This is because they feature *stereotypes of persecution*, conditions that always seem present when scapegoating occurs.[6] In *The Scapegoat*, Girard outlines four stereotypes. Six steps show how the process cycles:

Step 1: A society or culture is in its normal state. When we think about society in its normal state, a good analogy is the human body. Like a society, the body is a cohesive "system of anatomic differences."[7] It has several different parts, yet the parts all form and act as a single unit. The hand is different from the mouth and stomach, but they work together so we can eat. The tongue and teeth are different, yet their synergy allows us to sing. Likewise, a healthy society such as the city of Novigrad (well, let's pretend it's healthy) has numerous districts, differing due to their functions, who lives there, and what sociocultural backgrounds their inhabitants have. Yet they all form a cohesive system—a bustling trade city that Geralt and his companions adventure in.

Step 2: Something causes a generalized loss of social and cultural differences. Two major events of *The Witcher 3: Wild Hunt* throw Novigrad into mimetic crisis. First, Emhyr's and Radovid's pillaging armies displace hundreds of villagers who seek refuge in the city. We know this because Geralt passes by large crowds stopped at the Pontar River, and because of a guard's comments during the quest "A Deadly Plot":

GERALT: Why've you shut the city gates?

GUARD: So's we can clean it of mages, witches, and other scum that's crawled here since the war began. Aim to catch every last one of 'em, toss 'em on a flamin' pyre, like poxy livestock.

The armies compromise everyone's safety and security, resulting in the loss of social and cultural differences. They must all contend against one another for food, clothing, and shelter. Girard calls this an *external cause* of crisis because some force outside the society drives the conflict.[8] In this case, the cause is war. Other external causes could be plague, drought, flood, famine, natural disasters, giant griffins, or a dragon.

Second, gang wars within Novigrad pit citizens against each other. While looking for Triss Merigold, Geralt runs into the Blindeyes gang who are led by the King of Beggars. The Cutups, Whoreson Junior's gang, fight them for control of Lacehalls and The Bits. Meanwhile, witch hunters hired by the Church of the Eternal Fire scour the city for magic-users and nonhumans. In the game, players encounter such hunters when a merchant named Brandon reports on Triss and Geralt. "My friends ... begged me to notify them if I encountered a mage, sorceress, what have you," he says. "Didn't have the heart to refuse." Since these gang wars originate inside Novigrad's society, they are called *internal causes* of crisis. Religious, political, and social conflicts count as internal causes, too, namely Dandelion's sleeping around and Zoltan's beef with rare Gwent card collectors.

These internal and external causes of crisis lead to "an extreme loss of social order evidenced by the disappearance of the rules and 'differences' that define cultural division."[9] After a certain point in the game, no one can be trusted. The slightest grudge could result in accusation, arrest, or even murder. Everyone is potentially an enemy to everyone else. This, Girard says, is the ideal condition for mob formation. And when people form mobs, adopting a "mob mentality," things get really bad.

Step 3: Someone is accused of committing crimes that eliminate differences, and often of causing the crisis itself. Girard suggests that people place blame rather than identify and resolve the causes of crisis (perhaps because they're unable to):

Men feel powerless when confronted with the eclipse of culture; they are disconcerted by the immensity of the disaster but never look into the natural causes.... Since cultural eclipse is above all a social crisis, there is a strong tendency to explain it by social and, especially, moral causes.... But, rather than blame themselves, people inevitably blame either society as a whole ... or other people who seem particularly harmful for easily identifiable reasons.[10]

In other words, when people confront a crisis, they wrongly identify the cause and cast blame on the scapegoat rather than on the mimetic dynamic in which everyone plays a part. They think putting a name or face to the problem will give them control over it.[11] One common way of doing this is to claim a disaster was sent as divine punishment for wrongdoing. Then, through priests or other holy oracles, the guilty party is made "so generally known" that they can be identified and punished for causing the crisis.[12] This happened in 2020 when COVID-19 crippled the global economy, killed 350,000 people, and infected millions more.[13] One Ukrainian priest suggested the pandemic was God's punishment for allowing same-sex marriage.[14] Although that idea was denounced, he was not the only person to claim COVID was divine retribution. Earlier that year, *USA Today* reported religious leaders throughout the Abrahamic traditions—Christianity, Judaism, and Islam—fielding similar concerns from their congregants.[15] Many believed that there must have been some violation of God's laws. Interestingly, the priest in the opening of *The Witcher 3: Wild Hunt* claims Emhyr's and Radovid's battles "are the gods' whip, chastisement" for the sin of not rejecting magic when it was introduced during the Conjunction of the Spheres.

When divine retribution is not claimed, mobs call for scapegoats using more human-centered reasons. They accuse their victims of crimes to rationalize blaming and punishing someone other than themselves. Most often the alleged crimes transgress normal divisions of society. Girard explains:

> First there are violent crimes which choose ... people whom it is most criminal to attack.... [A] king, a father, the symbol of supreme authority, and in biblical and modern societies the weakest and most defenseless, especially young children. Then there are sexual crimes: rape, incest, bestiality. The ones most frequently invoked transgress the taboos that are considered the strictest in the society in question. Finally there are religious crimes, such as profanation of the host. Here, too, it is the strictest taboos that are transgressed.[16]

In *The Witcher*, mages are thought to enslave kings with their unnatural craft, while witchers are considered abominations against nature who prey upon the helpless. Both are believed to steal children from their parents. In the novels, witchers infamously invoke the "Law of Surprise," which demands fathers give as payment "that which they already have but do not know," and, in the Netflix series, a mage named Tissaia de Vries purchases Yennefer from her family for less than half the price of a pig.

An important point for Girard is that the victims being blamed—the scapegoats—need not be completely innocent. They may be guilty of other specific crimes, and even of some crimes they are accused of, but they are innocent of causing the crisis. The mob, however, is not.

"This was inevitable ... because you're different. And killing is easier than tolerating"

One appalling aspect of scapegoating is that while victims may be chosen at random, they may be singled out because of an abnormality. "Sometimes," states Girard, "the persecutors choose their [scapegoats] because they belong to a class that is particularly susceptible to persecution."[17]

Step 4: The people accused have specific marks which suggest they're victims. Every society has standards of normalcy. We can never get rid of them, and under many circumstances, they are good to have. It's considered normal, for example, to be at work on time, to wear clothes in public, and to maintain decent grades. Standards of normalcy can, however, be used for wrongful discrimination, especially when a particular person or group doesn't meet prevailing physical, religious, or social benchmarks. One could be justly punished for being late to work but not for having more or less melanin, or for believing differently about God.

Returning to our analogy of the body as a cohesive system of differences, we see that it is a closed system. A normal human body has two legs, two arms, and one head. So if someone had seven arms or five heads, that would be abnormal and we might say the person has a deformity. This also goes the other way: poor mental health, sickness, injury, and disability all single someone out for "discriminatory measures that make them victims ... to the extent to which their presence disturbs the ease of social exchange."[18] Witchers, mages, dwarves, elves, and halflings all fail to meet the prevailing benchmark of "being human," so they are more likely to be blamed for bad events even if they have nothing to do with them.

The notion of a closed system of differences extends into religious and social spheres, too. "One of the criteria by which victims are selected," says Girard, "though relative to the individual society, is transcultural in principle. There are very few societies that do not subject their minorities, all the poorly integrated or merely distinct groups, to certain forms of discrimination and even persecution."[19] That is to say, because religious or ethnic minorities are different, they're often first to be singled out as scapegoats. But "minority" here does not just refer to ethnicity or religious affiliation. Any extreme characteristic attracts the possibility of collective destruction. The extremely rich and powerful are as likely to be scapegoated as the meager and the meek. The most beautiful and the most virtuous are apt targets, just like the ugliest and most wretched.

Step 5: Violence against the accused. Once a mob has chosen a scapegoat, they enact any variety of punishments. In general, the most successful punishments are the most public and violent. Torture, exile, public humiliation, and death are historically common, and they are pervasive in The Witcher universe. During the quest "Count Reuven's Treasure," Caleb Menge commands his Temple Guard to rip off Triss's fingernails.

Geralt is banned from Blaviken in both the novels and the Netflix series. Willis, the dwarven blacksmith of White Orchard, is shunned by his fellow villagers.[20] And Moritz, a mage in Novigrad, is publicly burned at the stake.

The key factor here is that the mob must unanimously believe they're doing the right thing—that the scapegoat is guilty, and that the punishment is righteous. Caleb, the Temple Guard, and the villagers all seem convinced that their causes are just. In the real world, however, there can be grave consequences: if the slightest hint of the victim's innocence emerges, the crowd's unity is lost, and the scapegoat cannot be used to fulfill its purpose.

Step 6: The mimetic crisis is resolved. A society or culture returns to its normal state. The purpose of scapegoating is to reunify a society torn apart by mimetic desire and the resulting crisis of all against all. "Mimeticism," Girard states, "is the original source of all man's troubles, desires, and rivalries, his tragic and grotesque misunderstandings, the source of all disorder and therefore equally of all order through the mediation of scapegoats."[21] He means that the same imitative processes which cause people to fight against each other later unite them in heaping all their anger and hostility onto a single victim. After the punishment is complete, there is a cathartic purge, and the mimetic crisis is over.

Note, however, that this does not mean the problem has been solved. While they may have resolved the social crisis, the internal and external causes of it remain. No matter how many mages are burned and regardless of whether Novigrad is cleansed of nonhumans, Emhyr's and Radovid's armies are still camped outside, and gang wars still boil beneath the streets. Whatever peace is bought with the life of a scapegoat is tentative and fragile at best. It can never last. Inevitably, another must be found.

"Can we chart a course back into the light?"

At Pavetta's birthday ball, we saw mimetic desire transform first into rivalry and then into violent crisis. If things had not been interrupted by Pavetta's use of magic and the sheer absurdity of Coodcoodak strangling a bagpipe, Geralt and Duny would have been blamed for the conflict despite their innocence. All the stereotypes of persecution were present in that story, just as they were present in the Novigrad situation:

- It was a normal party.
- Sociocultural differences disappeared when everyone began fighting.
- Duny and Geralt would have been accused of causing the crisis.[22]
- A monster and a mutant, they both have marks suggesting them as victims.

- They would have been killed.
- Things would have returned to normal and Pavetta would have been married off.

Moreover, like the Church of the Eternal Fire, Calanthe preyed on Duny and Geralt rather than recognize her own ambition as causing the problem.

The good news is that knowing how scapegoating works in *The Witcher* better equips us to solve problems in the real world without perpetuating a vicious cycle. First, it enables us to choose better models to imitate. We can be more wary of people trying to seduce us into groupthink or mob mentality, especially when it polarizes us against a specific person or group. Second, we can recognize that placing blame doesn't actually solve anything. By not victimizing others to make ourselves feel better, we are not only being respectful, but we are also freeing up resources to identify and perhaps remedy the internal or external causes of a crisis. Lastly, we can resist objectifying people as "enemies" or "prizes" by forestalling the drives to prevail and possess.

By showing restraint and engaging Duny as a person rather than a monster, Geralt turned a rival into a friend. Near the end of the story, Duny says:

> When I found out who you were, there in the hall, I hated you and thought very badly of you. I took you for a blind, bloodthirsty tool, for someone who kills coldly and without question, who wipes his blade clean of blood and counts the cash. But I've become convinced that the witcher's profession is worthy of respect. You protect us not only from the evil lurking in the darkness, but also from that which lies within ourselves.[23]

Shouldn't we all aspire to do the same?

Notes

1. Andrzej Sapkowski, *The Last Wish: Introducing the Witcher* (New York: Orbit Books, 2022), 136.
2. René Girard, *Deceit, Desire, and the Novel: Self and Other in Literary Structure* (Baltimore: The Johns Hopkins University Press, 1966), 10–15.
3. Sapkowski, *The Last Wish*, 161.
4. René Girard, *Evolution and Conversion: Dialogues on the Origins of Culture* (London: Continuum, 2010), 64.
5. René Girard, *I See Satan Fall Like Lightning* (Maryknoll: Orbis Books, Kindle, 2001), 12–13.
6. René Girard, *The Scapegoat* (Baltimore: The Johns Hopkins University Press, Kindle, 1989), 39.
7. Girard, *The Scapegoat*, 21.
8. Girard, *The Scapegoat*, 12.

9. Girard, *The Scapegoat*, 12.
10. Girard, *The Scapegoat*, 14.
11. Girard, *The Scapegoat*, 4.
12. Girard, *The Scapegoat*, 2–3.
13. "2020 Final Death Statistics: COVID-19 as an Underlying Cause of Death vs. Contributing Cause," *CDC National Center for Health Statistics*, April 18, 2023, at https://www.cdc.gov/nchs/pressroom/podcasts/2022/20220107/20220107.htm.
14. Harmett Kaur, "Ukrainian Church Leader Who Called Covid-19 'God's Punishment' for Same-Sex Marriage Tests Positive for Virus," CNN, April 18, 2023, at https://www.cnn.com/2020/09/09/europe/ukrainian-leader-covid-same-sex-marriage-trnd/index.html.
15. Lindsay Schnell, "Is the Coronavirus an Act of God? Faith Leaders Debate Tough Questions Amid Pandemic," *USA Today*, April 18, 2023, at https://www.usatoday.com/story/news/nation/2020/04/02/coronavirus-god-christain-jewish-muslim-leaders-saying-deadly-plague/5101639002.
16. Girard, *The Scapegoat*, 15.
17. Girard, *The Scapegoat*, 16.
18. Girard, *The Scapegoat*, 18.
19. Girard, *The Scapegoat*, 17.
20. Granted, this depends on choosing the story option to turn in the arsonist.
21. Girard, *The Scapegoat*, 165.
22. After the battle ends, Calanthe admits that she would have blamed Geralt and had him killed if things turned out differently.
23. Sapkowski, *The Last Wish*, 178.

POSTMODERNISM

19

The Witcher as Postmodern Fairytale

Emily Vega and Walter Barta

"Another fairytale," says the Professor, the villain of the first CD Projekt Red *Witcher* videogame, as he kills Leo, a friend and fellow witcher to Geralt of Rivia. The Professor shoots Leo just to see if a witcher can catch an arrow in midflight, like the "fairytale" says. This moment and many others are self-conscious of *The Witcher*'s place in, but also critical of, the fairytale tradition. Such moments make Andrzej Sapkowski's *The Witcher* saga and related media—the stories, shows, and games—a special case of the fantasy genre. On the one hand, the tales of *The Witcher* saga have the forms of fairytales; on the other hand, they take the philosophical form of a postmodern criticism of its genre. In this way, *The Witcher* might be said to be a "postmodern fairytale."

"Folklore is a valuable *brand*"

In *The Postmodern Condition: A Report on Knowledge*, Jean-Francois Lyotard (1924–1998) defines "postmodernism" as an "incredulity towards meta-narratives."[1] This "incredulity," or disbelief, often takes the form of self-referential and self-critical themes, sometimes offered ironically. Lyotard's "meta-narratives," the grand, authoritative stories that form our worldviews, include the sacred parables from holy books, classic stories—like fables and fairytales—grand philosophical systems—like those of Plato and Aristotle—and today, even novels, television shows, or video-games. In Lyotard's work and others', the characteristic postmodern move is to shed doubt (and new light) on stories and worldviews (not unlike what a "Philosophy and Pop Culture" book tries to do). So, by Lyotard's definition, a postmodern fairytale would be a fairytale that is incredulous toward fairytales.

Fairytales are a subgenre of folklore, which is the "lore," or expression of shared identity through traditions, of the "folk," persons with common traits. Folklore, then, consists of the texts, tales, stories, and practices that

The Witcher and Philosophy: Toss a Coin to Your Philosopher, First Edition.
Edited by Matthew Brake and Kevin S. Decker.
© 2025 John Wiley & Sons, Inc. Published 2025 by John Wiley & Sons, Inc.

have been shared and passed down since the beginning of human connection and communication. In his work *The Folkloresque: Reframing Folklore in a Popular Culture World*, folklorist Michael Dylan Foster applies postmodernism to analyze modern fairytales; he suggests that the fantasy genre, of which *The Witcher* saga is a part, has become postmodern through its repetitions of folkloric "tropes," or significant, recurrent themes.[2] In explaining the strange relationship between new media and old stories, Foster, following postmodern philosophers like Lyotard, describes how mass marketing picks through and reassembles folklore for contemporary audiences, particularly those who have been socialized by digital mediums and communication:

> Simply put, the *folkloresque* is popular culture's own ... perception and performance of folklore ... it refers to creative, often commercial products or texts (e.g., films, graphic novels, video games) that give the impression to the consumer ... that they derive directly from existing folkloric traditions.[3]

Whether a *Witcher* fan watches the Netflix series, plays through the video games, or reads the original novels and short stories, they're interacting with folklore as represented by different creators. The original fairytale has been divorced from its original context to be reshaped and reformatted for new audiences and new media presentations.

In this manner, the folkloresque relates contemporary work to older work; the original folk create and disseminate the various folkloric elements (creatures, monsters, events) that later works like *The Witcher* will incorporate. The writers of *The Witcher* universe borrow from these folklores to craft their vision of the stories' worlds, creating a "text" that, although reliant on folklore, does not represent a singular tradition, national, generational, or otherwise. Foster affirms, "the folkloresque signals popular culture's recognition that folklore is a valuable *brand*," to be rebranded and resold like other products.[4] However, though *The Witcher*, a commercial product, is not a real work of folklore, it feels "real" enough to consumers because of the many traditions it draws from, particularly through the many familiar monsters and folk figures that populate its narrative. The reader, viewer, or player of *Witcher* media consumes these texts and is introduced to new permutations of old traditions, promoting their relevance for new generations of folk. But, as Lyotard would point out, this whole cultural and technological process is postmodern in the sense that it fundamentally changes the meanings of these grand stories, and their associated worldviews, which puts into question the very idea that such grand stories can be authoritative in guiding our lives.

As folkloresque form of media, *The Witcher* can be thought of as a series of altered fairytales, each one an instance of Lyotard's postmodern "incredulity." This incredulity is directed toward *internal meta-narratives*, grand stories within the story-world of the text; *external meta-narratives*, grand stories brought in from the real world outside the text; and *adaptive/ interactive media experiences*, varieties of different storytelling formats enabled by modern telecommunications technologies—formats that Lyotard points out have transformative effects on the way tales are told. Each of these we'll discuss in more detail as they appear in *The Witcher*.

"Why look for truth in a ballad?"

Throughout *Witcher* media, we frequently see the creators' incredulity toward meta-narratives internal to the story-world. For example, the bard Jaskier, Geralt's long-term friend and travel companion, is a character who often represents the role of stories and the storytelling process. In the novels, Jaskier's songs show how stories function within the *Witcher* universe. Geralt uses Jaskier's services as advertising for his witcher profession, having him spread the good word about witchers across the Continent. In fact, on their first meeting, Jaskier excitedly tells Geralt about the Witcher's own adventures, wrongly citing several species and breeds of monsters that Geralt has supposedly defeated. Hearing this, Geralt clarifies the facts about his work and the monsters he's actually killed. This self-conscious reference to lore, supernatural species, and oral transmission through folk song makes *The Witcher* especially folkloresque. In one violent incident in the city of Blaviken, Geralt himself becomes an infamous figure of urban legend, earning the moniker "The Butcher of Blaviken." He is thus acutely aware of how his public image is informed by the stories and songs created in praise or admonition of his work. Because of this unwanted, if genuinely earned status as a figure of legend, Geralt is partially defined by the tales that precede him. As Lyotard might observe, Geralt and Jaskier have a postmodern awareness of their world's lore, its role in their world as worldview-forming, and the ways in which stories both act as forms of marketing and represent (or misrepresent) people, places, and professions.

Jaskier's stories also have the greater role of both referring to and participating in the greater story of *The Witcher* saga. This is evidenced by Jaskier's own oral dissemination of Geralt's life and work and "past adventures" through crafting folk songs (and thus dissemination of folklore within the *Witcher* world).[5] For example, at the beginning of the novel *Blood of Elves*, Jaskier sings about Geralt and Ciri's previous adventures. Jaskier thereby both informs the reader and also informs another character, the villainous sorcerer Rience, of the whereabouts of the heroes.[6] This internal self reference, using the role of internal narrative as both plot summary and plot device, is a distinctive postmodern move, in that it shows how narratives are operating even within the greater narrative that the audience of *Witcher* media is consuming. In this way, Jaskier's role throughout the series expands to become a stand-in for the audience in both the narrative world inside of and the real world outside of *Witcher* media as he witnesses Geralt's feats of greatness while also spreading elaborate, even hyperbolic tales of these feats through song. In other words, Jaskier is the postmodern agent on the textual level, the level of the narrative itself, and the meta-textual level, the level outside of the text of the narrative: he is a character in the series who spreads stories about other characters in the series, while also illustrating to the audience of *The Witcher* series how stories work.

Elsewhere, Jaskier even serves as commentary on the relationship between narrative, meta-narrative, and truth. Highlighting the incredulous (postmodern) relation between Jaskier's ballads and the facts, another character comments, "Truth is one thing, poetry another."[7] As Geralt describes it, "A story is a largely false account, of largely trivial events, fed to us by historians who are largely idiots."[8] Again, Jaskier is the Continent's postmodern agent, a stand-in for the author in a way, but also a stand-in for the greater awareness of the novel as a narrative. As Lyotard might put it, postmodern self-awareness like this works in a story by revealing, not hiding, that it is a story in a tradition (not "truth").

Folklore plays another role in enriching and complicating the background of *The Witcher*'s story-world. Townspeople frequently describe monsters to Geralt when they hire him to fight them, and these descriptions are chock full of fairytale references, adding both world-building and allusion to the story-world, filling the story with the reader's own knowledge of the fairytale tradition. However, Geralt often corrects and contests these reports. This mimics the spread of real-world folklore, which is often spread orally and is full of variations and misrepresentations. For example, in "The Edge of the World," what the townsfolk describe as "devils" turn out just to be Sylvans, or goatlike humanoids.[9] In "The Lesser Evil," the wizard Stregobor wants to hire Geralt to hunt and kill a princess named Renfri, under the superstitious pretext that she was born under a bad moon and is cursed.[10] Always a skeptic, Geralt doubts but never learns whether Stregobor's story is true (in a fantasy world perhaps it could be). Geralt's skepticism (his incredulity) mirrors the reader's (and Lyotard's) skepticism, as we exist within the real world where moon curses do not exist and stories about them are false. Incidents like this force the reader's attention to the division of the story as story and our reality as reality, coaxing us in a postmodern manner to disbelieve Stregobor's worldview as presented.

Geralt also uses the lore of monsters, or what we think of as shared cultural knowledge of folklore, like a textbook in order to fight monsters scientifically. For example, in "The Bounds of Reason," Geralt references his monster encyclopedia when deciding how and whether to kill certain types of monsters.[11] In another example, in "A Grain of Truth," Geralt points out that fairytales, while not strictly "true," might have a "grain of truth" in that they are based in some reality.[12] This is in reference to the idea of "true love breaking a spell," which has nothing to do with "truth" per se but is a metaphor for the power of love to surmount obstacles. Ironically though, the narrative as a fairytale can make it "true" in that the story can be written in a way that makes it "true" in the story-world. This internal reference to the truth of "fairytales" is yet another instance of Lyotard's incredulity at work, poking holes in beloved stories and worldviews.[13]

This applies to fables as well. At their first meeting in "Sword of Destiny," Geralt tells Ciri a moralistic fable about a cat, in the tradition of Aesop's Fables and other animal tales.[14] True to the tradition, Ciri demands a moral at the end. Geralt offers her only the cryptic answer: "Survive." This "moral" has two effects, operating as a form of Geralt's meta-awareness of the role of fables in the world. First, "Survive" gestures toward the ultimate meaning of life in Darwinian nature: there is no morality, just whatever a creature does in the struggle for survival. This is a subtle reinterpretation of Aesop's intelligent animals and their moralism through a modern scientific lens. Second, the moral of the fable also suggests itself as a meta-moral for Ciri's own situation in the frame narrative of "Sword of Destiny". It accounts for the fact that Ciri is in great danger and needs to stop listening to stories and attend to her personal safety. In both senses, the takeaway is a Lyotardian postmodern reevaluation of fable and suspicion toward its familiar functions.

The Witcher perhaps seems most postmodern when it criticizes the idea of "destiny." Destiny plays a large role in much fantasy and folklore. Many of its characters and consequences are "destined." But, destiny is arguably another term for meta-narrative in that destiny is the story that we tell ourselves or that has been told to us about how life is supposed to go, which we use to navigate life. Readers also use fairytales and other stories to inform their thoughts about their own destinies. So, references to destiny in a story function as an internal acknowledgment of the meta-narrative of that story. The Witcher novels seem quite aware of this trope: Geralt begins the Saga with strong anti-destiny opinions and is reluctant to face his destiny, criticizing the idea by examining its pressure upon social expectations and impact on those who are "destined." To the characters within a story, the events may be their "destiny," but the reader is always aware that it is just the "story." Lyotard's postmodern criticism works in such a manner as well, pointing out the role of "destiny" as "story": destiny isn't so much "true" in advance as it is the worldview through which we look back at events.[15] Of course, a story proceeds according to some destiny or other; it cannot help it because that's the plot the author wrote. The books of the Witcher saga notably question destiny, and in bringing attention to destiny, they lay bare the trope in a manner that allows the readers to evaluate their own views against the characters' views. By reconsidering how characters blindly follow destiny in stories, we can assess whether we are similarly led by meta-narratives in our own lives. Furthermore, the shared "destiny" of

Geralt and Ciri is actually unclear. In *The Lady of the Lake*, many characters attempt to use Ciri to fulfill some grander destiny. Nilfgaard and the Lodge of Sorceresses want Ciri to breed a magical empire.[16] Even people of parallel dimensions attempt to use her for her powers. However, Ciri evades all these attempts to claim her power and ends up subverting what seemed to be her destiny. So, was destiny fulfilled after all?

"It isn't a fairy story, it's real life"

Stories of *The Witcher* media are also situated within the real-world tradition of fantasy meta-narratives. The *Witcher* saga is populated with frequent allusions to the wider world of fairytales—Grimm's, Anderson's, and others'. Immersion in the events of the *Witcher* tales requires the reader to already have some fantasy literacy. Readers have to know about elves, dwarves, sorcerers, princesses, and monsters of the week; to understand some of the "rules" of stories involving magic; and to recognize certain references to the real-world literary canon—like the Arthurian legends. The *Witcher* tales even allude to real-world places and events. For example, Jaskier attends the Academy at Oxenford, a not-so-subtle reference to the real-world Oxford University.[17] Through the Conjunction of the Spheres, a world-merging event, and Ciri's dimension-hopping magical powers, these stories further imply that the *Witcher*'s story-world is actually just one universe in a multiverse of many other fantasy universes: one of Arthurian Legend and one our very own (real) universe, from which it's implied the original humans on *The Witcher*'s Continent migrated.[18] Ciri's story is described by people in other dimensions *as* a story, acknowledging the *Witcher* narrative as existing in the larger context of other worlds which are ambiguously internal but also external to the text.[19] As Lyotard would point out, all of this draws attention to the way the *Witcher*'s story-world is operating in our real world as a story with a worldview.

The *Witcher* stories themselves also frequently take on the structures of familiar fairytales in order to critique them. Throughout our real-world history, fantasy stories—folktales, fairytales, and fables—have followed certain story structures. They often have a hero, a villain, a three-act plot, and in the end provide practical wisdom, that is, lessons and "morals of the stories," answering questions about how a life should be best lived. The stories in *The Last Wish* and *The Sword of Destiny* are structured as fairytales in this way: most have a monster and a moral, follow the course of a typical "Hero's Journey" arc, and often end with the familiar, resolved feeling of a fairytale (i.e., good ultimately wins over evil).[20] Later in the series, starting with *Blood of Elves*, Sapkowski's story structures expand toward the epic, another familiar story structure.[21] But as a contemporary reinterpretation of old monster stories, *The Witcher*'s stories attempt to provide a new angle on the genre, and often comment on and criticize the simplicity of these older tales, while also updating and complicating the practical wisdom they offer for more mature and keen eyes. In this way, the *Witcher* stories end up embodying fairytales, even as this is the genre that they are critiquing. And while the stories are *influenced* by fairytales, they don't necessarily deliver a *fairytale plot*, nor do they allow themselves to be limited to being *merely a fairytale*, which allows more room for postmodern critique.

Furthermore, the *Witcher* stories are also eclectic in their incorporation of multicultural sources. Though the novels and stories are Polish in origin, the saga marshals a wide variety of monsters, legends, events, and figures from world folklore. From the various witches and wizards who populate the stories, to the monsters Geralt fights, to events and celebrations like The Great Hunt, folklore enriches *The Witcher*'s many story-worlds, but without shifting focus away from the main narrative of Geralt's, Yennefer's, and Ciri's trials and triumphs. The series grounds its world-building not just in Geralt's literary and literal role as monster hunter, his character affirmed through his folkloric function as hero, but also through the diverse cast of monsters ripped straight from the pages of global folklore's fairytales: the Sylvans call back to Greek and English satyrs, horned goatmen who dwelled in the forest; the djinn, whom Geralt and Yennefer battle, originates in South Asian and Middle Eastern folklore; the dragons notably evoke both Western and Eastern iconography. This self-conscious representation and performance of plural folklores rather than one national folklore (of Sapkowski's Poland) makes the series distinctively diverse, like the real world, which is something Lyotard would point to as a feature of our times, as *The Witcher* is a product in a globalizing community, unified by telecommunications technologies, which can increasingly draw upon its many cultures, traditions, and worldviews in the grand stories that it tells.

"In the library are all the legend's versions and adaptations ..."

The various media forms of *The Witcher*'s extended universe also allow for many versions of the same stories to coexist. The books, shows, and games represent the same narratives, but they do so in different media, and any adaptation in form necessarily alters features of the original. Lyotard would identify this as a postmodern technique because one cannot change the telling without questioning what is important in the tale.

The television show, for example, is a semi-, but not quite, faithful adaptation of the books. The show changes, rearranges, and outright estranges some aspects of the books. For example, Geralt meets Ciri in the Dryad forest in the books, but in the Netflix show Geralt meets Ciri only after she has fled the Dryads ("Of Banquets, Burials, and Bastards," season 1, episode 4).[22] Furthermore, some features of reading (like mental imagery) simply cannot be replicated in film: a reader's mental image of book-Geralt is probably not Henry Cavill.

In what sense then can the *Witcher* fandom call the shows or games "canonical," part of the "true" lore? The answer is that the narrative variations between books, shows, and games allow multiple retellings that undermine a singular "canonical" and "true" telling of the Witcher's life story. Lyotard would likely further suggest that we should be skeptical of the very idea of a "canonical" or "true" telling of any tale.

The *Witcher* novels also reject a "canonical" reading through their open-endedness. Infamously, the final book in the series, *The Lady of the Lake*, ends with an ambiguity.[23] Here we offer a spoiler alert ... but do we need to, since it's not obvious what actually happens? Do Geralt and Yennefer die? Are they rescued? Some clues point to the former, some to the latter. Characters in the book comment upon these differences in the accounts of "versions and adaptations."[24] So, the open-endedness of *The Lady of the Lake* resists being treated as one unified, canonical narrative. No one knows how it ends. And, whether we think our heroes die or not, the extended universe resurrects them for videogames that function as pseudo-sequels. Yet should we count the games as part of the "true" *Witcher* canon or not? In a sense, the games are not canonical because Sapkowski did not write them; in another sense, the games are arguably more popular and better known, and therefore more canonical in the sense of being more popularly accepted. If noncanonical, what are they?

Worse still, *The Witcher* videogames explode the very idea of a "canon" in enabling player choices.[25] In *The Witcher 3: Wild Hunt*, most of the quests in the game have minor or major choices. Do you side with one faction or another? Who do you decide to rescue from death? Who do you decide to kill? Do you favor mercy or punishment? None of these choices can be the "true" narrative for Geralt because every player's game will have a different and unique combination of these options. The player can even make romantic decisions for Geralt. Although the canonical witcher-girl of the novels is Yennefer of Vengerberg, in the videogame a player can pick a different girlfriend for Geralt: Triss Merigold. This choice of side-girl is ultimately a difference in side-quests and their respective explicit cutscenes, but the player is actively engaged in altering the narrative as part of the gameplay, effectively annihilating the notion that there is any one "true" narrative, since every individual player's narrative will be different. Even the ending sequence of the main quest of the game changes depending upon player choices—specifically, how the player treated Geralt's adopted daughter Ciri during the game. So, far from relegating player choices to minor aesthetic decisions, the game rejects having a canonical main quest and required outcome. Consistent with Lyotard's postmodern incredulity, it becomes more difficult to believe in a single grand and authoritative account of the world when all we have are conflicting versions of events. And yet, even this interactivity seems to reassert that there's a "moral to the story," in a manner that casts the critical postmodern eye on the players themselves, since the player must *choose the story* for Geralt and face the happiness or unhappiness of the outcome.

"And is that the end of the story?"

So, like Galahad at the end of *The Lady of the Lake*, wondering whether he has heard the "end of the story," where are we readers left in the post-modern condition? According to folklorist Bob Trubshaw in *Explore Folklore*, "the genres reflect back on each other like a kaleidoscope," and for the casual reader, viewer, or gamer, hopefully this allows for some level of philosophical self-reflection.[26] Through internal textual elements, external textual references, and self-conscious media choices, *The Witcher* saga simultaneously presents the trappings of a traditional fairytale and the meta-narrative skepticism so definitive of postmodern philosophy: showing us how the story-world is formed through textual elements, how it reflects features of real-world cultures, and how it changes depending on how it is told. Thus, *The Witcher* saga is the ultimate postmodern fairytale, giving us familiar fantasy tropes we know and love, while also thrusting us into philosophical engagement with the storytelling.

Notes

1. Jean-Francois Lyotard, *The Postmodern Condition: A Report on Knowledge*, trans. Geoff Bennington and Brian Massumi (Manchester: Manchester University Press, 1984), xxiv.
2. Michael Dylan Foster and Jeffrey A. Tolbert, *Folkloresque: Reframing Folklore in a Popular Culture World* (Denver: Utah State University Press, 2015).
3. Foster, *Folkloresque*, 5; emphasis added.
4. Foster, *Folkloresque*, 5; emphasis added.
5. Andrzej Sapkowski, *Blood of Elves*, trans. Danusia Stok (New York: Orbit Books, 2008), 168.
6. Sapkowski, *Blood of Elves*, 34–35.
7. Sapkowski, *Blood of Elves*, 17–19.
8. Andrzej Sapkowski, *The Season of Storms*, trans. David French (London: Orbit Books, 2018), chap. 13.
9. Andrzej Sapkowski, *The Last Wish*, trans. Danusia Stok (New York: Orbit Books, 2007), 213–215, 220 221, 233.
10. Sapkowski, *The Last Wish*, 95–144.
11. Sapkowski, *The Last Wish*, 229; *The Sword of Destiny*, trans. David French (New York: Hachette, 2022), 10; *Blood of Elves*, 221.
12. Sapkowski, *The Last Wish*, 88.
13. Sapkowski, *Blood of Elves*, 71.

14. Sapkowski, *The Sword of Destiny*, 270–272.
15. Sapkowski, *Blood of Elves*, 52, 72–73.
16. Andrzej Sapkowski, *The Lady of the Lake*, trans. David French (New York: Gollancz, 2017).
17. Sapkowski, *Blood of Elves*, 243.
18. Sapkowski, *The Lady of the Lake*, 4, 529.
19. Sapkowski, *The Lady of the Lake*, 20–21.
20. Sapkowski, *The Last Wish*; *The Sword of Destiny*.
21. Sapkowski, *Blood of Elves*.
22. Sapkowski, *The Sword of Destiny*, 247–313.
23. Sapkowski, *The Lady of the Lake*, 493, 528–531.
24. Sapkowski, *The Lady of the Lake*, 22.
25. CD Projekt Red, *The Witcher*.
26. Bob Trubshaw, *Explore Folklore* (Nottingham: Heart of Albion Press, 2002, revised 2010), 85.

Shocks of Destiny
The Witcher's Unlawful Surprise

Corry Shores

A witcher, something between a mage and a beast hunter, yet something monstrous all its own, is Andrzej Sapkowski's intriguing new twist on the sorcerer figure. Surely a witcher like Geralt of Rivia is pure fantasy, something only possible in our imaginations. Or is it? Maybe there's something to learn from the weird ways of the witcher. Gilles Deleuze (1925–1995) crafted his own unique conception of the witch or sorcerer in his philosophy. His sorcerers are agents of "becoming-other," of mutation. Their existence requires us to affirm that people have unpredictable and uncontrollable fates, reminding us of how witchers often invoke the Law of Surprise. We might wonder: Can Deleuze's philosophy of *sorcerous becoming* shed light on the unique traits of witchers? And could Deleuze, who was called the "Great Sorcerer" by his students, instead be better known today as the *Great Witcher*?[1]

Creatures Contrary to Nature

Witchers are mutated aberrations, but they begin as human children given specialized training in combat, survival, and spell ("sign") casting. Then comes a fateful day of horrific medical interventions called the Trial of Grasses. They're administered herbs, hormones, and viruses that'll end their normal lives one way or another.[2] These nasty experiments can last for a week and are often lethal; out of ten children, six to seven are likely to die in the process.[3] Even Russian Roulette has better odds! Their brains might burst during their fits of delirium, or their eyes might "rupture and gush forth."[4] With such high stakes, becoming a witcher is a deadly gamble with fate, not to mention all the lethal risks that'll soon come with the job even if they survive the trials. But the payoff is great: an extended lifespan, heightened reflexes and physical abilities like night vision, along with enhanced sexual prowess and romantic desirability. With their unique and valuable skills and abilities, witchers can live adventurous, eventful lives as monster hunters.

The Witcher and Philosophy: Toss a Coin to Your Philosopher, First Edition.
Edited by Matthew Brake and Kevin S. Decker.
© 2025 John Wiley & Sons, Inc. Published 2025 by John Wiley & Sons, Inc.

However, the transformation comes with costs: witchers become aberrant, beastlike monstrosities, with cat- or viper-like vertical pupils and albino hair, and they can undergo further, if temporary, extra-human alterations by drinking potent elixirs.[5] Witchers have been described as "the offspring of foul sorcery and devilry," "true diabolic creations, fit only for killing," and "Mutant. Monster. Freak. Damned by the gods, a creature contrary to nature."[6] As the cursed Nivellen remarks, witchers eat "magic herbs" to be "turned into monsters in order to kill other monsters."[7] Their loss of human form also results in changes in how witchers relate to others. A witcher like Geralt must exist on the fringes of society, being always an "outsider."[8] "Due to their *otherness*, unusual abilities, and magical skills, Witchers are treated as *outcasts* and sometimes even met with hatred."[9] And they often become vagabonds; Geralt says, "I'm a *wanderer*, a witcher, a mutant, who travels the world and slays monsters for money."[10] Yet all the while, witchers can serve the same societies that marginalize them, acting as mediators and protectors and operating in accordance with a strong moral compass and code of honor.

Deleuze's "sorcerer"—which he developed with his co-author, Félix Guattari (1930–1992)—shares many philosophically important similarities with the witcher. Deleuzian sorcerers, like witchers, must mutate, not just once but repeatedly, and this always involves reconfigurations and changes in how they relate to, and interact with, all the things, creatures, and people in the world around them. These new "alliances" and alignments can cut across different species and kingdoms of creatures and might even involve nonliving partners: what Deleuze and Guattari call "unnatural participations" or "nuptials against nature."[11] Since sorcerers constantly initiate new configurations within and outside themselves, they're anomalies that exist at the borders: "Sorcerers," Deleuze and Guattari write, "have always held the anomalous position, at the edge of the field or woods. They haunt the fringes. They are at the borderline of the village, or *between* villages."[12]

The mutations of Deleuzian sorcerers don't have a preset outcome. Mutations imply a movement away from what one is, but not a movement toward *something else in particular*. The outcomes can never be foreknown, because they can't be predetermined.[13] For this reason, Deleuze generally prefers the term "deformation" instead of "transformation" to characterize this sort of becoming.[14] In order to begin *becoming-other*, we must take a gamble because we can't know in advance who or what we'll later become as a result. Assuming we even survive at all.

Dicing with Destiny

Given that the Trial of Grasses often makes witchers infertile, they can try to obtain new recruits by invoking the Law of Surprise as a payment for their deeds or services. When fate permits, this enables them to adopt a child for witcher training. Coodcoodak (Baron Eylembert of Tigg) describes the Law of Surprise in the following way:

> Of the price a man who saves another can demand, of the granting of a seemingly impossible wish. "You will give me the first thing that comes to greet you." It might be a dog, you'll say, a halberdier at the gate, even a mother-in-law impatient to holler at her son-in-law when he returns home. Or: "You'll give me what you find at home yet don't expect." After a long journey, honorable gentlemen, and an unexpected return, this could be a lover in the wife's bed. But sometimes it's a child. A child marked out by destiny.[15]

Queen Calanthe of Cintra notes this element of uncertainty and gambling when she tells Geralt that the Law of Surprise is "a game! A game with chance, a game with destiny!"[16]

There's yet another risk that comes with this custom. A person gambles *destructively* with fate if they deny what the Law of Surprise demanded. Coodcoodak cites one case: Zivelena, Queen of Metinna, promised the gnome Rumplestelt her first born through the Law, but when Rumplestelt returns to retrieve the child, Zivelena uses magic to thwart him. "Not long after that," Coodcoodak continues, "both she and the child died of the plague. You do not dice with Destiny with impunity!"[17]

This is remarkable! On the one hand, the outcome of the Law of Surprise is unpredictable, a "game with chance," but on the other hand, whatever it proves to be, the outcome is considered necessary and unalterable, since it's also a "game with destiny." Somehow, *before* the fate is sealed, the outcome could be anything, but *after* the surprise, it couldn't have been otherwise. So, when we fully commit to the Law of Surprise, we affirm—*in advance*—both that our fate is undecided and, at the same time, that whatever it proves to be was destined from the beginning.

As paradoxical as this might sound, it's exactly how Deleuze characterizes what we might call the "affirmation of fated chance" in becoming-other. Deleuze, drawing from Friedrich Nietzsche (1844–1900), writes that the "game of becoming ... has two moments which are those of a dicethrow—the dice that is thrown and the dice that falls back."[18] In the first moment, we throw the dice of becoming up to the gods in the sky, in order to leave it to their powers to cast the dice back down, when they fall to the earth with the force of destiny and decide the outcome with their roll.[19] In other words, we consign our fate to blind chance, but in that very same act, we also commit ourselves to embracing the outcome whole-heartedly, regardless of whatever it is. As Deleuze puts it, "the dice which are thrown once are the affirmation of chance, the combination which they form on falling is the affirmation of *necessity*."[20] This doesn't involve a passive resignation to the whims of fate but is rather a full *affirmation* of destiny—it's a *love* of fated chance, or what Nietzsche called *amor fati*.[21] We don't say, "Oh, well!" to the outcome or, "Better luck next time." We must rather say "Yes!" no matter what it is.

For Deleuze, to affirm becoming as fated chance means treating every outcome as *putting things back into play*. Deleuze writes, "It is sufficient for the player to affirm chance once in order to produce the number which brings back the dicethrow."[22] In other words, loving fated chance means that we see the outcomes as creating new uncertainties, new becomings to take risks on. Queen Eithné of Brokilon says to Geralt, "I want to show you what destiny is. I want to prove to you that nothing is ending. That everything is only beginning."[23] To love fated chance means to treat each outcome, no matter how bad or good, as creating a new game to play, with its own unforeseeable and undecidable possibilities.

Besides the chaos of chance, another reason that outcomes cannot be predetermined is "co-fatality" or "co-destiny." For something to be fated, often other things must be true as well, and so they're all co-fated together, a notion held by the Stoic Chrysippus of Soli (c. 279–206 BCE). Using examples from Chrysippus's time, if it was fated that Laius would have a son, Oedipus, then it must also be fated that Laius will sleep with a woman to conceive him. The first fate is linked co-fatally with the second; it can't happen without the other. Or consider this prophecy: the great athlete Milo will wrestle at Olympia. Although this is fated to be, we can't reason from this that "he will wrestle whether he has an opponent or not."[24] This is important: no matter how much Milo might affirm his fate to compete at Olympia, another person, his opponent, must *also* make a complementary affirmation, too. Only if they *both* do this can their fates become bound into a shared co-destiny.[25] Even when Geralt fully affirmed Princess Cirila of Cintra as his destiny, that wasn't enough to seal her fate to his. She had to affirm him as her destiny, too, which she does when she confirms to Lady Eithné, "I wish to follow my destiny" by going with Geralt, "for he ... is my fate."[26] Eithné, who can see their destinies merging co-fatally through their mutual affirmations, says to Geralt, poetically, "The Sword of Destiny has two blades. ... You are one of them."[27] When we cast the dice of fated chance and affirm, in advance, whatever will come up, we know that the ultimate outcome also rests on the actions and commitments of others who are rolling their own dice simultaneously.

Cries of Chaos

This picture shows that every event has many players, each struggling and gambling on one or another future, although most don't align. Since all these paths of potential future development are in play, with conflicting forces actively pushing the event in various, often opposing, directions all at once, incredible tensions exist between the futures under contest. Deleuze portrays these potent tensions as "diabolical powers of the future" that impinge upon the present, disrupting it and enhancing its uncertainty by injecting even more chaos into it. Deleuze gives the name "cry" or "scream" for the moment when the future demonic powers explode into the present and scramble the already chaotic sea of conflicting forces, thereby further increasing the undecidability of the event. It's an "outburst" of sorts, which can manifest in various ways. In some of his examples, it can be an audible (or visible) cry, like the cries in Alban Berg's operas *Wozzeck* and *Lulu*, or the screams portrayed in Francis Bacon's (1909–1992) paintings, which express the forces that disrupt and deform the painted imagery.[28]

We find such a scream in the chaotic engagement banquet of Princess Pavetta of Cintra, an event that also illustrates the other Deleuzian ideas mentioned above. Lord Urcheon of Erlenwald, one of Pavetta's suitors, once saved the life of her father, King Roegner. For his reward, Urcheon invoked the Law of Surprise. Upon Roegner's return home, he found that his wife Calanthe was pregnant. She was pregnant with Pavetta, who became claimable via the Law of Surprise by Urcheon, although Calanthe would make efforts to obstruct this fate.

Years later, at Pavetta's betrothal ball, Urcheon arrives for his lawful claim, resulting in a stand-off with Calanthe and her court. Geralt tries to disarm the tensions by invoking the *co-fatal* requirements of the Law of Surprise, saying, "You will win her only when ... the princess herself agrees to leave with you. This is what the Law of Surprise states. It is the child's, not the parent's, consent which confirms the oath, which proves that the child was born under the shadow of destiny."[29] In other words, Pavetta must affirm this as her fate, too—which she does—thereby fusing together the two "blades" of their double-edged "sword of destiny."

Despite the lovers' wishes, Calanthe and her guards turn on Urcheon. With Geralt's aid, he holds them off as best he can, despite being heavily outnumbered. Pavetta grows more and more distraught; all the while, Geralt senses an overpowering "Force" that's increasingly "condensing in the air," until finally Pavetta lets out an "even, monotonous and *vibrating cry*."[30] With its elemental force, it sends the room into sustained, violent chaos, scattering furniture and food all about, with tables "rising and spinning" in the air, while "heavy chairs were flying around the hall and shattering against the walls." Calanthe's throne, with her still sitting in it, "sprang up and flew across the hall like an arrow, smashing into the wall with a crash and falling apart," as Calanthe "slid to the floor like a ragged puppet."[31] Could this be a consequence of Calanthe's not loving fate?

Pavetta's cry produces even more chaos and uncertainty within an already uncertain situation by injecting the diabolical forces of the future into the present, as Deleuze might see it. As Mousesack the Druid proclaims, "It's pure, primordial Force!... She's got no control over it!"[32] This was like a toss of a coin or of dice, or the rolling of the roulette ball along the wheel, overpowering all other forces trying to determine the outcome, with its even greater unstructured power.

This chaos continues only until Mousesack and Geralt intervene during an opportune lull. In the aftermath, Calanthe, having learned her lesson, comes around and finally affirms this fate, too, by blessing the union of

Urcheon and Pavetta. This seals everyone's co-fatal destiny, but Geralt further affirms it with a true love of fate—he puts everything back into play by invoking the Law of Surprise for his own reward, which (unknown to many present) is the child that pregnant Pavetta now carries, Princess Cirilla.

Isn't all this just fantasy? Perhaps, but there's a lot at stake philosophically. What Deleuze has in mind—and what Sapkowski portrays—is something we face more frequently in our lives than we might realize. Life, we often find, is full of surprises, "plot-twists," moments of uncertainty with unknowable outcomes. And whether we like it or not, we're often changed by these events, be it from traumas, losses, realizing we can't go on with our lives as the same self, or simply learning something new that alters our perspective, attitude, and behavior in fundamental ways.

But to affirm fated chance doesn't imply living recklessly. Rather, it asks us to see the potential for certain events to create the world and ourselves anew through a mutation parallel to that which creates witchers. As the sorceress Triss Merigold of Maribor reminds us, "everyone, absolutely everyone, is a mutant to a certain degree."[33] Variation is our given and ongoing state: it's our destiny to change, one way or another. Deleuze and Sapkowski invite us to wonder, "Can I *now* affirm the me who will appear—or who might even die—when the dice of fate soon strike the earth?"[34]

Notes

1. Michel Cressole, *Deleuze* (Paris: Éditions Universitaires, 1973), 103.
2. Andrzej Sapkowski, *The Last Wish*, trans. Danusia Stok (New York: Orbit Books, 2017), 131.
3. Andrzej Sapkowski, *Blood of Elves*, trans. Danusia Stok (New York: Orbit Books, 2017), 97; Andrzej Sapkowski, *Sword of Destiny*, trans. David French (New York: Orbit Books, 2013), 339.
4. Sapkowski, *Sword of Destiny*, 339.
5. Sapkowski, *Blood of Elves*, 97.
6. Sapkowski, *Blood of Elves*, 53, 64.
7. Sapkowski, *The Last Wish*, 58.
8. Sapkowski, *The Last Wish*, 3.
9. Shyama Krishna Kumar, "Netflix's 'The Witcher' Explained," Gulf News, December 25, 2019, at https://gulfnews.com/entertainment/tv/netflixs-the-witcher-explained-1.68664234; emphasis added.
10. Andrzej Sapkowski, *Time of Contempt*, trans. David French (London: Gollancz, 2013), 142; emphasis added.
11. Gilles Deleuze and Félix Guattari, *A Thousand Plateaus*, trans. Brian Massumi (London: Continuum, 2004), 266; Gilles Deleuze and Claire Parnet, *Dialogues II*, trans. Hugh Tomlinson and Barbara Habberjam (New York: Columbia University Press, 2007), 14.

12. Deleuze and Guattari, *A Thousand Plateaus*, 271; emphasis original.
13. Deleuze and Parnet, *Dialogues II*, 2.
14. Gilles Deleuze, *Francis Bacon: The Logic of Sensation*, trans. Daniel W. Smith (London and New York: Continuum, 2003), 42.
15. Sapkowski, *The Last Wish*, 160.
16. Sapkowski, *Sword of Destiny*, 342.
17. Sapkowski, *The Last Wish*, 160.
18. Gilles Deleuze, *Nietzsche and Philosophy*, trans. Hugh Tomlinson (New York: Columbia University Press, 2006), 24–25.
19. Deleuze, *Nietzsche and Philosophy*, 25.
20. Deleuze, *Nietzsche and Philosophy*, 26; emphasis original.
21. Deleuze, *Nietzsche and Philosophy*, 27.
22. Deleuze, *Nietzsche and Philosophy*, 26.
23. Sapkowski, *Sword of Destiny*, 293.
24. Cicero, *De fato*, trans. H. Rackham (Cambridge, MA: Harvard University Press, 1942), 224–227.
25. Cicero, *De fato*, 227.
26. Sapkowski, *Sword of Destiny*, 295, 292.
27. Sapkowski, *Sword of Destiny*, 295.
28. Gilles Deleuze, *Two Regimes of Madness: Texts and Interviews 1975–1995*, ed. David Lapoujade, trans. Ames Hodges and Mike Taormina (New York: Semiotext(e), 2006), 324; *Logic of Sensation*, 43.
29. Sapkowski, *The Last Wish*, 164.
30. Sapkowski, *The Last Wish*, 167, 169; emphasis added.
31. Sapkowski, *The Last Wish*, 169.
32. Sapkowski, *The Last Wish*, 170.
33. Sapkowski, *Blood of Elves*, 168.
34. I would like to thank Matthew Brake, Kevin Decker, and William Irwin for making substantial improvements to this chapter's content and style.

21

Post-Apocalyptic Prognostications in *The Witcher*

Matthew Crippen

Catastrophes are cross-cultural themes in ancient stories.[1] Similar motifs can be found in the off-balance mythical past of *The Witcher*. The narrative is set in a continent undergoing a climate crisis known as the Great Frost, which started after the Conjunction of the Spheres, an event that opened a cosmic gateway that allowed humans to leave a dying world and enter a new one. In a way, this development parallels that of the paleolithic Sahara desert, which had wet spells. These allowed our ancestors northward passage through this normally impenetrable barrier, letting them branch out of Africa.[2] Lurking in the background of all of this and imprinted in humanity's genes is an ache in people to perpetuate themselves and their communities, a desire molded further through cultural experiences of contending with apocalyptic situations. In *The Witcher*, too, this desire drives many individuals.

There's also a figurative sense in which apocalyptic impulses are in our DNA. Aristotle (384–322 BCE) claimed that all people "by nature desire to know," and the word "apocalypse" has meanings that relate to truth-seeking.[3] The term is a compound of the Greek "apo- *'un-'* + *kaluptein* 'to cover.'"[4] So "apocalypse" literally means uncovering or revealing. In the hands of Greeks like Plato (c. 429–347), knowledge seeking takes on deathly tones because the sought-after truths are perfect, unchanging, and immaterial—in short, the opposite of messy, ever changing, and material biological ways of living. We see this deathly Greek ideal personified in Yennefer because her nearly ageless beauty and otherworldly wisdom are achieved at the cost of her ability to have children.

The word "apocalyptic" has ruinous tones in no small part because of biblical books like Revelation (called *Apokalypsis* in its original Greek title). The Book of Revelation may have partly been an allegory for the persecution that was occurring in Rome.[5] The scripture further suggests that humans have a destructive nature. This book describes an erosion of

The Witcher and Philosophy: Toss a Coin to Your Philosopher, First Edition.
Edited by Matthew Brake and Kevin S. Decker.

the barrier between earthly and otherworldly realms, allowing entrance of monsters such as a seven-headed dragon and an army of locust-lion-horse-human-scorpion hybrids.[6]

The Witcher has its own apocalyptic monsters in the form of its mutant creatures that appear when the barrier between worlds ruptures, with environmental crises further driving these beasts to migrate into human-populated areas. The series also has characters experimenting in an effort to create a transhuman superspecies, echoing the aspirations of Nazis as well as recent companies that try to perfect bodies through interventions ranging from steroids to cosmetic surgery to electronic brain implants.

In *The Witcher*, biological changes are implemented in humans through a mix of magic and science, leading to a breakdown of customary ways of classifying things. Geralt doesn't consider himself human anymore, even though that's what he was as a child. Paralleling this classificatory breakdown is something close to a post-truth erosion of moral concepts, which often just become whatever the powerful want, causing political mayhem. *The Witcher* captures these points. It frames environmental catastrophe, war, refugee migration, and ethnically based atrocities as interconnected problems, confronting us with a post-apocalyptic, post-truth, and transhumanist chaos that shadows the situation that's brewing in our own world.

Familiar Bedfellows

On the one hand, sex and death seem pretty far apart. On the other, they're familiar bedfellows. As the elf Avallac'h says to Geralt, "Sex totally governs you," adding that it's "more powerful even than the survival instinct. To die? Why not, if one can fuck around beforehand. That is your entire philosophy."[7]

Though these remarks are glib, they get at pervasive realities that appear in culture and nature. The Japanese have myths of their volcanic islands ripping up—almost apocalyptically—from the ocean through a kind of erotic coupling. And the ancient Greeks told about how Aphrodite—their goddess of sex and love—emerged from the bloody froth of Uranus's severed genitals hitting the sea.[8] Television nature shows feature rutting animals fighting to the death or expending their last bit of strength to mate. As humans, we aren't that different. We exhaust enormous energy in prestige games that probably shorten our lives out of stress. We do this even if we're celibate, which is likely because we can't escape sexually competitive social instincts hardwired into us. Sexual temptation has destroyed the lives of many prominent people.

Most of us aren't willing to die for sex. Rather, it's because we will die that we've got a strong sex drive: our children will replace us. But a break in the last part of this equation motivates many characters in *The Witcher*.

Factions in Sapkowski's books condemn contraception, abortion, and oral sex, similarly to certain religious traditionalists from history who hold that nonprocreative lovemaking is wrong.[9] This is a polite way of saying that individuals should stick to sex that has the potential to spread genes, though it doesn't matter for witchers and magic users since they are infertile. It's the price they pay for gaining their superhuman powers, and we're also told they'd make bad parents. For the witchers and those they protect, the situation is dire because they've lost the ability to transform humans into members of their order, meaning their kind is on the edge of apocalyptic destruction.

Especially haunted by her inability to conceive children, Yennefer plans to kill a highly intelligent and endangered dragon in hopes of trading its valuable tissues for a cure. Later, though, she turns sympathetic because the dragon's protecting an egg—an unborn youngling, the very thing she wants. The elves, who are oppressed and are victims of bigotry, are similarly infertile; their effort to rectify this motivates many of their actions. Interestingly, the elf king is obsessed with Ciri's Elder blood—a name for genes she carries that contribute to her magical powers.[10] He plans to impregnate her, believing that a child with her Elder blood will save all races from a world nearing apocalyptic demise. Ciri's father wants to do the same, and he's revealed to be the emperor of the Nilfgaardians, ancestral enemies of Ciri's clan who violently massacred many of her people.[11]

Withering Heights

A problem for many characters in the *Witcher* is that they grow to be what Friedrich Nietzsche (1844–1900) described as individuals "who lack every-thing, except one thing of which they have too much."[12] These people, he goes on to say, "are nothing but a big eye or a big mouth or a big belly or anything at all that is big. Inverse cripples I call them."[13] We see something similar in *The Witcher*. Geralt, for example, curses his overdeveloped eyes that allow him to see imperfections in the magically perfected bodies of sorceresses, and Avallac'h bemoans that the long lives of elves make sex "boring."[14]

Discussions with Socrates, who's a character in Plato's *Phaedo*, lead to the conclusion that philosophers ought to separate themselves from bodily distractions like excessive emotion, uncontrolled lust, and greed, which impede the pursuit of truth.[15] Witchers partly follow these prescriptions since they suppress emotional feelings that would distract them from fighting, additionally adhering to restrictions about the kinds of jobs they can take for pay. Characters in the *Phaedo* conceive of "truth" as perfect and unchanging, free from the vagueness of the material world, and they regard philosophy itself as a preparation for death, defined as the separa-tion of soul from body.[16] Though not exactly as in the *Phaedo*, witchers likewise train with the expectation of dying for their profession, with Geralt remarking, "No witcher has yet died of old age, lying in bed dictating his will."[17]

Nietzsche diagnosed the views of the *Phaedo* as flowing from a hatred of the living body, leading philosophers to pursue what is contrary to it. "All that philosophers have handled for thousands of years have been concept-mummies,"[18] he complained. By this, he meant philosophers worship what doesn't change. We see this in Plato's notion of truth, which borders on the apocalyptic because it's devoid of life. To some extent, this idea is personified in Yennefer, whose magic prevents her from aging. The idea also shows up in the way that various characters fixate on Ciri as a vessel of the Elder blood of long-dead individuals. Ralph Waldo Emerson (1803–1882), who influenced Nietzsche, analogously grumbled that intellectuals of his era lived in "the sepulchers of the fathers."[19] By this, he meant that too many people of his day obsessed over the biographies of their dead predecessors.

Another intellectual admired by Nietzsche was Fyodor Dostoevsky (1821–1881), and some of what he wrote gets close to capturing Yennefer's barrenness. He remarked that it's a burden for us to be human "with real bodies and blood; we're ashamed of it, we consider it a disgrace."[20] He added that "we're stillborn" and that "soon we'll contrive to be born somehow from an idea."[21] The words "idea" and "ideal" connect closely. We often use the term "ideal" in Plato's apocalyptic sense to indicate something that's so perfect as to not exist. This gets at another way that Yennefer lives as if dead: because she pursues otherworldly standards of magical power and beauty.

Transhumanist Entanglements

The predicament faced by Yennefer and Geralt gets at the issue of transhumanism, which is an agenda aimed at "changing and improving natural human characteristics through biological, technological, and cognitive modifications."[22] This can lead to a situation that philosophers characterize as "posthuman," a term that designates the view that we're moving to a condition where the category of "human" no longer applies.[23]

Classical prescriptions advocate for a balance between our rational, emotional, and desiring aspects (including reproductive capacities).[24] But these functions are all out of whack in Geralt, who doubts that he is even human. His encounter with Dudu in *Sword of Destiny* illustrates this point. Unlike the doppler, or shape- and mind-mimicking creature, in the TV series, Dudu is not evil and can only "copy what is good." Geralt hints at his own bad sides by warning Dudu: "I am what you are unable of copying."[25] It's not that Geralt is evil. He does noble things, but his tasks require an inhuman hardness. His job is to kill nonhuman monsters, but when an innkeeper asks him to murder Dudu on these grounds, he responds, "I would like to point out that that non-human hasn't harmed anybody else, only me. And incidentally, I'm also a non-human."[26] Geralt's lack of humanity does not stop him from acting according to a strict moral code. He can also behave altruistically. He refuses to kill harmless creatures for pay, and he often protects people at great risk to himself without expectation of being tossed a coin.

Others, however, severely violate conventional morality, doing this partly because of their transhumanist obsessions. The worst is probably Degerlund, "an outstanding scientist, a specialist in the field of genetics, boasting immense, simply incalculable accomplishments in transhumanism, introgression and speciation."[27] The magical community considers Degerlund's work "pivotal for the development and evolution of the human race" and its "genetic modification."[28] By "hybridization and combination of the gene pool," the wizard hopes to create a more powerful transhuman to "dominate non-humans and subdue them utterly."[29] Degerlund gleefully details other possibilities like "creating a woman with a perfectly flat back, so you can fuck her from behind and have somewhere to put a glass of champagne and play solitaire at the same time."[30]

Part of the transhumanism in Degerlund's specific schemes comes from the fact that his modifications of people treat them as if they're less than human. In Immanuel Kant's (1724–1804) language, they're reduced to mere things to be used.[31] Degerlund's wish to subjugate and perhaps cause the apocalyptic extinction of other races is morally problematic from most ethical standpoints, including the Kantian perspective that we ought to respect rational individuals' right to self-govern.

Though not nearly so sinister, entrepreneurs in our society—like Elon Musk—expressly advance a transhumanist agenda through ventures aimed at implanting electronics into the brain to enhance it. There's also talk of uploading minds. Although the feasibility is doubtful, the enterprise is marketed as a path for transcending human limits of mortality. In a posthumanist vein, accordingly, the intent seems to be to transgress boundaries previously imposed on our species by nature and also to move us beyond classical conceptual bounds of what it is to be "human." Similarly, Degerlund wishes to transgress human limits, though he's also just a sadist. He wants to cut out Geralt's eyeballs, which have a reflective tissue that enhances night vision, in hopes of leaving "the whole of humanity with the ability to see like cats."[32]

Post-Apocalyptic Post-Truths

A different concern about transhumanism and posthumanism comes from conservative quarters. It's the concern that we're eroding notions of "man" and "woman" and that the next step in the progression is to explode the concept of "human beings." Some religious people see these social changes as signs that the end times are nigh since Western society is falling into moral relativism by ignoring divinely ordained boundaries. Ironically, however, conservative political leaders have been instrumental in spreading post-truth relativism through what are sometimes called "alternative facts." This is even more interesting when we remember that the word "apocalypse" means "revelation," which is close to "truth." Seen in this light, a post-apocalyptic world is a post-truth world.

Geralt's morality, on the one hand, is far from post-truth relativism in that he exhibits old-fashioned virtues such as loyalty to friends and willingness to protect those who can't defend themselves. But Geralt's traditional commitments do not preclude progressive attitudes. His ideas about sex are liberal, he closely associates with outgroups like dwarves, and he befriends those who'd normally be his enemies, like the Nilfgaardian officer Cahir and the kindhearted vampire Regis. But Geralt's reason for these friendships is precisely the opposite of post-truth relativism. Regis, for example, repeatedly proves he's not a monster despite belonging to a monstrous species. He's given up sucking blood, and repeatedly uses his knowledge and skill to help his companions and even strangers. Regis dies protecting Geralt in *The Lady of the Lake*. In the same book, Cahir meets his end when attempting to rescue Ciri.

One of Geralt's strengths, then, is that he grasps the substance of individuals—their genuine character based on what they actually do. This is why he's eventually able to see beyond Regis's and Cahir's superficial identities and welcome their companionship. In this regard, he aligns with the Book of Revelation's acceptance of multitudes "from every nation, tribe, people and language."[33] Elsewhere, Jesus welcomes society's moral outcasts and says whoever is not actively fighting his followers is supporting them (a statement that classifies even people holding contrary religious views as friends as long as they aren't attacking).[34] From this perspective, we might say Geralt is both orthodox and heterodox. He accepts values that we find in old sources like the Bible. Yet he breaks norms by upholding inclusive principles that many religious adherents have historically ignored, meaning they have applied post-truth and in this sense post-apocalyptic thinking to their own scriptures.

Geralt especially becomes baffled by morality supplanted with economic calculations. When he offers to remove a bridge troll who brutalizes people for refusing to pay a toll, the town's alderman objects: "Who will repair the bridge if the troll's not there?"[35] The troll does "solid work, first rate. It's cheaper to pay his toll."[36] Geralt also complains about a man who wanted him to slay a harmless beast because of a false belief that its bones cure impotence. Similarly, people try to hire him to kidnap various nymph-like creatures, presumably for sex, even when "the villages are teeming with girls."[37] In both the books and Netflix series, Geralt declines mercenary soldiering jobs. Despite declaring that he works for money, most of his battles and quests are unpaid, taken up for principled reasons. He's disoriented in a post-truth world where moral values shift according to individual self-interest.

World Wounds

Perspectives ranging from ancient Greek and Neoplatonic traditions to Indian Vedic and Chinese Daoist philosophies held that the world has a proper balance or equilibrium.[38] The Greek formulation of the idea is *psukhe kosmou*. *Psukhe* connotes "psyche," "soul," "breath," and "life," and *kosmou* means "world," "cosmos," or "harmonious system."[39] If the world is alive and breathing, it can get wounded when things fall out of balance—a description that characterizes the apocalyptic situation that's brewing in *The Witcher*.

The Witcher series portrays an ecologically unbalanced world on the edge of environmental cataclysm. It has ghoulish mutants and also creatures violating their normally reclusive natures to retaliate against people who are causing their extinction. In *The Sword of Destiny*, the mage Dorregaray advises that everything has "natural equilibrium."[40] He says each creature is the natural enemy of others, and that all nonhumans are the foe of people, adding that this is for the better, since struggle leads to improvement.

Though Dorregaray's ideas are dubious, they stress connections between sex and destruction: overall improvement requires both the death of weaker individuals and continuing the genes of the stronger ones. His claims also orbit the notion of planetary equilibrium. In both the books and the Netflix series, magical tampering rips fissures in the earth that breed new and deadly mutants. Climate change is a reality in the *Witcher* stories, as it is in our world, where ruptures in equilibrium from altered weather coincide with the increasing numbers of invasive species. And as with monsters in *The Witcher*, the COVID-19 virus itself is a deadly mutation that seemed apocalyptic at times, and it was generated and spread because of human-made conditions.

The title of Sapkowski's *Baptism of Fire* has an ominous apocalyptic tone, and alludes to a New Testament verse.[41] The novel recounts how an elf long ago "prophesied the climatic changes" that came to be "known as the Great Frost" and were seen as "a sign of the end of the world."[42] *The Tower of Swallows* has another elf telling Geralt, "And then suddenly comes the Conjunction of the Spheres and you, people, appear here. Human survivors, come from another world" that "you managed utterly to destroy."[43] A message is that the environmental calamity is not just due to nonhuman forces in nature. It's also a consequence of an apocalyptical post-truth scenario in which selfish interests lead to ruin.

Social Apocalypses

These apocalyptic tones match Hebrew, Islamic, and especially Christian scriptures. The fact that humans migrated to new lands where others were already living also mirrors Indigenous American history and is captured in a divination that circulates among the Anishinaabe First Nations tribes: "Beware if the light skinned race comes wearing the face of death."[44] The parallels between *The Witcher* and colonial history are stronger in light of the fact that European migration to the Americas occurred for environmental reasons like famine. Indeed, Sapkowski appears to model the predicament of the elves after the plight of Indigenous and other colonized populations. This allusion is fitting for another reason. As one scholar notes, if we are presently triggering cataclysms on our own planet, then there are lessons to take from "Amerindians who, nonetheless, have managed to abide, and learned to live in a world which is no longer their world 'as they knew it'."[45]

Like Indigenous people of the Americas, who had advanced textiles, metal working, mathematics, palaces, crop domestication, and possibly one of the earliest writing systems, the elves are also sophisticated.[46] Because the elves do not farm, but take only what the land gives them, they resemble hunter-gatherer Indigenous communities. As an elf named Filavandrel elaborates, unlike humans, elves "never cultivated the land" and "tore at it with hoes and ploughs. To you, the earth pays a bloody tribute." But "for us, the earth gave birth and blossomed because it loved us." Filavandrel says that these days his people "are starving" and "threatened with annihilation." Because of cataclysmic environmental changes, "the things we used to eat, made use of, are dying."[47]

Filavandrel complains that when humans talk about living with elves, they mean on terms that acknowledge human sovereignty. He asks, "Cohabit as what? Slaves? Pariahs? Cohabit with you from beyond the walls you've built to fence yourselves away in towns? Cohabit with your women and hang for it? Or look on at what half-blood children must live with?"[48] These comments recall the removal of Indigenous people from their lands to be confined to reservations, which was part of a cultural apocalypse. The remarks also echo Jim Crow laws and social rules preventing intermingling, whether in America, Nazi Germany, apartheid South Africa, or colonial India. And together with the claims about how human appetites destroyed the land, Filavandrel is presenting cultural and environmental apocalypses as two sides of the same coin.

Despite the abuses they suffer, the elves have a proposition, involving Ciri having a child with the elf king, to save everyone from the dying planet. Though mostly human, Ciri is the descendant of a powerful elf, which explains her magical gifts. As Avallac'h explains, were Ciri to have a baby with the elf king, their child would have a genetically bestowed supernatural capacity that could open an escape from the world, a "permanent Gateway, through which everyone would pass."[49] It's debatable that this is a solution, however, since the apocalyptic situation in *The Witcher* is at least partly caused by people, who seem likely to destroy their new world too.

Bad Endings

In the Netflix series, cities and forests are tinted gray, often crumbling or dying, recalling Soviet-era industrial cities as well as the polluted stretches of centers of capitalist industry that look like post-apocalyptic wastes. The visuals demonstrate that worlds—and cities in them—can get sick.

A conversation from *The Sword of Destiny* brings this into relief. Yennefer claims women want town walls and protection from dragons so they can bear children at the "proper rhythm" of one a year.[50] Dorregaray counters that "it is filth and lice—and not dragons—which threaten your splendid cities," spreading disease so that only one in ten babies survive.[51] This once again ties the ideas of social and environmental apocalypses.

In today's world, cities are key to a sustainable future because they're more efficient than rural settlements in many ways. Yet because of crowding and pollution, diseases in urban areas can be worse. Cities also fuel the environmentally destructive attitude that we're separate from nature, a belief Yennefer perpetuates when she talks of settlements as havens from the wilderness.

The failure of people within communities to cooperate is another kind of sickness. The dwarf Zoltan Chivay says to Geralt, "I predict a bad end for your race."[52] He explains that almost every other conscious creature "cleaves to his own" in desperate periods "because it's easier to survive the bad times in a group, helping one another." But humans "just wait for a chance to make money from other people's mishaps."[53]

A last thing to remember is that ancient concepts of city-soul like Plato's were modeled after "just individuals," said to have a healthy equilibrium between rationality, emotions, and appetites, all of which are unbalanced in most *Witcher* characters. Overwhelming lust for power or wealth drives many individuals. Others are absorbed in rational calculation without love for others. Again, the Greek word *apokalypsis* can almost be translated as "truth," and *The Witcher* reiterates the link between these terms. We get mage-scientists seeking solutions irrespective of ethical implications. We see greed driving people to act without compassion. In short, we are presented with a post-apocalyptic scenario that's partly grounded in a post-truth collapse of moral reasoning, and this gets close to the trajectory of our own history.

Notes

1. David Leeming, "The Flood," in *World Mythology: A Very Short Introduction* (New York: Oxford University Press, 2022), at https://doi.org/10.1093/actrade/9780197548264.003.0004 (accessed April 23, 2023).

2. Robert Beyer, Mario Krapp, Anders Eriksson, and Andrea Manica, "Climatic Windows for Human Migration out of Africa in the Past 300,000 Years," *Nature Communications* 12 (2021), art. 4889, at https://doi.org/10.1038/s41467-021-24779-1.

3. Aristotle, *Metaphysics*, trans. William David Ross, in Richard McKeon ed., *The Basic Works of Aristotle* (New York: Random House, 1941), 1.980a22.

4. Angus Stevenson ed., *The Oxford Dictionary of English* (Oxford: Oxford University Press, 2010), 72.

5. Francis Moloney, "The Book of Revelation: Hope in Dark Times," *Religions* 10 (2019), 239.

6. Revelation 12:3 and 9:7–10, in *Holy Bible (New International Version)* (Grand Rapids: Zondervan, 2011).

7. Andrzej Sapkowski, *The Tower of Swallows*, trans. David French (New York: Orbit Books, 2016), 228.

8. Matthew Crippen, "Review" of Richard Shusterman, *Ars Erotica: Sex and Somaesthetics in the Classical Arts of Love, Society* 60 (2023), 279–284.

9. Andrzej Sapkowski, *Season of the Storms*, trans. David French (New York: Orbit Books, 2018), interlude 1; Andrzej Sapkowski, *Baptism of Fire*, trans. David French (New York: Orbit Books, 2014), chap. 7; Richard Shusterman, *Ars Erotica: Sex and Somaesthetics in the Classical Arts of Love* (Cambridge: Cambridge University Press, 2021), chap. 3.

10. Sapkowski, *Baptism of Fire*, 249–250; Andrzej Sapkowski, *The Lady of the Lake*, trans. David French (New York: Orbit Books, 2018), 334.

11. Sapkowski, *The Lady of the Lake*, chap. 9.

12. Friedrich Nietzsche, *Thus Spoke Zarathustra*, in Walter Kaufman ed. and trans., *The Portable Nietzsche* (New York: Penguin, 1954), 250.

13. Nietzsche, *Thus Spoke Zarathustra*, 250.

14. Sapkowski, *Tower of Swallows*, 227.

15. Plato, *Phaedo*, trans. David Gallop (Oxford: Oxford University Press, 1975), 64–84a.

16. Plato, *Phaedo*, 64–84a.

17. Andrzej Sapkowski, *Blood of Elves*, trans. Danusia Stok (New York: Orbit Books, 2008), 96.

18. Friedrich Nietzsche, *Twilight of the Idols*, in Kaufman ed. and trans., *The Portable Nietzsche*, 479.

19. Ralph Waldo Emerson, *Nature* (Boston: James Munroe & Co, 1836), 5.

20. Fyodor Dostoevsky, *Notes from Underground*, trans. Richard Pevear and Larissa Volokhonsky (New York: Vintage, 1993), 130.

21. Dostoevsky, *Notes from Underground*, 130.

22. S.S. Merzlyakov, "Posthumanism vs. Transhumanism: From the 'End of Exceptionalism' to 'Technological Humanism,'" *Herald of the Russian Academy of Sciences* 92, Suppl. 6 (2022), S475.

23. Merzlyakov, "Posthumanism vs. Transhumanism," S475.

24. Plato, *The Republic*, trans. Allan Bloom (New York: Basic Books, 2016), book 4.

25. Andrzej Sapkowski, *Sword of Destiny*, trans. David French (New York: Orbit Books, 2015), 161.

26. Sapkowski, *Sword of Destiny*, 133.

27. Sapkowski, *Season of the Storms*, 240–241.

28. Sapkowski, *Season of the Storms*, 241, 236.

29. Sapkowski, *Season of the Storms*, 241.

30. Sapkowski, *Season of the Storms*, 150.

31. Immanuel Kant, *Groundwork of the Metaphysic of Morals*, trans. Mary Gregor (Cambridge: Cambridge University Press, 1997), 429.

32. Sapkowski, *Season of the Storms*, 152.

33. Revelation 7:9.

34. Matthew 9:10–17, Mark 2:15–22, Mark, 9:40, Luke 5:29–39.

35. Andrzej Sapkowski, *The Last Wish*, trans. Danusia Stok (New York: Orbit Books, 2007), 249–250.

36. Sapkowski, *The Last Wish*, 250.
37. Sapkowski, *The Last Wish*, 250.
38. Harold Coward, "Hindu Views of Nature and the Environment," in Helaine Selin ed., *Nature across Cultures* (Manchester: Springer 2003), 411–419; Matthew Crippen, "Chinese Thought and Transcendentalism: Ecology, Place and Conservative Radicalism," *Religions* 14 (2023), 570; Matthew Crippen and Alice Cortés, "Ecology and Technological Enframement: Cities, Networks, and the COVID-19 Pandemic," in Debra Mutnick, Margaret Cuonzo, Carole Griffiths, Timothy Leslie, and Jay M. Shuttleworth eds., *The City Is an Ecosystem* (London: Routledge, 2023), 13–24.
39. Alice Cortés and Matthew Crippen, "Phenomenology and Ecology: Art, Cities, and Cinema in the Pandemic," *The Polish Journal of Aesthetics* 61 (2021), 27–41.
40. Sapkowski, *Sword of Destiny*, 42.
41. Matthew 3:11.
42. Sapkowski, *Baptism of Fire*, 263.
43. Sapkowski, *The Tower of Swallows*, 227.
44. Edward Benton-Banai, *The Mishomis Book: The Voice of the Ojibway* (Haward: Indian Country Communications), 90.
45. Eduardo Viveiros de Castro, "Who Is Afraid of the Ontological Wolf?: Some Comments on an Ongoing Anthropological Debate," *The Cambridge Journal of Anthropology* 33 (2015), 2–17.
46. Charles Mann, *1491: New Revelations of the Americas before Columbus* (New York: Knopf, 2005); Frank Salomon, *The Cord Keepers* (Durham, NC: Duke University Press: 2004).
47. Sapkowski, *The Last Wish*, 183.
48. Sapkowski, *The Last Wish*, 183.
49. Sapkowski, *The Lady of the Lake*, 169.
50. Sapkowski, *Sword of Destiny*, 43.
51. Sapkowski, *Sword of Destiny*, 43.
52. Sapkowski, *Baptism of Fire*, 147.
53. Sapkowski, *Baptism of Fire*, 147.

POLITICAL PHILOSOPHY

22

King Foltest, John Locke, and Political Sovereignty in Temeria

John P. Irish

There is one way more whereby such a government may be dissolved, and that is, when he who has the supreme executive power, neglects and abandons that charge.... This is demonstratively to reduce all to anarchy, and so effectually to dissolve the government.[1]

John Locke, *Two Treatises of Government*

The story "The Witcher" from *The Last Wish* introduces us to the main character of the series.[2] Geralt of Rivia is looking to cash in on a reward from Foltest, the King of Temeria, who wants someone to lift a curse put on his daughter, Adda. The girl was born a striga (a vampire-like creature) due to Foltest's incestuous relationship with his sister. Geralt's challenge is to lift the curse without killing the girl, and the witcher believes he knows how: he must survive one night in her crypt without being killed—a daunting task, even for a witcher!

This story raises important philosophical questions about the nature of political sovereignty, which is defined as the authority to govern a state or nation. Critical questions about political sovereignty concerning King Foltest include: Does Foltest hold legitimate political power over his subjects? Has Foltest violated his political obligation to protect the citizens of Wyzim/Vizima by allowing the striga to remain alive? If his actions violate his responsibilities toward his subjects, what recourse do they have in demanding justice from Foltest? Does his refusal to act—a failure to protect their lives, liberty, and property—justify their actions against him— even regicide, the murder of a king?

To help us explore these difficult questions, let's turn to John Locke's (1632–1704) seminal work in political philosophy, the *Two Treatises of Government*.[3] This influential piece has left an indelible mark on Western political thought, serving as a cornerstone text for social contract political theory. It will serve as a valuable resource as we delve into the inquiries surrounding Foltest and his claim to the Temerian throne.

The Witcher and Philosophy: Toss a Coin to Your Philosopher, First Edition.
Edited by Matthew Brake and Kevin S. Decker.
© 2025 John Wiley & Sons, Inc. Published 2025 by John Wiley & Sons, Inc.

Foltest and the Divine Right of Kings

Hereditary monarchs across the Continent acquire authority "through the usual conquests, treatises, marriages, bribery, blackmail, and assassinations. Stronger realms consumed the weaker ones, uniting them under their dynasties."[4] Through his father, King Medell, and his mother, Queen Sancia of Sodden, Foltest inherited the throne of Temeria, making him part of the Temerian Dynasty. "He inspires both fear and respect in his subjects. [It is said that] Foltest rules with an iron fist; he is decisive and hot-headed."[5] Under his rule, though, Temeria has become one of the most powerful Northern Kingdoms.

Foltest understands the importance of culture in making his political authority legitimate, especially the role of the relationship between politics and religion. He's not particularly religious, but he understands the relationship between the two. He erected a new temple and demanded a tithe, which significantly drained the royal treasury. Although he doubts the existence of the gods, he recognizes the priests' power and their influence on his subjects; any attempts to limit the priest class might provoke their wrath.[6] Religion's influence on his subjects' daily lives and the priests' limited power bolsters his political legitimacy.

One of the churches, the Cult of Kreve, is very influential in the Northern Kingdoms and often serves as a prop to strengthen the bond between the church and the state. "The cult's priests hold no disdain for political influence and worldly concerns.... They usually spend their time droning on ... about the divine origins of rulers."[7] In our world, the "divine right of kings" theory claims that God granted earthly power to the monarch, just as he granted spiritual authority to the pope. This grant provided legitimacy to political sovereignty in the minds of many of those supporting the hereditary monarchy. Foltest rose to the throne of Temeria as a result of his birth. Still, his continued legitimate rule rests partly upon the collaboration and coordination he fosters between the church and the state.

The Continental Monarchs' Embrace of Absolutism

When Locke published his *Two Treatises of Government* in 1689, Sir Robert Filmer (1588–1653) had been dead for almost 40 years. Filmer's most important book on political philosophy, *Patriarcha*, was a vigorous defense of the system of absolute political authority. The fact that Filmer couldn't defend his ideas didn't stop Locke from focusing his attack on Filmer's defense of the "divine right of kings."[8] Influenced by Aristotle (384–322 BCE), Jean Bodin (1530–1596), and the Bible,[9] Filmer developed a nuanced political philosophy combining the "divine right of kings" as allowing monarchs to rule with absolute power with a new twist—that of patriarchy, the belief that the "power of government is settled and fixed by the commandment of 'honor thy father.'"[10]

The French jurist and political philosopher Jean Bodin was known for his theory of absolute sovereignty.[11] He argued that political sovereignty had to be defined according to some essential characteristics: every state must have a single sovereign who alone must make all the laws; the sovereign is not subject to those laws and is accountable only to God; the sovereign is absolute and indivisible, and his subjects are, under no circumstances, permitted to resist him.[12] Bodin and Filmer both believed that a political theory of absolute sovereignty was the only practical solution to questions about political order, given the nature of humanity. Since the biblical "Fall of Man" (the transition of humans from a state of innocent obedience to a state of disobedience to God), an absolute political order was necessary to ensure human society did not collapse into anarchy.

The monarchs on the Continent openly embrace these principles about human nature and political sovereignty, governing according to the observation of the golden dragon Villentretenmerth that "human history is invariably filled with conflict."[13] Conflict, they believe, can only be controlled by absolute rule. Despite their differences, monarchs of the Continent act according to their unwavering belief that it's their destiny to enlarge their power and their domains through any means possible and that, as heads of their state, they are the absolute power within their domain—their sovereign rule is law and beyond question. Villentretenmerth, in *The History of the World*, records that King Niedamir of Caingorn "hanged, beheaded, and quartered all opposition for as long as it took the local nobility to officially recognize him as the leader."[14] He also discusses "the realm of Jamurlak, which for a long time was ruled by a psychopath ... [whose] cruelty was as legendary as his lustfulness."[15] He notes the Northern Kingdom of "Kaedwen's quarrelsome nature and history of conflict."[16] And after King Demavend of Aedirn's death, "social disturbances, peasant revolts, ... and a growing separatist movement"[17] broke out, according to Villentretenmerth.

Filmer added the idea of patriarchy to Bodin's political theory by saying that monarchs must wield the "natural authority of a supreme father."[18] Filmer believed patriarchy to be consistent with the biblically based social theory that emphasized the divinely appointed duty of children to obey their fathers. The first father was Adam; hence, male monarchy was the original form of government. The law of primogeniture ensured that Adam's heirs would continue the political line of sovereignty; primogeniture is a system of inheritance in which a person's property passes to their firstborn legitimate child upon their death. Filmer argues that humanity's initial state was not characterized by freedom, liberty, and equality. Instead, he posits that the opening book of the Bible, *Genesis*, shows how human history, starting from Adam, entailed a state of subordination to Adam's descendants.[19]

Temeria's Right to a Social Contract

Filmer's and Bodin's view that some persons are *naturally* subject to the political authority of others fits the view of Foltest and the other monarchs on the Continent. In contrast, Locke advocated political *voluntarism*, the idea that sovereignty is based on each individual's free choice to be part of a particular political organization.[20] Such a free choice is based on social contract theory, the belief that "political legitimacy, political authority, and political obligation are derived from the consent of the governed, and are the ... product of the voluntary agreement of free and equal ... agents."[21]

Locke believed humanity grew up in an original state of freedom, equality, and liberty. Political societies began when individuals moved out of this state of nature. Locke states, "To understand political power ... we must consider what state all men are naturally in, and that is, a state of perfect freedom to order their actions, and dispose of their possessions, and persons as they think fit," he continues "within the bounds of the law of nature, without ... depending upon the will of any other man."[22] Locke undercuts the Bodin/Filmer argument that superior and inferior political positions are natural by arguing that, initially, humans are equal and free. The move from the state of nature into political society demonstrates that political authority is *artificial*, something created. Locke goes further to say that those who employ political power legitimately do so only as trustees of the people: "Political power then I take to be a right of making laws ... for the regulating and preserving of property [including life, liberty, and possessions] ... for the public good."[23]

This theory of political voluntarism would have significant consequences for the monarchs on the Continent if it were acted upon. Locke argues there's no single form of legitimate government; instead, Locke focuses on the process by which a government originates. Foltest and the other monarchs hold legitimate political authority as long as their rule has the consent of the people governed, preserves order and property, and is used for the public good. However, Foltest's political power is actually inherited and used to benefit himself, his monarchy, and the expansion of his kingdom. There is no evident social contract in Temeria, so according to Locke, Foltest's rule is illegitimate.[24] But all is not lost for Foltest! If monarchs use political authority correctly (to protect their subjects' lives, liberties, and property), they might be able to claim legitimate political sovereignty, even without origin in a social contract.

Foltest's Breach of the Sovereign Trust

"Foltest," claims Lord Ostrit, "showed us what he was capable of, and he was capable of a great deal."[25] He was, in fact, unable to control himself in "matters of the flesh."[26] Shortly after his coronation, Foltest surpassed himself by demonstrating there was no limit to his selfish desires and utter disregard for the public good. He got his sister pregnant with a child, a blatant violation of cultural and institutional norms leading to a breakdown of social order. Adda the White, the striga and King Foltest's daughter, preys upon the citizens of Wyzim, creating a perpetual state of fear and insecurity. Foltest's action puts the citizens of Wyzim on high alert as they fear for their lives.

"Foltest ... forbade any attempt to kill the striga and brought in charlatans from all corners of Wyzim to reverse the spell and turn her into a princess."[27] Foltest prohibited anyone from laying a hand on the striga and used force against those who tried to harm her in any way. Many tried to burn or invade the old palace during the day, but these attempts were thwarted and met with swift and harsh punishment. The existence of the striga represents an existential threat to the community, clearly threatening their lives, liberties, and property. Her presence and continued existence raise a critical Lockean question about sovereignty: Does Foltest's refusal to deal with the striga threat demonstrate a fundamental breach of the sovereign trust?

Locke argues that individuals leave the state of nature to better protect life, liberty, and property, and there are limits to sovereignty in the notion of political trust. Political figures hold and wield power from a trust that's part of the social contract: "with this express or tacit trust, that it shall be employed for their good, and the preservation of their property."[28] The striga represents a severe threat to the citizens of Wyzim and is the opposite of "protection." By allowing Adda to prey upon the citizens of Wyzim, Foltest is guilty of violating the Lockean principle of sovereign trust. This makes Foltest responsible for the terror, fear, and insecurity of the citizens. So Foltest not only wields illegitimate authority (because his power is not a result of a social contract) but also violates the duty and obligation on which all legitimate sovereignty exists—protecting the lives, liberties, and property of Wyzim's citizens. Since Foltest is violating his sovereign duty, what recourse do the citizens of Temeria have to protect themselves?

The Miners' Uprising

A new twist is added to the story in the Netflix episode "Betrayer Moon" (season 1, episode 3). The year is 1243, and Temeria is on the brink of anarchy. A group of miners is inciting a revolution; they've collected 3000 coins for anyone who'll come and kill the striga. Lord Ostrit confronts the angry mob and dispatches them. Secretly though, Ostrit bribes individuals who come to kill the striga not to kill her because he wants revenge on Foltest. Ostrit had been in love with the king's sister, Adda, and he blames Foltest for interfering with their romantic relationship. Ostrit hopes that if enough fear and anger over the presence of the striga build up in the community, they'll overthrow and kill Foltest. This episode raises our final Lockean question about the nature of sovereignty: Are the miners justified in fomenting a political rebellion in Temeria?

Locke explains that political power has the potential to degenerate into tyranny through two different means. Firstly, when the ruler bases decisions solely on their self-interests, effectively governing "not for the good of those under it, but for his own private separate advantage. When the governor ... makes not the law, but his will, the rule."[29] This occurs when the ruler does not adhere to the law but imposes their own will as the guiding principle. Secondly, tyranny arises when the sovereign wields power beyond what is justifiable, or in other words, resorts to force without legitimate authority. As Locke expressed it, "Tyranny begins, if the law be transgressed to another's harm ... [and] whosoever in authority exceed the power given him by the law, and makes use of the force he has under his command."[30]

Locke says those with political authority are the actual transgressors for violating that sovereign trust, not the citizens who attempt to right the wrong. Since sovereign power is given from the social contract, society can take back that power when that trust is violated. Locke says this won't happen for frivolous or arbitrary reasons. It will take many examples of abuse and hardship before individuals rise and take back the sovereign power granted to their leaders: "[When] the people are made miserable, and find themselves exposed to the ill usage of arbitrary power,"[31] Locke continues, "great mistakes ... and all the slips of human frailty will be borne by the people.... But [after] a long train of abuses ... [they] may secure to them the ends for which government was at first erected."[32]

Foltest violates the political trust granted to him as part of his sovereign responsibility. The miners, with Lockean social contract theory on their side, are justified in overthrowing him by whatever means they feel necessary to restore legitimate political authority—as long as that new authority adheres to the political conditions for the legitimate sovereign rule: they must have the consent of the governed, they must protect the lives, liberty, and property of their citizen-subjects, and work toward the public good.

... And They Lived Happily Ever After—Sort Of!

Foltest holds illegitimate authority because his power doesn't rest upon a social contract between him and his subjects. Further, Foltest violates sovereign authority because he rules solely for his own benefit; his refusal to kill the striga leads to anarchy within Wyzim, establishing a crisis where none of the citizens' lives, liberties, or properties are safe. Finally, because Foltest violates the sovereign trust on which all legitimate political power rests, he's put himself at odds with his subjects, forfeiting his sovereign power and making himself subject to removal—even through a revolution that could include violence and even the king's death.

Sapkowski's story *The Witcher* grants us a glimpse into a realm teeming with adventure, monstrosities, sorcery, and malevolence. However, its significance extends beyond mere escapism, serving as a cautionary tale for those in positions of political power, illuminating the essence and limitations of sovereignty. Our political leaders have immense authority, entrusted by us to safeguard our lives, liberties, and property. In turn, they pledge to fulfill their assigned duties. Their governance remains legitimate only as long as they prioritize the common good. Any failure to uphold this ideal breaches the trust bestowed upon them, inviting severe consequences. Locke implores our leaders to wholeheartedly embrace this social contract—or face the repercussions. Thankfully, for King Foltest and the citizens of Wyzim, Geralt emerged victorious, dispelling the curse, rescuing the girl, and rightfully receiving his reward—just another day's labor for a witcher!

Notes

1. John Locke, *Two Treatises of Government*, ed. Peter Laslett (New York: Cambridge University Press, 1988), 411. I have modernized Locke's text throughout this chapter.
2. Andrzej Sapkowski, *The Last Wish* (New York: Orbit Books, 2021), 5–39.
3. John P. Irish, "Brief Lives: John Locke (1632–1704)," *Philosophy Now: A Magazine of Ideas* 138 (June/July 2020), 36–39.
4. CD Projekt Red, *The World of the Witcher: Video Game Compendium* (Milwaukie, OR: Dark Horse Books, 2015), 14.
5. "Foltest," The Official Witcher Wiki, November 21, 2022, at https://witcher.fandom.com/wiki/Foltest.
6. CD Projekt Red, *The World of the Witcher*, 14.
7. CD Projekt Red, *The World of the Witcher*, 103.
8. James Daly, *Sir Robert Filmer and English Political Thought* (Toronto: University of Toronto Press, 1979).
9. Julian H. Franklin, *Jean Bodin and the Rise of Absolutist Theory* (New York: Cambridge University Press, 2009).
10. Robert Filmer, *Patriarcha and Other Writings*, ed. Johann P. Sommerville (New York: Cambridge University Press, 1991), 238.
11. Jean Bodin, *Six Books on the Commonwealth*, abridged and trans. M.J. Tooley (Oxford: Basil Blackwell, 1955) and Jean Bodin, *On Sovereignty*, ed. Julian Franklin (New York: Cambridge University Press, 1992).
12. John N. Figgis, *The Divine Right of Kings* (Bristol: Thoemmes Press, 1994).
13. CD Projekt Red, *The World of the Witcher*, 13.
14. CD Projekt Red, *The World of the Witcher*, 28.
15. CD Projekt Red, *The World of the Witcher*, 29.
16. CD Projekt Red, *The World of the Witcher*, 30.
17. CD Projekt Red, *The World of the Witcher*, 33.

18. Filmer, *Patriarcha*, 11.
19. Johann P. Sommerville, "Absolutism & Royalism," in J.H. Burns and Mark Goldie eds., *The Cambridge History of Political Thought: 1450–1700* (New York: Cambridge University Press, 1994), 347–373.
20. A. John Simmons, "Locke on the Social Contract," in Matthew Stuart ed., *A Companion to Locke* (Malden, MA: Wiley Blackwell, 2016), 413–432.
21. Patrick Riley, "Social Contract Theory and Its Critics," in Mark Goldie and Robert Wokler eds., *The Cambridge History of Eighteenth-Century Political Thought* (New York: Cambridge University Press, 2016), 347.
22. Locke, *Two Treatises*, 269.
23. Locke, *Two Treatises*, 268.
24. Locke does allow for a difference between an "explicit" and "tacit" agreement to the social contract. Tacit consent can be conferred upon a monarch if the subject voluntarily resides within the kingdom and receives the benefit of their sovereign protection or other benefits within political society.
25. Sapkowski, *The Last Wish*, 10.
26. "Foltest," The Official Witcher Wiki.
27. Sapkowski, *The Last Wish*, 12.
28. Locke, *Two Treatises*, 381.
29. Locke, *Two Treatises*, 398–399.
30. Locke, *Two Treatises*, 400.
31. Locke, *Two Treatises*, 414.
32. Locke, *Two Treatises*, 415.

23

Stolen Mutagens and Frustrated Neutrality
Carl Schmitt and "the Political" in *The Witcher*

Florian R.R. van der Zee

The first *Witcher* video game starts off by disorienting the player. Wounded and on the run, you collapse. You wake up to find yourself at the witcher fortress of Kaer Morhen, the closest thing you have to a home. You are Geralt of Rivia and your name is legend, but, suffering from amnesia, you can't remember why. Nursed back to a degree of health, your recovery is interrupted as brigands attack Kaer Morhen and steal the witcher mutagens, the very precondition for witcher existence.

As you assume Geralt's skin and set out to retrieve the mutagens, the disorientation continues. This is partly due to the fact that Geralt often has to make choices whose consequences remain uncertain. But that's not all. As Geralt, a sizeable part of your confusion results from an inability to stay true to witcher neutrality: witchers are supposed to simply slay monsters while keeping their noses out of politics. This plagues Geralt throughout the novels, games, and Netflix series, and it plays a particularly central role in the first game. As Geralt traverses Temeria, a kingdom besieged by plague and civil war, he's inevitably forced into taking sides. Two philosophical questions arise: Why can't Geralt remain neutral? What does this say about neutrality and politics? As we'll see, the ideas of the German political theorist Carl Schmitt (1888–1985) on the nature of "the political" can help us find answers.

Choices and Consequences

What "neutrality" means according to a witcher like Geralt is partly revealed by an event early in the game. Geralt has tracked the "Salamandra" brigands who raided Kaer Morhen to the outskirts of Temeria's capital, Vizima. He soon discovers that a priest of the Church of the Eternal Fire,

The Witcher and Philosophy: Toss a Coin to Your Philosopher, First Edition.
Edited by Matthew Brake and Kevin S. Decker.

known simply as "the Reverend," is his only hope for finding out more about the Salamandras' whereabouts. But the Reverend won't enlighten Geralt for free. He insists that Geralt must first gain the trust of three of the most respected inhabitants of the rural Outskirts area outside Vizima.

One of these is the shady merchant Haren Brogg. For Brogg, Geralt's arrival is most opportune. Living close to the river separating Vizima and the Outskirts, Brogg uses the riverbank as his warehouse. But the riverbank is plagued by nightly visits of water-dwelling necrophages— drowners—that have taken a liking to his stores. Since this is precisely the sort of problem a witcher could fix, Brogg asks Geralt to liquidate the watery fiends.

Geralt readily agrees and disposes of several drowners, but matters become complicated when a band of Scoia'tael arrive on the scene. These nonhumans—mainly elves and dwarves—are waging a guerrilla war against human powers. They also claim to be trading with Brogg, and wish to take the goods he has promised them. Geralt is now faced with a choice: Will he allow the Scoia'tael to take the goods, or will he prevent them from doing so?

Neither choice seems particularly neutral at first. If Geralt allows the Scoia'tael to take the goods, he won't have actively aided the rebels, but he *will* have failed to thwart their activities while in a position to do so. Preventing the Scoia'tael from taking the goods means bloodshed. Geralt's options seem to be either passive aid or active opposition.

But remaining neutral can be treated as a matter of principle rather than an isolated stance on a particular conflict. And if we do that, this dilemma might distort things. Witcher actions might be guided by "neutralism"—by the "intention to remain neutral in any eventual conflict, and to treat the parties to that conflict with total impartiality," as Roger Scruton (1944– 2020) put it.[1] If so, then their neutrality might lie in the principle guiding their actions, not in the consequences of their acting or failing to act. So witcher neutrality would commit Geralt to the refusal of active aid to any side in any conflict. That refusal could still benefit one side or another, but it would be wrong to treat the resulting good or bad consequences as a violation of neutrality. The neutral actor only chooses to refuse active aid; they have not chosen who, if anyone, will benefit from that refusal.

On the sense of "neutrality" as principled-refusal-of-active-aid, it would seem that Geralt should allow the Scoia'tael to take the goods. In doing so, he would swing his steel sword for neither side. However, Geralt seems to see things differently. What he doesn't know before deciding is that letting the Scoia'tael take Brogg's goods will lead to the gang's assassination of Coleman, a Viziman fisstech trader. Learning of Coleman's death and realizing that the weapons that killed him came from Brogg's stock, Geralt reflects on his choice in the Outskirts. He concludes: "I know where the weapons that killed Coleman came from. I need to avoid those situations, remain neutral, not get involved."

Perhaps Geralt takes the stricter, principled-refusal-of-benefit view on neutrality after all. Or maybe there is an aspect to his neutrality we have yet to uncover. Carl Schmitt aids us by asking why it's so difficult for people like Geralt to remain neutral in the first place.

The Burdens of Group Existence

To get a grip on the political disorder of his day, Carl Schmitt coined the term "the political" (as distinct from "politics"). For Schmitt, the political is about an attachment to group existence: something counts as political if it has to do with the "specific political distinction ... between friend and enemy," a distinction which "denotes the utmost degree of intensity of a union or separation."[2] In turn, the "utmost degree of intensity of union or separation" is the possibility of war: no group is ever more united than the one willing to defend itself to the death, and it is most separate from the group against which it might defend itself.

The political is also about order. Groups can be enemies if they embody mutually exclusive ways of existing. As Schmitt put it, the enemy is "the other, the stranger" and "in a specially intense way, existentially something different and alien."[3] To live together, many alternative ways of living together must be excluded as they cannot be realized simultaneously. For example, in Temeria, nonhumans can either be wholly excluded from society, or treated as tolerated noncitizens, or respected as equal citizens able to occupy the same posts and professions as other people. A combination is impossible. King Foltest must choose.

The Scoia'tael have made their choice. They loathe their inferior position in human-dominated societies and are willing to wage war against them. At times, it seems they are even more radical, regarding human–nonhuman coexistence as impossible by definition.

Scoia'tael like to remind Geralt that he's a member of a group, too: Geralt is a witcher. That makes him neither human nor a member of the Elder Races. Given this, the Scoia'tael sometimes try to persuade Geralt to join their cause as a fellow excluded person. But although an opposition between human and nonhuman can become *the* basis for political opposition, it need not do so (not in the first place, anyway). Political groupings can, but don't need to, follow racial lines.

A central insight of Schmitt's concept of "the political" is that any principle animating group existence can become politically decisive, but that no specific principle is necessarily so. The closer that a difference between groups edges them toward war, the *more political* the difference and the groups are.[4] And the crucial question, "To which group do we ultimately belong, and what does that mean?" can only be answered during cases of actual conflict and by "the actual participants"—not by distant observers, whether philosophers or political scientists.[5] How the lines are drawn cannot be determined purely in theory. Those whose identities depend on it draw the lines. But this means that *anything* can be political.[6]

For the Scoia'tael, the political operates along racial lines. But even though the witcher way of existing will always involve either accepting or rejecting the principle of interracial coexistence on equal terms, the principle of racial self-rule, or the principle of Elder Race dominance, there is no one principle among these that necessarily makes witchers like Geralt tick. So, what does? And is a witcher a witcher first, or does their allegiance lie elsewhere in the end? Are witchers a political group?

Of Mutagens and Mutilated Principles

Central to *The Witcher* is the fact that the continued existence of witchers is under threat. Things haven't been looking good for them for quite some time. Witcher numbers are dwindling. That makes sense. Witchers come into existence by submitting young boys to a harrowing process of undergoing mutation, and the knowledge of how to perform the process has been lost. But a proper nail in the coffin opens the story of the first *Witcher* game, as we noticed earlier: the witcher mutagens—the secret substances required to turn boys into witchers—are stolen when Kaer Morhen is raided.

Responding to the theft, the witchers steal away "in search of the stolen secrets—classically, to the four corners of the world."[7] The witchers are attached to their group existence and to having control over their mutagen-dependent fates. From this point on, they're no longer neutral. Confronted with a group, the existence of which threatens their own—the Salamandra—they fight.

Schmitt would argue that this loss of witcher neutrality shows something important about the political. In the end, a principle like neutralism cannot be a political principle as Schmitt understands such principles. It cannot have the last word. Taken to its extreme, a group's commitment to the avoidance of conflict must lead to one of two ends: it may defeat itself by being violently defended,[8] or the conflict-shunning group must surrender its fate to other powers that don't back away from a fight:

> It would be a mistake to believe that a nation could eliminate the distinction of friend and enemy by declaring its friendship for the entire world. ... The world will not thereby become depoliticalized. ... If a people is afraid of the trials and risks implied by existing in the sphere of politics, then another people will appear which will assume these trials by protecting it against foreign enemies and thereby taking over political rule.[9]

Regardless of how a group defines itself, it ultimately can't uphold its way of existing unless it's willing to defend itself. A political group can still "solemnly declare that it condemns war," but such a declaration is necessarily "subject ... to specific reservations"—like the reservation that their rejection of war ceases when the group's continued, autonomous existence is threatened.[10] If their specific way of living is something witchers are willing to fight for, then witcher neutrality must take second place. Geralt's journey through Temeria suggests this is the case.

The meaning of this loss of neutrality is largely beyond the witchers' control. When they set out from Kaer Morhen, the witchers hardly know the enemy they face. They're ignorant that the true master behind Salamandra's activities, including the mutagen heist, is none other than Jacques de Aldersberg, Grandmaster of the Order of the Flaming Rose. Aldersberg believes he needs the witcher mutagens to create a new class of superhuman warriors to stave off the apocalypse he expects, as well as to fight the non-humans he detests. The witchers don't understand the web of schemes, allies, and enemies in which Salamandra is entangled. But the implications of what it means for a witcher to exercise self-defense are caught in this web. Geralt will need the help of the wealthy merchant and influential schemer Declan Leuvaarden (the enemy of my enemy), he'll have to thwart the coup plans of Foltest's daughter, Princess Adda, and he'll come face to face with the Order of the Flaming Rose. So much for neutrality, indeed!

Schmitt would say that Geralt experiences the specific logic of political existence. As soon as a group is willing to defend its existence to the end, the "real battle is ... of necessity no longer fought" according to fixed self-definitions alone, "but has ... its political necessities and orientations, coalitions, and compromises, and so on."[11] To maintain their existence, witchers may need to forge alliances and to further their allies' ends. These ends may be alien to their own: witchers may want to simply exist as unpolitical monster slayers, but a successful defense of that existence may depend on, say, their willingness to favor one or another pretender to the Temerian throne. Put differently, if "the political" is about the intensity with which differences produce opposing groupings, then "politics" is about finding out which differences are more and which are less important. What are we willing to die for? What are we willing to at least temporarily sacrifice, and in what order? For example, does it matter more that we are there to slay monsters, or that we never favor any side in any conflict? Such questions must be answered by any political group. It turns out that witchers answer them, too.

Of Monsters and Men

In *The Witcher*, the commitment to sustain the witcher form of existence must ultimately inhibit Geralt's attempts to remain neutral. How Geralt understands witcher neutrality, though, depends on how we view his reflections on Coleman's death. Perhaps Geralt's thinking here most clearly defines witchers as a group.

Witchers are very different from the state, the kind of political group that Schmitt wrote most about, fearing its dissolution. Schmitt realized that the state was a modern development, an entity that monopolizes the political decisions within a given territory.[12] For him, the modern state is the entity that tamed the political by prioritizing order over just order, existing in some way over existing in the right way. Schmitt feared that attempts to realize mutually exclusive views of just order in the same society would bring nothing but chaos and squalor. If people disagree about what constitutes a just order, continued peaceful coexistence may be better served by a somewhat arbitrary decision on how to order society than by everyone demanding that they should be able to perceive the social order as the right one. This was Schmitt's ultimate fear: if everyone tries to push through their view of justice, society may perish in civil war. In short, what matters for Schmitt is that political order is defended to stave off chaos; what that order looks like is of secondary importance.[13] In his view, the choice is more important than the outcome.[14]

Witchers aren't concerned with the imposition of order on "their" territory. Witchers are wanderers: they spend their time on "the Path," fighting monsters across territorial bounds. That partially explains why neutralism matters so much to them. The voice of reason seems to dictate that if crossing borders to do a job that transcends political division is your thing, then it would be wise to remain neutral. Antagonizing people you still have to work with is simply impractical.

But does slaying monsters really transcend all political divisions? Demonstrating Schmitt's point that anything is potentially political, Geralt meets many who want to make witchers do their dirty work of killing what they define as "monsters." In *Blood of Elves*, commander Vilfrid Wenck tries to subtly recruit Geralt to protect a convoy against possible Scoia'tael attacks, saying, "One can come across certain evil creatures in Kaedwen forests, lately incited by other evil creatures. They could jeopardise our safety. King Henselt, knowing this, empowered me to recruit volunteers to join our armed escort. Geralt?"[15] Geralt refuses, clearly skeptical of Wenck's characterization of Scoia'tael and Nilfgaardians as "evil creatures." "Please don't count on my sword. I have no intention of killing those, as you call them, evil creatures on the order of other creatures whom I do not consider to be any better," he replies.[16]

Schmitt would approve of Geralt's reluctance to expand the boundaries of the concept of "monster." As we've seen, Schmitt criticized the idea of "neutrality" in two ways: First, the supposedly "neutral" group's belief that it can truly avoid conflict can be incapacitating. Second, a group is never fully neutral, because any way of existing collectively always excludes alternatives. Denying this can lead to a horrifying intensification of conflict. For this reason, Schmitt reproached the use of power in the name of "humanity": "To confiscate the word humanity, to invoke and monopolize such a term probably has certain incalculable effects, such as denying the enemy the quality of being human and declaring him to be an outlaw of humanity; and a war can thereby be driven to the most extreme inhumanity."[17] For Schmitt, saying that your group is impartial and represents humanity won't eliminate the possibility of conflict, but it will obscure it—rendering that group either toothless or ruthless.

If there were a name for the group opposite to what Schmitt called "humanity," it would probably be "monsters." Monsters are beings that one may, and that witchers aim to, exterminate. So, when monster-slayers opt for neutralism, something important is at stake. They are preventing the radicalization of politics that may come from a denial of the political, that is, from denying that ways of existing collectively can be the reason for disagreement and conflict. For, by refusing to take part in certain conflicts, they refuse to brand one group "monsters" that witchers should exterminate, and that are unworthy of humane consideration.

In his later thought, Schmitt focused on the "politics of politics." This meant that our concepts of politics are themselves always political. Schmitt argued that modern Europe developed unwritten laws of political cohabitation saying that enemies were to be respected as equals. They weren't monsters to be wiped out. They were "others," to be pushed back. Thus, conflict was tamed. This remains a political position, however.[18]

Maybe witchers are similar. They belong in a world in which monsters are slain "outside" of the normal arenas of politics, and they feverishly guard the meaning of what "monsters" are, and at least Geralt seems to favor narrowing rather than broadening the definition. Theirs is a world in which enemies are political enemies, and so not treated as monsters. That is the only world capable of accommodating witcher neutrality.

This might help us understand why, reflecting on the Coleman assassination, Geralt thinks that "neutrality" entails active support for established powers against the Scoia'tael. Witcher neutrality is not neutral without exception; it accommodates, for example, the continued and self-determined existence of witchers. Another accommodation is that they must not let conflicts turn enemies into monsters to be exterminated. Because Nilfgaard and the Scoia'tael are waging such a war of annihilation, their plans are incompatible with a world in which witchers can exist. Opposing them might be part of the politics of witcher neutrality.

A Clearly Defined Side of the Palisade?

In the short story, "The Bounds of Reason," Geralt has a conversation with Borch, who inquires about Geralt's views on the witcher occupation. Unconvinced about the occupation's neutrality, he remarks:

> But at the root of it lies some idea, Geralt. The conflict between the forces of Order and the forces of Chaos, as a sorcerer acquaintance of mine used to say. I imagine that you carry out your mission, defending people from Evil,

always and everywhere. Without distinction. You stand on a clearly defined side of the palisade.[19]

Does Geralt find himself on a particular side of the palisade? He responds as if he doesn't, as if witchers are unpolitical professionals. Perhaps he does believe in the view of neutrality as refusing to benefit any side in a conflict. But any course of action is potentially beneficial to some parties. And any way of existing is potentially political. So any group could find itself on some side of a palisade and have to face the question of whether to defend it. The political may return with a vengeance when that is denied.

Or perhaps Geralt views witcher neutrality in the same way as Schmitt. In that case, he clearly finds himself on one side of a palisade. Witcher neutrality is often blamed as a lack of interest in the world. But that might miss the bigger picture. Witcher neutrality may well prevent the transmutation of enemies into monsters: a fight against chaos, indeed.

Of course, whatever is the true meaning of witcher neutrality or Geralt's interpretation of it, Geralt may also find it difficult to remain neutral on grounds of personal conviction or feeling. Geralt ends up defending the convoy he insisted he would not defend, probably to save those he cared for. The person playing Geralt in the games is frequently tempted to prevent injustice. This reveals the tragic nature of a world in which neutrality is ultimately impossible. The question of what one is willing to sacrifice for "greater goods" is inescapable—and can always be asked anew.

Notes

1. Roger Scruton, *The Palgrave Macmillan Dictionary of Political Thought* (Basingstoke: Palgrave Macmillan, 2007), 473.
2. Carl Schmitt, *The Concept of the Political: Expanded Edition*, trans. George Schwab (Chicago: The University of Chicago Press, 2007), 26.
3. Schmitt, *Concept of the Political*, 27, 28–29.
4. Schmitt, *Concept of the Political*, 29, 35–36.
5. Schmitt, *Concept of the Political*, 27.
6. Schmitt, *Concept of the Political*, 38.
7. *The Witcher: Enhanced Edition*, PC version (CD Projekt Red, 2008).
8. Schmitt, *Concept of the Political*, 36.
9. Schmitt, *Concept of the Political*, 52.
10. Schmitt, *Concept of the Political*, 50.
11. Schmitt, *Concept of the Political*, 37.
12. Carl Schmitt, *The Nomos of the Earth in the International Law of the Jus Publicum Europaeum*, trans. G.L. Ulmen (New York: Telos Press Publishing, 2006), 126–129.
13. Carl Schmitt, "Ethic of State and Pluralistic State," trans. David Dyzenhaus, in Chantal Mouffe ed., *The Challenge of Carl Schmitt* (London: Verso, 1999), 207–208.

14. Carl Schmitt, *Political Theology: Four Chapters on the Concept of Sovereignty*, trans. George Schwab (Chicago: The University of Chicago Press, 2005), 5–6, 9–10.

15. Andrzej Sapkowski, *Blood of Elves*, trans. Danusia Stok (New York: Orbit Books, 2017), 165–166.

16. Sapkowski, *Blood of Elves*, 166.

17. Schmitt, *Concept of the Political*, 54.

18. Schmitt, Nomos *of the Earth*, 140–142.

19. Andrzej Sapkowski, *Sword of Destiny*, trans. David French (London: Gollancz, 2020), 8.

24

Sometimes You Have to Pick Sides
Against Geralt's Neutrality

Matthew Brake

At the beginning of *The Witcher 3: The Wild Hunt*, the player, as Geralt, rides through White Orchard with Geralt's mentor Vesemir. As the two look upon the destruction caused by the war between the Nordlings and Nilfgaard, Vesemir expresses support for the Nordlings against Nilfgaard. This is an odd sentiment for Vesemir to express, given that witchers usually avoid picking sides, preferring to stay out of the political affairs of humanity. Geralt wryly notes, "So we're choosing sides now?" In Netflix's *The Witcher*, Geralt recalls that it was Vesemir himself who taught Geralt to stay out of such affairs. He tells his horse Roach, "You know what Vesemir would say? 'Witchers shouldn't play at being white knights. We shouldn't try and uphold the law. We don't show off. We get paid in coin'" ("The End's Beginning," season 1, episode 1). Across the Netflix show, the video games, and the novels by Andrzej Sapkowski, Vesemir as someone who advises witchers to stay out of human political affairs is consistent, which makes his comment at the beginning of *The Witcher 3* so striking. Yet Vesemir's own preference for a political winner indicates that even witchers can recognize that though perfect justice may be impossible to attain in politics, one political option can still be better than another.

Friends and foes try to enlist Geralt to their causes. In light of Vesemir's stance, at least in *The Witcher 3*, we might expect Geralt to pick sides. Yet Geralt remains reluctant to involve himself in the moral ambiguities of human politics. Of course, part of Geralt's hesitation might stem from his views on humanity's low morality and selfishness, springing in part from the personal rejection he suffered at the hands of humans. This low view of human character is accompanied by the Witcher's own moral simplicity, which puts Geralt at odds with the political intrigues of the Continent, intrigues so complicated they could tempt anyone toward political apathy. All the plotting and planning by political actors and factions—even those

The Witcher and Philosophy: Toss a Coin to Your Philosopher, First Edition.
Edited by Matthew Brake and Kevin S. Decker.
© 2025 John Wiley & Sons, Inc. Published 2025 by John Wiley & Sons, Inc.

with the most noble intentions—reek of self-interest, whether the actors be Dijkstra, Stefan Skellen, or Philippa Eilhart.

Looking at our world, philosopher and theologian Reinhold Niebuhr (1892–1971) addressed the problem of ethics and the moral ambiguity of politics. Niebuhr's "Christian Realism" says that the political options we have to choose from are choices between greater and lesser evils. This need not lead to political apathy, but we shouldn't expect the same degree of moral rigor in political life that we expect of individuals in their ethical decision making. Politics by its collective nature is messy, but that doesn't mean we should sit by while a tyrannical dictator takes over the world.

Geralt's biggest hang-up about human politics is the problem of ethical purity. But from Niebuhr's perspective, it's unrealistic to expect full moral clarity in social and political life. Despite this, there's much merit in political involvement, both for Geralt and for those of us in the real world, despite the fact that clear moral choices may not be available to us. Nor is there a promise of perfect justice—only perhaps an approximately better justice.

Ethics, Politics, and Lesser Evils

Geralt expresses an overall pessimism about the Continent and its people, but he treats all its political actors and factions as equally moral (or immoral). As he tells the wizard Vilgefortz at the Banquet on Thanedd, "Set out on your chessboard, the kings, queens, elephants and rooks, and don't worry about me, because I mean as much on your chessboard as the dust on it. It's not my game."[1] This is what politics is to Geralt—a game where it doesn't matter who wins. For Geralt, things always end up the same way, as he says to the wizard Stregobor in "The Lesser Evil":

> Stregobor, that's the way of the world. One sees all sorts of things when one travels. Two peasants kill each other over a field which, the following day, will be trampled flat by two counts and their retinues trying to kill each other. Men hang from trees at the roadside; brigands slash merchants' throats. At every step in town you trip over corpses in the gutters. In palaces they stab each other with daggers, and somebody falls under the table at a banquet every minute, blue from poisoning. I'm used to it.[2]

This is a bleak picture of the world, which Geralt thinks is made bleaker by the over-clever plans and flowery speeches of those with political ambitions. In the opening story from *The Last Wish*, "The Witcher," Geralt says to Lord Ostrit, "But I ... do not care about politics, or the succession to thrones, or revolutions in palaces." His next comment to Lord Ostrit offers some clarity about why he sees things this way: "Have you never heard of a sense of responsibility and plain honesty? About professional ethics?"[3] Here, Geralt seems to be differentiating between a plain and straightforward sense of ethical responsibility, on the one hand, and the intrigues of politics on the other.

Geralt's desire for moral clarity and dislike of politics is also on display in his conversation with Stregobor.

> "Geralt," said Stregobor, "when we were listening to Eltibald, many of us had doubts. But we decided to accept the lesser evil. Now I ask you to make a similar choice." "Evil is evil, Stregobor ... Lesser, greater, middling, it's all the same. Proportions are negotiated, boundaries blurred. I'm not a pious hermit. I haven't done only good in my life. But if I'm to choose between one evil and another, then I prefer not to choose at all."[4]

This is the problem of politics for Geralt—it always involves choosing between greater and lesser evils. Geralt's view of good and evil is dualistic, as he notes to Yarpen Zigrin: "The evil I fought against ... was a sign of the activities of Chaos, activities calculated to disturb Order. Since wherever Evil is at large, Order may not reign, and everything Order builds collapses."[5] Good and evil simply can't exist together in Geralt's mind, for they are utterly opposed to each other. Evil causes good to crumble. Thus, if there is evil in politics, the whole enterprise is corrupt. He continues telling Yarpen:

> The reason for existence ... and the raison d'être of witchers has been undermined, since the fight between Good and Evil is now being waged on a different battlefield and is being fought completely differently. Evil has stopped being chaotic. It has stopped being a blind and impetuous force, against which a witcher, a mutant as murderous and chaotic as Evil itself, had to act. Today Evil acts according to rights—because it is entitled to. It acts according to peace treaties, because it was taken into consideration when the treaties were being written.[6]

Politics involves compromises with evil, and Geralt's picture of evil is too stark to be able to tolerate these compromises. Geralt's stance makes it difficult to make complex ethical decisions, let alone political decisions, which are even more complicated because they involve the fates of entire nations of thousands or even millions of people. If we must choose the lesser of two evils, is it even possible to choose between the Nordling kings and Emperor Emhyr of Nilfgaard? While Emhyr is power hungry, a Nordling king like Foltest (particularly in the Netflix series) shows himself willing to allow his people to suffer and die rather than sacrifice his daughter, who's a striga. Does that make him a better option than Nilfgaard? Or, when Foltest advocates for killing Ciri in order to keep her out of Emhyr's hands, does this make him a better king? Is this decision more or less noble than Emhyr's plan to incestuously marry and impregnate his own daughter? Geralt's principle of not picking lesser evils would seem to rule out an ability to discern the difference in moral quality between two imperfect political options.

Here, Niebuhr can come to the witcher's rescue. Niebuhr understands that "the facts of human collective life can rob people of their confidence in the human enterprise" and that "individuals have a moral code which makes the actions of collective man an outrage to their conscience" given the "inability to conform collective life to individual ideals" and the "hypocrisy of [human] group behavior."[7] Because humanity is made in God's image, we are capable of transcending many of our limitations. So we are capable of some progress, but humans are also sinners, with souls marred by egoistic self-interest. So Niebuhr would caution Geralt that the moral vision of the individual will never be fully brought forth in collective, but some type of imperfect approximation is possible. One needs a more modest goal than perfect justice—perhaps "enough justice."[8] This would help to temper Geralt's dualistic notion that things are either wholly good or wholly evil. To truly defend humanity from evil, a person has to be realistic about the mixture of good and evil within humanity.

Nation-states seek to reconcile the competing egos and interests within themselves, so they're incapable of approaching the moral purity that an exceptional individual or saintly figure may be capable of. Beyond this, citizens of a nation who give themselves unselfishly to a national cause, such as war, support the "selfishness" of nations themselves in their geopolitical battles. To speak of national selfishness is to acknowledge that nations are always going to look after the interests of their own sovereignty, where any sort of saintly altruism would call for the overruling of such selfishness at the level of the individual. Thus, the moral standards that apply between individuals don't necessarily hold between groups: there's a disconnect.[9] Niebuhr says, "The most significant moral characteristic of a nation is its hypocrisy," so "the best that can be expected of nations is that they should justify their hypocrisies by a slight measure of real international achievement, and learn how to do justice to wider interests ... while they pursue their own."[10] However, Niebuhr points out, "No society has ever achieved peace without incorporating injustice into its harmony."[11] Moralists in search of purity, like Geralt, "have placed too great an emphasis upon the value of honesty as a method of escape from injustice."[12] We cannot attain perfect peace, but we can attain more perfect peace, "a progressively higher justice."[13]

Conflict Is Not Equal for Everyone

Of course, Geralt would find the very idea of "approximate" justice problematic, as well as the hope that the world "might" grow progressively more just. Niebuhr addressed why we must be realistic about what political society is able to achieve ethically, but Geralt acts like the world will be "the same" no matter who wins the war on the Continent. Who wins and who loses, though, affects the people he loves in very real ways. Niebuhr himself would say that a war of emancipation is "a different moral category" than that to maintain privilege.[14] As Triss tells Geralt in *Blood of the Elves*, witchers avoid war because to them it can be a choice, but for others like her, it's a matter of survival. Before the Battle of Sodden, Triss wondered whether she should concern herself with more or less competent rulers. After her experiences on the battlefield, she understands that what's a privilege for some is a matter of life and death for others.

Niebuhr would be sympathetic to Triss's argument against witcher neutrality. He writes, "Now capitulation to tyranny in the name of non-resistant perfection may be very noble for the individual. But it becomes rather ignoble when the idealist suggests that others besides himself shall be sold into slavery and shall groan under the tyrant's heel," when isolationism and political pacifism become mere "connivance with tyranny."[15] Niebuhr encourages us to try and see the difference between the relative virtue of a decent scheme of justice and the real peril of tyranny. In his day, he says it would be a "perverse judgment that Hitlerism is really preferable to British imperialism because it is 'more honest.'" Niebuhr tells his readers that there's "no vantage point in history where conscience can come easy," and those who can't accept that either resign themselves "to historical futility" or presume themselves sinless because they haven't risked making the "wrong" choice.[16] While it is tempting for a moral purist to seek "to evade their responsibility for maintaining a relative justice in an evil world," Niebuhr is adamant that the Allies "were certainly righteous when we fought the Nazis, that is, righteous by comparison."[17]

Geralt even comes to question whether his neutrality is right. After the coup on Thanedd and Nilfgaard's advance into the Northern kingdoms, Geralt recognizes that even though the world was bad and disappointing before, it's now gotten worse both for him and for those he loves. Ciri told Geralt that his neutrality was contemptible, and if anyone had the right to be politically cynical, it's Ciri: she was a pawn in a number of people's political schemes. When the war with Nilfgaard is over and she's apprehended by the Lodge, she recognizes that she is a pawn for them as well. Yet she knows that they are a better choice than Vilgefortz. Whereas Vilgefortz wanted to rob her of her dignity and impregnate her with a syringe, at least the Lodge respected her dignity and wanted to train her. This is a lesson that Geralt has a harder time grasping.

The War with Nilfgaard and the Evils of Peace

Nilfgaard was ruthless as it moved northward. While war on the Continent had been waged according to the truism, "War to the castles, peace to the villages," certain Nilfgaardian regiments disregarded this principle. Peter Evertsen, chief chamberlain of Nilfgaard's army, tells his men: "From tomorrow a different principle applies, which will now be the battle cry of the war we are waging. ... War on everything alive. War on everything that can burn. You are to leave scorched earth behind."[18] This approach's brutality is shown throughout the *Witcher* books as refugees of the Nordling kingdoms flee and are chased down and slaughtered. Once upon a time, restraint might have been shown to peasants in the villages, but now they're subject to the violence of war, resulting in death or enslavement. Such brutality causes even the apolitical Geralt to recognize that sometimes it's preferable that one political opponent should be vanquished in favor of another. Indeed, Nilfgaard is defeated, a cause for undisputed celebration.

And yet, even overcoming an evil political power does not make the victors righteous. About the Allies after the defeat of the Nazis, Niebuhr says, "But how quickly our righteousness runs out, not only because we have destroyed the evil with which we compared ourselves, but also because we inherited some of the irresponsible power through victory, which tainted them with evil."[19] The righteousness of the victors quickly runs out, and we're once again thrust back into the problem of everyday, relative evil, like on the Continent after the victory over Nilfgaard. As Geralt and Dandelion make their way to Rivia, they pass a column of haggard people being driven by Nordling soldiers. They're Nilfgaardian settlers who came to claim the Nordling land after Nilfgaard invaded. Having been encouraged by their country to migrate, they now find themselves being cruelly driven back out of the land. The soldiers beat the migrants and make hateful, xenophobic comments about the Nilfgaardians, but the most brutal part of the encounter is found in how the women of the group are treated. Sapkowski doesn't shy away from showing the aftermath of sexual violence perpetrated against the Nilfgaardian women. Dandelion takes note, "Many of the empty-eyed women and girls walking like automatons had torn garments, swollen and bruised faces, and thighs and calves marked by trickles of dried blood. Many of them had to be supported as they walked."[20] The pride of victory went to the Nordlings' heads, and now they find themselves perpetrating atrocities of their own against Nilfgaardian civilians.

Is this progress? When the "better" nation wins in war, are they justified in carrying out cruel acts against their former foes? Is this what relative justice looks like? Are these "the good guys"? For his part, Geralt seems more disillusioned than ever before. While Dandelion is afraid that Geralt will get involved and rescue the Nilfgaardians, his forlorn companion tells him, "Get involved? Intervene? Rescue somebody? Risk my neck for some noble principles or ideas? Oh, no, Dandelion. Not any longer."[21] While Geralt acknowledged how bad things were because of Nilfgaard's invasion, after his journey to rescue Ciri and seeing the Nilfgaardians on the road, he's once again come to see the world as a place where it's futile to hope for progress.

Is Political Progress Possible?

As Geralt awaits Yennefer and Ciri in Rivia, he drinks with Dandelion and Yarpen Zigrin and they discuss whether progress is truly possible. Despite Geralt's notion that trying to help is like pissing into the wind, Yarpen tells Geralt:

> Progress ... is like a herd of pigs. That's how you should look at progress, that's how you should judge it. Like a herd of pigs trotting around a farmyard. Numerous benefits derive from the fact of that herd's existence. There's pork knuckle. There's sausage, there's fatback, there are trotters in aspic. In a word, there are benefits! There's no point turning your nose up at the shit everywhere![22]

Niebuhr would agree with Yarpen. The inevitability of shit in the world doesn't go away, but that doesn't mean there isn't progress. Yet progress is always accompanied by a brand new set of problems owing to humanity's morally ambiguous nature, as Niebuhr believed. The fight, though, is still worth fighting for a better form of justice, which is essential for those whose very survival depends on such justice. Yarpen tells Geralt that progress requires us to fight through life's moral ambiguities:

> Progress ... will lighten up the gloom, for that is what progress is for, as—if you'll pardon me—the arsehole is for shitting. It will be brighter and brighter, and we shall fear less and less the darkness and the Evil hidden in it. And a day will come, perhaps, when we shall stop believing at all that something is lurking in the darkness. We shall laugh at such fears. Call them childish. Be ashamed of them! But darkness will always, always exist. And there will always be Evil in the darkness, always be fangs and claws, death and blood in the darkness. And witchers will always be needed.[23]

Yarpen doesn't deny that bad things happen in the world or that evil exists. As he tells Geralt, "Everyone's seen things. Everyone's been pissed off."[24] But this doesn't entail giving up on the world, because sorting through the moral problems of political life is often messy and morally complex. We should see it as a challenge. Evil will always be present, and the world will always need people who are willing to face evil and work for a slightly brighter tomorrow.

Notes

1. Andrzej Sapkowski, *The Time of Contempt*, trans. David French (New York: Orbit Books, 2013), 146.
2. Andrzej Sapkowski, *The Last Wish*, trans. Danusia Stok (New York: Orbit Books, 2007), 94–95.

3. Sapkowski, *The Last Wish*, 26.
4. Sapkowski, *The Last Wish*, 104.
5. Andrzej Sapkowski, *The Lady of the Lake*, trans. David French (New York: Orbit Books, 2017), 505.
6. Sapkowski, *The Lady of the Lake*, 505.
7. Reinhold Niebuhr, *Moral Man and Immoral Society: A Study in Ethics and Politics* (Louisville, KY: Westminster John Knox Press, 1960), 8–9.
8. Niebuhr, *Moral Man and Immoral Society*, 22.
9. Niebuhr, *Moral Man and Immoral Society*, 91, 172–173.
10. Niebuhr, *Moral Man and Immoral Society*, 95, 108.
11. Niebuhr, *Moral Man and Immoral Society*, 129.
12. Niebuhr, *Moral Man and Immoral Society*, 136.
13. Niebuhr, *Moral Man and Immoral Society*, 256.
14. Niebuhr, *Moral Man and Immoral Society*, 234.
15. Reinhold Niebuhr, *Love and Justice: Selections from the Shorter Writings of Reinhold Niebuhr*, ed. D.B. Robertson (London: Forgotten Books, 2012), 277–278.
16. Niebuhr, *Love and Justice*, 270–271.
17. Niebuhr, *Love and Justice*, 162.
18. Sapkowski, *Time of Contempt*, 216.
19. Niebuhr, *Love and Justice*, 162.
20. Sapkowski, *The Lady of the Lake*, 481.
21. Sapkowski, *The Lady of the Lake*, 481.
22. Sapkowski, *The Lady of the Lake*, 506.
23. Sapkowski, *The Lady of the Lake*, 508–509.
24. Sapkowski, *The Lady of the Lake*, 505.

MONSTERS

25

Origin and Desires as Monster Makers in *The Witcher*

Julie Loveland Swanstrom and Victoria Lyle

Geralt of Rivia has one of his worst days in "The End's Beginning" (season 1, episode 1) when he is given a "Sophie's choice." As a witcher, he is paid to kill monsters, and normally, Geralt would be happy that his attempt to sell a kikimora results in not one but two offers. However, each comes with a catch: both supposed monsters appear human, having been born of human parents, and both supposed monsters are accused of actual or potentially truly monstrous deeds. Killing either is presented as selecting the lesser evil, so Geralt must answer the question, "What makes a monster?" in order to decide.

Geralt's choice: kill Renfri of Creyden, a young woman who allegedly suffers the Curse of the Black Sun, or kill a sorcerer who certainly tortured and autopsied almost sixty potentially mutated young girls born around the first full eclipse in 1200 years. The eclipse supposedly marks the return of Lilit, a demon sent to exterminate the human race. To make way for Lilit, the curse goes, sixty women wearing golden crowns will fill the valleys with blood, and Renfri's birth during the eclipse supposedly reveals her as one of them. The sorcerer is Stregobor, who survives Falka's rebellion and seeks to prevent additional rebellions but who pathologically doubts whether women and girls have good natures. Stregobor's paranoia runs deep enough for him to seek out, imprison, and arrange for the murder of Renfri, who survives by building a life as a violent outcast. Renfri understandably wants Geralt to deliver Stregobor to her, but Stregobor insists that Geralt kill Renfri; Stregobor believes she has the power to destroy all of humanity by paving a way for the demon Lilit. Geralt must decide: Who lives, and who dies? Who is the monster: the one whose birth may mark them as a mutant, something unknowable until after her death, or the one who has systematically exterminated all girls born around a rare eclipse?[1]

Stregobor introduces one of many ancient or medieval philosophical explanations for monstrosity. Some philosophers and theologians have called members of various human groups "monsters" for their physical traits, ethnic

The Witcher and Philosophy: Toss a Coin to Your Philosopher, First Edition.
Edited by Matthew Brake and Kevin S. Decker.
© 2025 John Wiley & Sons, Inc. Published 2025 by John Wiley & Sons, Inc.

heritage, gender, sex, or religious affiliation. In *The Witcher*, explanations for monstrosity include blaming celestial influence for mutation, blaming mutations on heritage, or blaming gender for monstrous physiology, specifically the presence of a uterus. And yet another explanation suggests that a person's choices and actions make them monstrous. Especially in the Netflix series, each of these explanations for monstrosity plays a role in *The Witcher*. As we'll see, those explanations fit within philosophical frameworks to some degree. Despite how *The Witcher* engages with these ancient and medieval conceptions of monstrosity, the best understanding of monstrosity in *The Witcher* is based on motivation. Geralt's role as either monstrous or good is complicated by this theory, but motivation-based monstrosity theory best explains the depth and range of the monstrosity encountered.

Monsters, Monsters, Everywhere

Stregobor's theory that Renfri's birth beneath the black sun makes her a monster feels jarring to us. Geralt and Renfri herself also doubt Renfri's monstrous nature. Her violent actions seem to aim at only self-defense and survival. An eclipse is a celestial event, not something that causes mutation! Her mutation is supposedly internal, and only someone knowing the girls' birthdays could suspect them of mutation or monstrosity. We share our birthdate on social media, on our driver's licenses and passports, and with our doctors, but we don't expect to be accused of having mutations simply based on that! Even astrology, which uses birthdates and celestial alignments, doesn't call people monsters; that wouldn't make for a fun daily horoscope column.[2]

Stregobor's rabid insistence seems irrational—even Geralt ridicules the foretelling about Lilit—but some past philosophers might have sided with Stregobor about Renfri. This approach illustrates the first type of monstrosity: monsters produced by celestial influence. Medieval philosophers such as Thomas Aquinas (1225–1274) referred to celestial influence to explain mutations and other oddities within species.[3] Ibn Sina (980–1037) saw the celestial region as more perfect than the earth, so if something odd happened among the stars, any poor schmuck born at that time didn't stand a chance.[4] Both Aquinas and Ibn Sina follow the ancient philosopher Aristotle (384–322 BCE), from whom they got the notion that celestial influence could sometimes explain visible mutations, especially in a fetus.[5] Stregobor goes further, insisting to Geralt that Renfri's birthday alone proves her to be a mutant. None of these philosophers would back Stregobor up because none appeal to specific celestial events as the supposed causes of mutation. For Aristotle, Ibn Sina, and Aquinas, celestial influence is a generic way to explain mutation. The eclipse might be powerful, and it might even be divinely influenced, but it can't prove that Renfri has something wrong on the inside.

But "wrong on the inside" doesn't describe all who are mutated or monstrous because heritage, rather than celestial influence, might cause monstrosity. Yennefer of Vengerberg, born with a twisted spine, could borrow Lady Gaga's anthem "Born This Way."[6] Yennefer blames her body on her half-elven father, and her stepfather happily sells her for four marks because of it. The Chapter uses her ancestry as an excuse to yank away Yennefer's promised post at Aedirn.[7] Her genetics held her back, but she won't pass them on to another generation—she paid for her transformation with the loss of her uterus.

Ugly and elven, or beautiful and barren, Yennefer might be a monster by medieval standards. The same philosophers who thought Renfri's eclipsed birthday could possibly make her monstrous might judge Yennefer the same way. Aquinas said that the movements of the heavens aren't the only ways that babies are corrupted, since parental contributions to the fetus, which he incorrectly thought were sperm and menstrual blood, may fail in some way.[8] It's not fair to blame him, since he didn't know what we know today about genetics. But his idea did begin to address the need for basic genetic compatibility. Yennefer's spine, he'd likely say, is truly due to her elven and human heritages failing to mesh. Young Yennefer's monstrous appearance comes from her heritage.

Mutant Monsters

Well known for his aesthetic—white hair, yellow eyes, and a steely gaze—Geralt of Rivia is called a monster, but his witcher mutations are neither celestial nor entirely genetic. Herbs, Elder blood, chemicals, and certain genetic predispositions best explain the survival rate of young boys through the witcher trials, fewer than half of Geralt's young peers.[9] Witchers are monsters created to hunt monsters, an evil tolerated by humans to protect themselves from greater evils.[10] Like Yennefer, witchers are unable to reproduce, so they rely on the Law of Surprise to collect their next generation.[11] These donated, won, or otherwise procured children were human when they arrived at Kaer Morhen, but they either leave as witcher-monsters or die.

Once witchers undergo their transformation, they share common traits and abilities. In a way, this makes them like a new subspecies of humanity. By now, it may be no surprise that Thomas Aquinas had thoughts on monstrosity and subspecies. Curious about the stability of animal species, Aquinas reflected on the mule, a horse–donkey hybrid. Though infertile and not the offspring of other mules, the mule counts as its own natural kind because it is distinct from horses and donkeys in specific ways.[12] However, mules are not naturally occurring, and their infertility prevents them from populating freely.[13] In a sense, Geralt is like a mule—a comparison that Jaskier would undoubtedly find apt! Like mules, witchers are created deliberately under the right circumstances, and they share common traits and abilities. They don't spontaneously arise in nature and can be grouped as a kind. Throw in Geralt's mulish nature, and we arrive at the conclusion that witchers are an engineered, unnatural subspecies just like mules are.

Don't Judge a Monster by Its Cover

Mules, Lady Gaga's anthems, and eclipses all begin to help us use ancient and medieval philosophy to categorize our friends from *The Witcher* tales as monstrous or not. Celestial influence, heritage, and mutation have only helped us start to plumb the depths of monstrosity we encounter on the Continent. Yet there must be more to the story, for we haven't found a place to put the horrid Stregobor, who murdered and "autopsied" young girls based on their birthdate.[14] We also can't categorize Nivellen, who was born a human but now has a boar-like appearance because of a curse.[15] Renfri, despite her birthday, wasn't born violent; her life struggles and choices helped make her who she is. Even Geralt must train, for the witcher mutagen doesn't automatically provide sword skills to accompany his speed and agility. Knowing that Yennefer was born with a twisted spine doesn't help us understand why she obsesses over her infertility and sees herself as a monster because of it.[16] These individuals' motivations may be the missing piece of the puzzle and may best explain why some of these characters are monstrous.

Princess Renfri's actions are motivated by the fact that Stregobor convinced her stepmother to cast her out, and as a result, the "kindly huntsman" rapes her. Stregobor offers evidence of her bad choices and evil motivations gathered from her stepmother, who has motive to remove the heir to the throne and clear the way for her own biological children. Renfri insists that she *could have* become so many things, but the trajectory of her life changed when the woodsman raped her, when she starved in the forest, and when she fought for her own survival. She swears by Lilit to take vengeance on Stregobor, for she views her revenge as justified.[17]

But Geralt isn't moved. Labeled a monster by others, Geralt knows that if he kills those who seek to hurt him, "[he] is what they say [he] is."[18] Furious, Renfri asks if she's a monster because she can't let go of her desire for revenge. Geralt's simple "yes" clarifies how motivation relates to monstrosity: Renfri isn't a monster because of her birthday, but she might be a monster if she won't drop it, won't leave Blaviken, and won't move forward. Her revenge doesn't actually solve any of her problems or make her whole—it is just bloodlust, and those are the sort of motivations that monstrous individuals give in to.

Monstrous Motivations

Geralt is onto something significant. Philosophers have debated about how motivations and decisions relate to our nature, and some agree that certain decisions and actions make people monstrous. For Aristotle, a pattern of significant bad choices become such strong habits that a person can't break away into new, good habits.[19] These people are "bestial"—and today we still use the word for those we see as morally irredeemable. Renfri may be bestial if she can't set aside her quest for retribution. Her potential inner monstrosity will be manifested in her outer "bestial" behavior. Geralt thinks she can still choose, that she has not yet gone past the point of ethical no return.

"Inner" and "outer" monstrosity may or may not align, though. Geralt isn't convinced that mutation makes someone monstrous, and he repeatedly emphasizes what people do (and why they do it) over how people look. Nivellen's boar-like appearance doesn't put off Geralt, even though he is surprised that his formerly human friend looks this way. But the Witcher does seem horrified by Nivellen's choice to rape the temple priestess of the Lionheaded Spider.[20] Similarly, Aristotle's approach to ethics focuses on individual habits and decision making; someone is moral or immoral based on their character, which can be revealed by a person's choices and responses to situations.

Aristotle's ethical approach is a form of "virtue ethics." Each person determines what is right to do by reasoning about the moderate way to feel, think, and behave—or, as Aristotle says, the "mean relative to us" between either too much (the extreme) or too little (the deficiency). This mean is calculated not according to each individual's whims but according to how a wise person would calculate it.[21] Relevant factors for establishing the "mean relative to us" include the intensity of his or her feelings and his or her situation in life.[22] But even though these factors matter, Aristotle still thinks there is a right thing to do and a right way to be. He's not a relativist; he doesn't think that morally right or wrong depend entirely on circumstances. Instead, he's aware of the ways that the "mean" for one person will be reached slightly differently than the "mean" for another person. If someone, let's call him Jaskier, has a propensity toward self-indulgence, then Jaskier must struggle to be temperate in a different way than someone who is well-practiced in self-denial (as rare as such a person may be). Jaskier's goal is to enjoy things moderately, desire things moderately, and not harm his own health in pursuit of such moderate enjoyments or desires.[23]

Aristotle's virtue ethics can explain Geralt's horror. Nivellen did the wrong thing! Even when we take life situations or intensity of feelings into account, we find it impossible to identify a situation or case where raping priestesses is the right thing to do. Nivellen revealed a serious character defect; raping priestesses isn't a mean—it is just extreme! Nivellen's beastly exterior reflects his bestial action, justifying Geralt's horror. Geralt doesn't judge Nivellen based on his appearance but based on his character.[24] By consistently approaching many monsters with suspended judgment or even opportunities to change, Geralt reasons like a virtue ethicist at times.

Aristotle thinks that a life of virtue has the same goal for everyone: happiness (human flourishing). Because humans alone possess advanced reasoning capacities, to be human is to use those capacities to live a flourishing life. This is what it means to be happy according to Aristotle. Living this way fulfills a human's function or *telos* (or "end").[25] All humans share the same basic nature, and so all humans have the exact same *telos*. Other creatures each have their own distinctive *telos*, too, and we judge a creature good or bad depending on whether it fulfills its *telos* or not.

So Geralt's status as a fledgling virtue ethicist means that he should be judging different creatures according to different standards. He does recognize when monsters aren't doing the typical "monster" thing. In "Four Marks," the "devil" that locals ask Geralt to stop from taking their grain and supplies is a Sylvan, whom Geralt tells to leave. The Elves, who are behind the Sylvan's theft, are paid by Geralt and told to leave. His vampiric friend, Regis, smells and behaves differently than other vampires, and so becomes a trusted comrade.[26] The monsters who act according to their expected natures can be killed with impunity, but ones like Nivellen's bruxa friend, who treats Ciri nicely and initially avoids conflict with Geralt, spark feelings of regret or reflection.[27] Some creatures fight the impulses of their nature to harm others, and Geralt seems to respect that.

Doubly Monstrous: Yennefer's Many Failures

Yennefer struggles with her own nature as a mage and a woman, but some ancient and medieval philosophers might judge her for her nature as a woman alone. For most of Netflix's season 1, Yennefer seeks to restore that which she spent: her womb. Perhaps it is hackneyed for a woman to feel incomplete without the part that has been used to define her for centuries, but Yennefer feels that without the ability to bear children, she's missing something important to being a woman.[28] Both Aristotle and Aquinas focus on the uterus as a defining characteristic of women.[29] But even Aquinas recognizes the basic humanity of infertile women. So Yennefer is more extreme than Aquinas when she feels incomplete without her uterus.[30]

Yennefer demonstrates another type of philosophical monstrosity: someone unable to conform to their nature. As a woman, Yennefer is a type of human that Aristotle and some medieval philosophers thought needed explaining.[31] Yennefer's womanhood varies from the expected, male human form for them. Aristotle and Aquinas believe that like produces like, and because both think that only sperm does any genetic work, male sperm should make only a male fetus.[32] So any female child is deformed because she's not male. Women are natural—even necessary for reproduction—but not ideal. Aquinas won't call women "monsters," but he won't quite call them ordinary, either. Others, like Tertullian (160–240), do call women monstrous, deformed, and defective.[33] How third century!

Despite how antiwoman this sounds, Yennefer's case helps show the value of including motivation in our understanding of monstrosity. Yennefer wants a child and will go to wild lengths, even attempting to house a djinn within herself, to get one.[34] Her motivation is growing her own flesh-and-blood child. Does that make her a monster? To Aquinas, it does not; it shows that she's doing a good job trying to conform to the womanly "side" of her nature.[35] But Aquinas also wouldn't overlook the fact that while Yennefer's motivations are good, how she carries them out can be, and often is, immoral. Unfortunately, that means Yennefer's a monster doubly-over: she's a woman (one without a uterus!), and she's acted immorally while trying to get a new one. Not only is she missing a key part of what enables her to fulfill her nature, but she's also got moral shortcomings the size of a kikimora. Poor Yennefer.

Maybe we can borrow from Aristotle's and Aquinas's pattern of reasoning—without thinking that the essence of womanhood is reproduction—and redeem Yennefer somewhat. If we replace talk of her nature as a woman with her nature or role as a mage, then she'd have a different frame of reference. Yennefer's twin motivations are to have a child and to have power. A mage's role is to advise rulers and ensure that chaos (not the chaotic type of magic) doesn't break out. Since Yennefer was assigned to Nilfgaard to stabilize and correct cruel King Fergus, she fails grossly: Nilfgaard's newest king, himself a usurper, caused the catastrophic Continent-wide war! And if Yennefer is judged based on her service to the Kingdom of Aedirn, she's also a catastrophic failure—she abandons that post entirely. Yennefer still fails the test.

A Motivated Monster-Hunter Turned Moralist

So much for Yennefer. What about Geralt's motivations, his nature, and his monstrosity? Over the course of Sapkowski's novels and stories, Geralt's motivations slowly change. He wants to fight evil. He wants to be a great witcher. He wants to keep Ciri safe. And Sapkowski teases us throughout, making us guess how witcher-like Geralt actually is. So if we consider Geralt's physical nature to be that of a witcher—remember the comparison to mules earlier?—then his motivation should match the *telos* of a witcher. A witcher's job is to be a monster that fights monsters to protect humanity from those monsters.[36]

As Geralt tells Roach, his first encounter with a human acting monstrously reinforced the lessons from Vesemir: deal with the monsters rather than getting involved in human affairs, and don't be a "white knight." Translation: don't save any princesses, Geralt! Stregobor helps make

Vesemir's advice convincing by saddling Geralt with the title "Butcher of Blaviken" after Geralt kills Renfri.[37] So, monsters it is! When he secures a Child Surprise, Geralt even renounces claim to her (in the Netflix adaptation) because the life of a monster-hunter is not for children.[38] Don't save that princess! Don't save the world! Just do your job!

Grinding away, Geralt projects an aura of a dangerous, successful monster-slayer, but his interactions with sentient monsters show his reluctance to kill. After encounters with Renfri, the Sylvan, Nivellen, and Regis, Geralt studiously questions whether the "monster" is always a monster. Queen Calanthe says that monster killing is the simplest thing in the world, but not for Geralt; monsters must pass his test before he's willing to kill them.[39] When others see monsters and want deadly action, Geralt still takes stock of the situation. For example, when Geralt is hired to kill the vukodlak in "Betrayer Moon," he plays detective. Given clearly biased information, Geralt needs to determine what the creature is, what abilities it has, and what to do with it. During this investigation, he realizes that the vukodlak is a striga, and a princess at that! After he sentimentally offers King Foltest a gift for his (currently monstrous) daughter, Geralt struggles to save her. When he breaks Princess Adda's curse, she thanks him by viciously attacking him while in her human form, showing that she may be human but not yet humane. Fortunately, Geralt's own virtuous development gives her the chance to unlearn her monstrous behavior. Oh, Geralt ... you saved the princess again, didn't you?

Saving princesses becomes an unbreakable habit where Ciri is involved. In the story "A Question of Price," Geralt plans to collect her at age six, and in the Netflix series, he arrives in Cintra requesting to save Ciri from the Nilfgaardian advance.[40] His quest to be reunited with Ciri, to protect her from the raging Nilfgaardian war, and from other threats leads to Queen Meve of Rivia knighting him Sir Geralt of Rivia.[41] Sir Geralt, despite his side-quests in Sapkowski's tales, steadfastly seeks out Princess Cirilla. His deepest desire is to keep her safe, and his motivation shifts from fighting monsters to protect humans, to fighting monsters to protect Ciri.

As Geralt's motivation shifts, he signals a shift in what he perceives to be his *telos*. The *telos* of a witcher is to kill monsters while protecting humans, but Geralt's new motivation is to protect Ciri.[42] It seems like he's leaving his identity as a witcher behind, and his friends and companions notice. When Geralt scares away a monster rather than killing it in *Baptism of Fire*, his traveling companion Zoltan tells him that "you're no longer a witcher, you're a valiant knight, who is hastening to rescue his kidnapped and oppressed maiden."[43] A changing identity matters because being a good person isn't the same as being a good witcher. A good person will use reason to act rightly, and a good witcher will use reason to kill monsters. Geralt becomes consumed with his need to protect Ciri, an ordinary parental response (usually with fewer gutted creatures in the process). The way he's dealing with monsters also shifts, since he leaves many alive who don't seem to threaten him or Ciri and kills many humans who do. Despite constant accusations that he's inhuman, Geralt begins to hold to the standards for good humanity. Whether Geralt becomes virtuous or not is, of course, debatable: he kills, maims, tortures, threatens, and harms anyone who harms those whom he loves.

Geralt's motivational shift helps show the weakness of understanding monsters in the story in non-motivation-based ways. Mutants are supposed to be monsters simply because they are mutants. But if this mutant can develop virtue, then monsters can be good in the same way that humans can. Mutants such as witchers can't be completely distinct—they can't be like mules—if witchers can have the same *telos* and virtue as humans.

The same holds true for Yennefer, whether we think of her quarter-elven heritage or her womanhood. Since her motivations drive her choices, those motives deserve additional scrutiny. Her desires for power and motherhood can lead to great choices and personal development, or they can lead to vice. Renfri's motivation of revenge leads her to destruction. Nivellen's quest to end his curse succeeds, but at the expense of his loving bruxa's life and the lives of the villagers. The elves' motivation in using the Sylvan is to survive in hiding, and Geralt talks them into leaving to rebuild for the future. Mutations, heritage, gender, or birth during a special celestial event don't cause monstrosity. Needlessly and carelessly bringing harm to self and others does make someone a monster.

Monsters in *The Witcher* should be categorized by their motivations and by their lack of virtue. Though *The Witcher* tales illustrate different philosophical definitions of monstrosity, in the end, the only understanding of monstrosity that makes sense is one based on motivation and purpose. Only then can we follow the intricate development of Geralt's own morality.

Notes

1. "The End's Beginning," season 1, episode 1.
2. Madeline Gerwick-Brodeur and Lisa Lenard-Cook, *The Complete Idiot's Guide to Astrology*, 2nd ed. (Indianapolis: Alpha Books, 2000), 256–261.
3. Thomas Aquinas, *Truth* 5.9 ad 9, trans. Robert Mulligan (Indianapolis: Hackett, 1994), 245; unfortunately, in this passage, Aquinas blames celestial influence to explain the putrefaction necessary for a fetus to be female rather than male. Because Aquinas thought of the default setting of humans as male, female fetuses needed to have some explanation. Women aren't monsters—we're natural, and we're even necessary—but we're also not quite as expected, either. For further discussion, see Julie Loveland Swanstrom, "Aquinas on Sin, Essence, and Change: Applying the Reasoning on Women to Evolution in Aquinas," *Zygon* 56 (2021), 470–471.
4. Avicenna, *The Metaphysics of the Healing*, trans. Michael Marmura (Provo: Brigham Young University, 2005), IX.4 and IX.5, 334. Ibn Sina's latinized name is Avicenna.

5. Aristotle, "Generation of Animals," 766b32–767b35, in Jonathan Barnes ed., *The Complete Works of Aristotle* (Princeton, NJ: Princeton University Press, 1984), 1186–1187.
6. "Four Marks," season 1, episode 2.
7. "Betrayer Moon," season 1, episode 3.
8. Aquinas, *Summa Theologiae* I.92.1 ad 1 and I.581 ad 6, trans. The Fathers of the English Dominican Province, at https://www.newadvent.org/summa (accessed February 7, 2024); Aristotle, "Generation of Animals," 766b32–767b35, 1186–1187.
9. *The Witcher: Nightmare of the Wolf*, directed by Kwang Il Han, screenplay by Beau DeMayo, aired August 23, 2021, at https://www.netflix.com/watch/81037868 (33:13). Boys receive the mutagenic elixirs during The Trial of Grasses, a process that kills almost every subject.
10. Andrzej Sapkowski, *Blood of Elves* (New York: Orbit Books, 2022), 209.
11. Andrzej Sapkowski, "A Question of Price," in *The Last Wish* (New York: Orbit Books, 2022), 178.
12. Aquinas, *Summa Theologiae* Ia.73.1 obj. 3 and response.
13. Aquinas, *Summa Theologiae* Ia.73.1 obj. 3 and response; Aristotle, "History of Animals," 773a17–18, 899.
14. "The End's Beginning."
15. "A Grain of Truth," season 2, episode 1.
16. "Bottled Appetites," season 1, episode 5.
17. "The End's Beginning."
18. "The End's Beginning."
19. Aristotle, *Nicomachean Ethics*, book 7, chap. 1, 5, trans. Terence Irwin (Indianapolis: Hackett, 2019), 1145b15–1145b22, 1148b15–1149b24.
20. "A Grain of Truth."
21. Aristotle, *Nicomachean Ethics*, book 2, chap. 6, 1107a1–1107a5. Rather than being an insufferable know-it-all like how Jaskier finds Yennefer to be, this "wise person" stands for one who has attained virtue and how such a person would reason.
22. Aristotle specifies some virtues for some walks of life, such as the virtue of magnificence for those who are wealthy enough to spend large amounts of money on the public good. To practice this virtue, someone already needs to be incredibly wealthy; Geralt seems unlikely to ever reach this capability. Aristotle also discusses a virtue for young people that falls between a sense of disgrace and shamelessness. See Aristotle, *Nicomachean Ethics*, book 4, chap. 2, 1122a17–1122a29 and book 4, chap. 9, 1128b10–1128b23.
23. Aristotle writes that finding the mean is difficult: "For in each case, it is hard to work to find the intermediate; for instance, not everyone, but only one who knows, finds the midpoint of a circle. So also getting angry, or giving and spending money, is easy and everyone can do it; but doing it to the right person, in the right amount, at the right time, for the right end, and in the right way is no longer easy, nor can everyone do it. Hence doing these things well is rare, praiseworthy, and fine." Aristotle, *Nicomachean Ethics*, book 2, chap. 9, 1109a25–1109a30.
24. "A Grain of Truth."
25. Aristotle, *Nicomachean Ethics*, book 1, chap. 13, 1102a5–1103b10.

26. Andrzej Sapkowski, *Baptism of Fire* (New York: Orbit Books, 2022), 219–221.
27. "A Grain of Truth."
28. This definition of "woman" leaves out women who are infertile and women who are transgender, among other types of women (such as possibly women who do not want to bear children).
29. Aquinas, *Summa Theologiae*, Ia.92.1 ad 1 and Ia. 99.2 ad 2.
30. "Rare Species," season 1, episode 6.
31. Perhaps to blunt the "pregnant in the kitchen" vibe, the writers in "Rare Species" have Yennefer tell us that what she wants is a *choice* instead of insisting that she wants a child.
32. Aquinas, *Summa Theologiae*, Ia.92.1 ad 1 and I.58.1 ad 6; Aristotle, "Generation of Animals," 766b32–767b35, 1186–1187; Aristotle, "History of Animals," 573b19–574a16, in Jonathan Barnes ed., *The Complete Works of Aristotle* (Princeton, NJ: Princeton University Press, 1984), 900.
33. Tertullian, *Disciplinary, Moral, and Ascetical Works* (Baltimore: Catholic University of America Press, 1959), 118.
34. "Bottled Appetites."
35. Aquinas is not willing to call women who are infertile monsters either, but he does assert that impotence, not infertility, is an impediment to marriage. Elderly people can still marry because, even though they may not be fertile, a man can still be potent (despite what commercials for erectile dysfunction seem to imply!). See Aquinas, *Summa Theologicae*, Ia.58.1 ad 4.
36. "The End's Beginning"; "What Is Lost," season 2, episode 3.
37. "The End's Beginning."
38. "Rare Species." Geralt intends the child to continue the Witcher lineage, as this is the ordinary way for Witcher children to be acquired. See Sapkowski, "A Question of Price," 179.
39. "Of Banquets, Bastards, and Burials," season 1, episode 5.
40. "Before a Fall," season 1, episode 7; Sapkowski, "A Question of Price," 179.
41. Sapkowski, *Baptism of Fire*, 343.
42. "Voleth Meir," season 2, episode 7.
43. Sapkowski, *Baptism of Fire*, 88.

26

The Witcher and the Monstrous Feminine

Yael Cameron

Tales of female monsters slaughtered by heroes are elemental to the great library of world literature. In retelling the engagement between the hero and the monster in female form, Andrzej Sapkowski becomes yet another storyteller in an ancient and much-honored brotherhood. Slain female monsters are scattered throughout literature as early as Tiamat of the Mesopotamian *Epic of Creation*.[1] The Grecian bestiaries of Ovid and Homer readily bring to mind the monstrous feminine, not least the Sphinx, Chimaera, Scylla, Charybdis, and the Gorgon Medusa. Nightmarish creatures like these are targets for gallant heroes like Geralt of Rivia. However, Sapkowski depicts Geralt in states of anguish, rather than gallantry, on account of these battles. The Witcher fears becoming less human and more monstrous with each encounter. This cost is made manifest as Geralt takes on the identity of outcast—a self-exiled loner, feared and reviled in village and town. This burden on the Witcher's soul appears in the Netflix adaptation of *The Witcher* from the very first episode.[2] In "The End's Beginning" (season 1, episode 1), marginalization and isolation become defining markers in his relation to civilization.

This anguish borne by the fighter of monsters is a curious phenomenon. It calls up a crumb of Nietzschean wisdom: "Those who fight with monsters should take care not to become monsters in the process ... if you gaze into an abyss for a long time, the abyss also gazes into you."[3] Friedrich Nietzsche (1844–1900), not unlike Geralt of Rivia, has a preoccupation with battling feminine horrors. Luce Irigaray writes that in Nietzsche's book, *Beyond Good and Evil*, there are several poignant moments of this kind of masculine hysteria.[4] Yet in the bosom of this same work exists a fascinating provocation for this exploration of the Witcher and the monstrous feminine, because Geralt of Rivia is such a hero, a monster fighter par excellence. Do Nietzsche's admonitions about monsters hold true for Geralt? What is the nature of the (feminine) abyss and what might it mean if she gazes back?

In Sapkowski's short story collection *The Last Wish*, the Witcher's conflicted relation to two female monsters is foundational to the

The Witcher and Philosophy: Toss a Coin to Your Philosopher, First Edition.
Edited by Matthew Brake and Kevin S. Decker.

establishment of Geralt's character, to his birth in a way, and to the labor of a savage maternity. A female monster, the striga, appears in the short story, "The Witcher," and the bruxa, another female creature, follows in "A Grain of Truth."[5] In both short stories, the femininity of these monsters is a critical element in the narrative beat. Inspired by a feminine rendering of Nietzsche's abyss, this chapter explores the relation of the Witcher to these two encounters with the monstrous feminine via the articulate language of French feminist theory. To this end, the chapter will draw on two thinkers: Heléne Cixous, who writes of the monstrous feminine in mythology in her essay "Sorties," and Julia Kristeva, on the maternal in *Powers of Horror*.[6]

A Game of Thrones

The striga is found in the anthology, *The Last Wish*, but also in the Netflix series episode "Betrayer Moon."[7] In the short story called "The Witcher," Sapkowski borrows a female monster from Polish lore: the strzyga. However, Sapkowski's "striga" draws on more than Polish mythology. The quest of the striga is set in the context of a disturbing family romance. Sapkowski paints an intriguing picture of the King of Wyzim, Foltest, who also happens to be the (un-)natural father of the striga. Sapkowski adds to this deviancy by giving Foltest what might be understood as a feminine appearance: "Foltest was slim and had a pretty—too pretty—face," he writes. The implication here is that Foltest is not quite manly. In the story, it is Velerad, the castellan of Wyzim, not Foltest, who tells Geralt the fuller context of how the striga came to be in the abandoned castle.[8] It turns out that Foltest got his younger sister, Adda, pregnant—it was a controversial union for reasons of indecency, that is, incest, and the future stability of the throne. The birth goes horribly wrong. The baby is terribly deformed in some unnamed way and quickly dies, along with one of the midwives (and the other midwife loses her mind). In the midst of this chaos, the child dies, then Adda. Foltest has his sister and daughter buried together in a tomb, and all is quiet for seven years. But one night, under a full moon, the child emerges as a striga. The striga has supernatural animalistic strength and wide jaws full of sharp teeth and fangs, two on each side. Her hands are clawed like a cat's. Or as Velerad describes, "Her Royal Highness, the cursed royal bastard, is four cubits high, shaped like a barrel of beer, has a maw which stretches from ear to ear and is full of dagger-like teeth, has red eyes and a red mop of hair! Her paws, with claws like a wild cat's, hang down to the ground."[9]

The short story concerns the deliberations between men, not over how to vanquish the striga, but who should be blamed for its existence. The consensus of this elite company is that the baby was cursed because of the evil of the incest between Foltest and Adda. Incest, even in the Witcherverse, breaks a core taboo and produces a tear in the social order. However, Sapkowski only toys with this possibility, posing doubt as to why incest in and of itself would manifest such a great evil. The truth of the identity of the malefactor is an additional twist in the plot. As it turns out, Lord Ostrit, a preening courtier, is the author of this curse—due to his jealous desire for Adda, as well as his hatred for Foltest (perhaps for getting to Adda first). Ostrit claims this curse issued from him, apparently without conscious forethought. We discover this just before the striga eats him.[10]

The first sighting of the striga through Geralt's eyes is poignant: she is all rage and hunger.[11] The battle that follows between Geralt and the creature is brutal and exhausting. Eventually, the Witcher seeks respite by hiding in the striga's own tomb. The end is in sight for the Witcher as he finds a skinny, naked, dirty girl lying beside the sarcophagus, assuming the curse has been broken. She rakes her remaining striga claw across his neck, and he begins to bleed out. The end of the fight is strange and unexplained. The Witcher responds by biting the half-girl/half-striga on the neck "until her inhuman howling became a thin, despairing scream and then a choking sob—the cry of a hurt fourteen-year-old girl."[12]

It may be an understatement to point out that this short story prioritizes the phallocentric order, that is, the order that has at its center the symbols and language of masculine power. Geralt, Velerad, Foltest, and Ostrit are all men engaged in seemingly important discourse with one another. This is patriarchal speech in an almost exclusively patriarchal setting. And of course, this is how it is in the world of *The Witcher*, structured as it is in terms of kingdoms and empires. This reproduction of a patriarchal feudal world is nothing new in fantasy. The "empire of the proper," defined by men, is as elemental to Sapkowski's new mythology as it is in many of the old myths—Ovid's *Metamorphoses* or Homer's *Iliad* and *Odyssey* are structured in the same way.[13]

What remains muted in the story is the voice of Adda. She never speaks for herself. Her speech is mediated and represented in the third person by the words of Foltest, Velerad, and Ostrit. She is presented as an object of desire for Foltest and Ostrit, who take from her body against their own rules of social order. Furthermore, Adda predictably appears as chattel in a greater game of thrones, a female piece available for economic exchange in the political will to power. Perhaps the only sound Adda can make is manifest in the howling rage of her monstrous daughter. But even with this concession, the daughter makes no comprehensible utterance, not even at the end. She can only speak in screams, choking sobs, and cries.

Love and Blood

Apart from the short bridging text where Sapkowski has Geralt rehabilitate in the womanly embrace of the Temple of Melitele, the next story in *The Last Wish* is "A Grain of Truth,"[14] a *Witcher* version of Madame de Villeneuve's old tale, *Beauty and the Beast*.[15] The short story begins with the Witcher and his horse Roach on the forest road; in the distance, birds are circling. When Geralt comes upon the death scene, he finds a pitiful tableau: "The woman in the sheepskin and blue dress had no face or throat, and most of her left thigh had gone."[16] On closer inspection of the body, he's pricked by a dark blue rose pinned to her dress. He catalogues the ravages of her body to find signs of unnatural bite marks. Traversing the forest toward the only building he can see, a conical tower, he feels the presence of the monstrous female other, "as if an invisible, soft creature had latched onto his neck."[17] Geralt comes upon a girl this time, a beautiful sprite on the distant hill. Catching glimpses of her through the trees, he's mesmerized by her long black hair, trailing dress of white, and enormous black eyes.

Unlike the striga, this girl-creature has a proper name, "Vereena," and Geralt's bestiary of monsters allows him to refine his thoughts on her species. A rusalka, a kind of vengeful aquatic nymph, is his first guess.[18] But Vereena is not a rusalka; she's a bruxa, which is apparently a much worse female nightmare in *Witcher* lore. Sapkowski's take on bruxa mythology is based in our own world's Portuguese vampire-witch stories. Vereena is bird-like and charming, but her savagery is held back by a thread. A higher vampire who can come out in the sun, she demonstrates an inhuman sentience. Her scream is a soundwave that can bruise and crush any threat. Additionally, she can morph into a black bat with horrendous claws and teeth.[19]

The irony in the story regards Nivellen, the other protagonist, also once a human and very much a classic archetype of toxic masculinity. As a youth, Nivellen was cursed for raping a priestess of the Church of Cora Agh Tera.[20] The curse turned him into a bear-headed humanoid with magical powers. Meeting Nivellen on the grounds of the tower, Geralt engages him in oddly convivial fashion, as if meeting a bear is matter of course. They partake in a banquet of food and wine together with considerable tête-à-tête. Perhaps twelve years of living like a beast is punishment enough for rape, because Geralt doesn't condemn Nivellen, apart from a matter-of-fact observation that the young man had the misfortune to rape the wrong woman. There is a curious omission here in the conversation that erases the brutality of that violation. This dismissal is even more vivid given that the bruxa's punishment as a matter of course will be terminal.

When Geralt departs the castle the following morning, he encounters Vereena in the courtyard. When his suspicions that she's a bruxa are confirmed by silver, the engagement escalates into a battle to the death. Vereena transforms into a bat, black and sleek, red in tooth and claw. The battle is vicious and both combatants are wounded. Finally, Geralt is pushed back and comes close to being routed, but Nivellen appears and saves Geralt by pushing a broken wooden pole through Vereena's chest. Geralt expedites Vereena's end by chopping off her head with his silver sword.

A strange twist in the story, the bruxa's last words express love for Nivellen. When Nivellen raises himself from the ground, his curse is broken, and the depth of the relationship between the two is laid bare. Nivellen and Vereena had a meaningful bond—a magical one. Over time, the two had become unlikely companions, sharing the lonely circumstances of their existence. However, the love they shared, while apparently real, does not seem equal: Nivellen readily sacrifices Vereena to save Geralt.[21]

What troubles us in this story is again the predetermination of the female character as the evil other. Vereena is always already the monster in relation to the masculine characters. Again, Sapkowski crafts a phallocentric scene: Geralt encounters Nivellen, and they sit and talk, man to man, for the evening. The prioritization of patriarchal discourse is central to the development of the plot. However, the story portrays the female other as a raging killer, but also, paradoxically, as living with such a degree of encompassing love that, on her death, Nivellen is freed from his curse by the magical properties of love and blood: "There's a grain of truth in every fairy tale.... Love and blood. They both possess a mighty power. Wizards and learned men have been racking their brains over this for years, but they haven't arrived at anything except that.... It has to be true love."[22]

Sapkowski's dying bruxa bears a tentative resemblance to the priestess of the temple of Church of Cora Agh Tera who died, brutalized and with a curse on her lips, all those years ago. In a shadowy echo, and perhaps what might be a kind of restorative justice over time, Sapkowski hints that Nivellen has cared for Vereena, this inhuman woman, for many years.[23] He's cared for her, surprisingly, given his venal youth, even allowing her to drink his blood. This represents an expiation of Nivellen's earlier sin that might, over time, have drained the poison from his body, allowing it to seep away in persistent service to the woman who can't help but live out her monstrous nature with him and others. It is altruism, and an evolution of Nivellen's character. It is as Sapkowski claims, "true love."[24] However, at the telling moment, Nivellen's first concern is not for Vereena, and not for their love. Geralt appears to eclipse all this: He stands in for a preeminent order, higher than love. His actions satisfy a particular construction of patriarchal justice, to which Vereena will be given up, utterly.

The Monstrous Feminine and the Tragic Hero

Nietzsche's maxim, "Those who fight with monsters ..." speaks to something serious at stake for the Witcher. Nietzsche makes synonyms of the pair: monster–abyss. In *Newly Born Woman*, Heléne Cixous writes that women have been "frozen in our place within two terrifying myths: between the Medusa and the abyss ..."[25] By "abyss" Cixous means the void, emptiness, the unknown, lack, castration (the absence of the phallus), the feminine. By "Medusa," she means the monster, which as we have seen is represented repeatedly by the feminine in mythology—Medusa the Gorgon, Chimaera, Sphinx, Scylla, Charybdis, Circe, not to mention sirens, harpies, and of course, the bruxa and the striga. In Greek mythology these female monsters seem to exist simply to provide a demonstration of the glory of a male hero (Jason, Perseus, Oedipus, Heracles, Theseus, Bellerophon). The endless battling of monsters functions toward reestablishing a semblance of equilibrium in the symbolic order. Unrest is settled through blood, and sometimes the actual culpability of the one put to the sword does not matter. All that matters is that one little girl is a sacrifice to the chaos that arises out of the abyss—the "fall girls" of bruxa and striga. The Witcher's function, then, is to ritually enact the reestablishment of civilization and law. Geralt mediates this balance in a violently chaotic world.

The Witcher has a conflicted relation to Kristeva's monstrous feminine: in gazing into Nietzsche's abyss, the abyss has gazed back at him. The escape available to Foltest and Ostrit, to Nivellen, that of misrecognition, is not available to Geralt of Rivia. In the quest for the striga, Geralt must face her without killing her. He must go down into the vault, and into the grave—into death itself. He has to battle with the striga through the night, standing in her place, lying in her own crypt and breathing her air. In the encounter of a Kristevan monstrous-feminine-abject and a somewhat monstrous, contaminated male (the Witcher is some other order of creature, one that only just passes as a man), the princess draws his blood with her claw and he draws hers with his teeth. In this blood-taking and blood-letting, the Witcher bears the girl's marks on his body and she bears his on hers. It might even be said that he shares with her the punishment of her father's sins, dragging them back across the binary where they belong. But in transforming the princess back to her humanity by draining her rage and anger, he's also restored the balance of a phallocentric order. This is a poor outcome for the princess. She is now available again to her father-uncle, should he desire her pretty eyes, and becomes again a marital prize to be brokered between kingdoms. Who knows what might happen to her?

The bruxa, having never been human in the lore of the Witcherverse, will not endure the fate of returning to a repressed human woman form like the striga. There is no way back for her, no way for her to fit into the social order, because she's a born monster. She is unrepresentable in language. In order to safeguard patriarchal domination, her feminine rage must be completely extinguished and erased. In the story, she's served her function as Nivellen's object of desire, an object upon which his salvation was hammered and shaped. In this story, the mold, once used, is broken. Nivellen has been restored to his manhood in the symbolic order and has taken up his old position, but Vereena now stands in the way of his full restoration. As Kristeva writes poignantly in *Powers of Horror*, "Death keeps house in our contemporary universe. By purifying us (from literature) it establishes our secular religion."[26] Vereena must die in order to restore the balance. Kristeva's "little mother" must be expunged from the record of Nivellen's life. The quasi-religious order of the patriarchy is thus reaffirmed.

Geralt has not been made into a magnificent hero in the way we might expect. He doesn't go like Perseus, appearing before the king bearing the

Medusa's head in a bag. After the striga, Geralt ends his story in the bosom of Melitele. In the goddess's temple, nursed by the abbess Nenneke, the Witcher recuperates from his life-threatening wounds.[27] Maybe Geralt has undergone a transformation, too. In coming face to face with the princess-striga, transforming her back into woman by lancing the venom of her rageful agonies, he has bled like a woman, and he has shown himself to be permeable and penetrable, destabilizing a fantasy of the hero's inviolability. The abyss represented by the feminine wrenches him out of the established patriarchal order, making him, like her, an abjection and abomination. He is presented in a state of degradation like that in which women are often cast in myth. In battling the striga and the bruxa, Geralt pays a personal cost for his proximity to what is archaic, maternal, and for which we have no words—the "unnamable otherness" of the monstrous feminine.[28] He has likely become a monster himself in the process, and perhaps is monstrous in their place. This sacrifice is made manifest in Geralt's continued self-alienation from society and his liminality with respect to gender, to woman, to evil, and the significance of this liminality in Sapkowski's fantasy world.

Notes

1. Stephanie Dalley, *Myths from Mesopotamia: Creation the Flood Gilgamesh and Others*, rev. ed. (Oxford: Oxford University Press, 2008), 228–278, 254.
2. *The Witcher*, season 1, created by Lauren Schmidt Hissrich, released December 20, 2019, at https://www.netflix.com/nz/title/80189685.
3. Friedrich Nietzsche, *Beyond Good and Evil* (London: Penguin, 2003), 102.
4. Nietzsche, *Beyond Good and Evil*; Luce Irigaray, *Marine Lover of Friedrich Nietzsche*, trans. Gillian C. Gill (New York: Columbia University Press, 1991).
5. Andrzej Sapkowski, *The Last Wish* (New York: Gollancz, 2020), 2–32, 39–74.
6. Hélène Cixous and Catherine Clement, *The Newly Born Woman*, trans. Betsy Wing (Minneapolis: University of Minnesota Press, 2008), 63–132; Julia Kristeva, *Powers of Horror*, trans. Leon S. Roudiez (New York: Columbia University Press, 1982).
7. *The Witcher*, season 1, episode 3.
8. Sapkowski, *The Last Wish*, 7.
9. Sapkowski, *The Last Wish*, 15.
10. Sapkowski, *The Last Wish*, 25.
11. *The Witcher*, season 1, episode 3.
12. Sapkowski, *The Last Wish*, 30.
13. Ovid, *Metamorphoses* (London: Penguin, 2015).
14. Sapkowski, *The Last Wish*, 39–69.
15. Maria Tatar, *Beauty and the Beast* (London: Penguin, 2015), 27. Villeneuve's novel was published in 1740. Gabrielle-Suzanne Barbot Gaalon de Villeneuve, *La Jeune Américaine et les contes marins* (La Haye: Aux dépens de la Compagnie, 1740–1741).

16. Sapkowski, *The Last Wish*, 40.
17. Sapkowski, *The Last Wish*, 42.
18. Anne-Gaelle Saliot, *The Drowned Muse* (London: Oxford University Press, 2019), 121.
19. Sapkowski, *The Last Wish*, 64.
20. Sapkowski, *The Last Wish*, 52, 58.
21. Sapkowski, *The Last Wish*, 68.
22. Sapkowski, *The Last Wish*, 68–69.
23. Sapkowski, *The Last Wish*, 69.
24. Sapkowski, *The Last Wish*, 68.
25. Cixous, *The Newly Born Woman*, 68.
26. Kristeva, *Powers of Horror*, 17.
27. Sapkowski, *The Last Wish*, 36.
28. Sapkowski, *The Last Wish*, 59.

27

The Dialectics of Monstrosity

Paul Giladi

In *On Film*, Stephen Mulhall describes monsters as "mutations or distortions of the human."[1] In one sense, Mulhall's conceptualization of monsters rings true, as it is neatly evidenced by fictional creatures such as strigas, plague maidens, and necrophages. However, in another sense, Mulhall's way of thinking about monsters appears to lack some bite. For monsters inspire horror in us because of how "monstrosity" points to something that is "an absolute danger ... which breaks absolutely with constituted normality."[2]

Taking this into account, strigas, plague maidens, and necrophages are not *just* mutations or distortions of the human—they are horror-inducing because they are *metaphysical* aberrations. Every aspect of these horrifying things' existence typically prompts human agents to freeze in fear upon seeing them. As Colin Milburn has observed, monsters are "denizens of the borderland ... extremities of transgression and the limits of the order of things ... with [their] unprecedented deformation of the norm and its threat to the boundaries of conventional thought."[3] By "transgression," Milburn refers to how the category of monstrosity points to something that is *wrong*, insofar as it breaks with established and ordered conventions. Indeed, thinking about monsters as metaphysical aberrations and extremities of transgression also goes some distance in helping explain why the saying "There is no God" is a common utterance when coming face-to-face with monstrous creatures.

In this chapter, I propose that perhaps the most sophisticated and powerful conceit in the worlds of *The Witcher* is the juxtaposition of the cultural propensity to construct the world in terms of strict dualities—"human" and "monster"—with what I call "the dialectics of monstrosity."

This strict distinction between "human" and "monster" is most clearly expressed by a witcher's two swords: a silver sword and a steel sword. The former is only used to slay monsters. The latter is only for fighting humans. A witcher's medallion also evidences the categorial separation of "human" and "monster" with respect to how it vibrates only around the presence of monsters and magic. In the video games, this fundamental division is woven into the programming; players, when combatting monster and

The Witcher and Philosophy: Toss a Coin to Your Philosopher, First Edition.
Edited by Matthew Brake and Kevin S. Decker.

human foes, *must* switch between silver and steel by pressing different buttons if they wish to land any hits on the target.

The dialectics of monstrosity is a challenging and "messy" conceptual space which subverts the propensity to construct the world in terms of dualities. It does so by blurring the distinction between "monster" and "human" in such a way that reveals the great extent to which the category of "monstrosity" is philosophically complex. The category can be used to not only refer to biologically deformed and frightening entities like necrophages, but also to ethically distorted and twisted human agents with abhorrent sensibilities and actions such that they are best seen as *moral monsters*. What distinguishes moral monsters from generically immoral agents is the way in which morally monstrous agents are cruel through and through, disparaging of vulnerability, contemptuous of compassion, and invested in practices of especially violent dehumanization.

"Killing Monsters"

The *Killing Monsters* trailer opens with just the sound of a male Nilfgaardian officer addressing someone convicted of morally heinous charges. The officer proclaims that the addressee is to be executed by hanging. We then see that the officer is addressing a visibly distressed and impoverished young woman. As two hooded male figures on horseback—later identified as witchers—slowly approach the officer and his crew, one of the witchers instructs his companion, "Don't meddle." The young woman sees both hooded figures on horseback. She reaches out to them and pleads, "Help me!" The witchers say and do nothing. As the witchers continue along their journey, the camera pans out and we see the young woman overpowered and a noose prepared for her by the Nilfgaardians. While the soldiers begin to string her up, the witchers have their backs to her. Suddenly, one of the witchers—Geralt—stops. He stares in the direction of the TV audience and dismounts. Before brutally killing all the Nilfgaardians except for the officer, Geralt gently instructs the young woman to close her eyes. The officer cowers away from Geralt, and stutteringly asks the Witcher what he is doing. In a cold and blunt tone, Geralt replies, "Killing monsters." The officer is then strung up by Geralt, who leaves his fate in the hands of the young woman.

Geralt's answer to the officer's question is especially salient for illustrating the dialectics of monstrosity. By saying "Killing monsters" Geralt identifies the man and his underlings as *moral monsters*. The soldiers are not aberrant and vile biological kinds in the way that necrophages clearly are. Rather, the men are morally hideous and transgressive agents, given their cruelty and violence. Geralt speaks on behalf of those of us watching the scene unfold; we are morally outraged by how the young woman has been treated. The lack of due process she receives in the pitiless exertion of power by armed and armored men is upsetting to see. For that matter, arguably the most arresting part of the trailer is the moment when the "camera" pans out to reveal the following scene: the young woman is overpowered by multiple Nilfgaardian soldiers, who prepare a noose for her while the two witchers face and move in the opposite direction away from her. This visual impression in the trailer encapsulates two dimensions of male violence against women that often work hand-in-hand and mutually support each other: active male violence against women together with the silent indifference to such violence. Were Geralt to obey Vesemir's original command—"Don't meddle"—he would be complicit in such male violence through his silent indifference. He could also, given his complicity, be judged a moral monster. Indeed, when the Nilfgaardian soldiers ask, "You like that, you bitch?" there is a disturbing inflection of sexual violence in their denigrating misogynistic speech. This only serves to make the men more morally monstrous. The way that Geralt suddenly stops and intensely stares directly at the "camera" before proceeding to deal with the men may reflect his "awakening" and the need to raise awareness of the multiple dimensions of male violence against women in contemporary society.

"You don't need mutations to strip men of their humanity"

While playing as Geralt in *The Witcher 3: Wild Hunt* and exploring the free city of Novigrad, the player can encounter a witch hunter, who has a brief but philosophically provocative conversation with Geralt.[4] The witch hunter, like so many people in the Continent, treats witchers as "Other." Human beings who survive the Trial of the Grasses are said to lose their emotional receptivity following their mutagenic transformation into witchers. Because of this, they can no longer be seen as part of the human community. Witchers are, therefore, commonly labeled "freaks," or even "monsters." In response to the witch hunter's othering remark, Geralt thoughtfully retorts, "[Y]ou don't need mutations to strip men of their humanity. I've seen plenty of examples."

Geralt's remark is an instance of the dialectics of monstrosity: losing one's humanity doesn't necessarily stem from the physiological transformation from human to witcher. Rather, losing your humanity, as evidenced by acts of immense cruelty, often consists in violating central norms of inter-subjective recognition. For Axel Honneth, the process of gaining recognition from, and according recognition to, people is identical to the journey of self-realization as a social agent. As he puts it, "practical identity-formation presupposes intersubjective recognition."[5] Taking inspiration from G.W.F. Hegel's (1770–1831) three forms of intersubjectivity—love, legal relations, and solidarity—Honneth draws distinctions between three forms of recognition: *self-confidence, self-respect,* and *self-esteem. Self-confidence* refers to the basic sense of the stability and continuity of one's bodily and psychological integrity. *Self-respect* comes from being recognized as part of an equal legal community, where being part of a legal community as an equal member under the protection of law enables social respect. And *self-esteem* comes from having one's traits and accomplishments positively recognized either by fellow members of one's individual community or by other communities. In his later work, Honneth expands his model of intersubjective recognition to include a form of recognition that is developmentally prior to self-confidence, self-respect, and self-esteem: antecedent recognition, which is sympathetic engagement with other people as human beings.

Geralt's point about *moral* monstrosity directly relates to Honneth's concern that abominable and dehumanizing moral practices involve "los[ing] sight of antecedent recognition."[6] By this, he means *forgetting* the primal, emotionally rich relations of sympathetic engagement with other people as human beings. In such cases, Honneth writes, "we are dealing ... with a retroactive denial of recognition for the sake of preserving a prejudice or stereotype."[7] Other people are no longer *automatically* viewed as emotional and intentional subjects with hopes, dreams, fears, and worries of their own. Instead, they are perceived as a "merely observable [object] lacking all psychic impulse or emotion."[8] Such a degrading and especially cruel form of nonrecognition demonstrates a pathological type of unlearning by people in social and political communities: a person who loses sight of antecedent recognition of another person intentionally looks past and denies the other's humanity from the very outset.

For Geralt, cruelty, the moral vice deemed by Judith Shklar as "the *summum malum*, the most evil of all the evil,"[9] is what makes a moral monster. For cruelty creates "objectively horrifying conditions"[10] that are designed to brutalize the targets of cruel acts. The wrong of cruelty consists in hurting agents in such a way that the pain inflicted "unmakes" them by breaking their ability to maintain a healthy self-conception, to the distressing extent that agents end up being "devastated."[11] Such agents invariably no longer see their world as facilitating and encouraging *trust*, a concept central to our socialization as human beings.

"People ... like to invent monsters and monstrosities. Then they seem less monstrous themselves"

One of the most philosophically rich moments in Sapkowski's novel, *The Last Wish*, is Geralt's reflective and critical take on the intellectual origin of monstrosity. At one point in a conversation with Dandelion, Geralt offers a psychological-genealogical take on the category. Specifically, he thinks the category has been conceptualized in a static and simple way that not only radically divides "human" from "monster" but also plays an important role in reproducing the value system of the Continent:

> People ... like to invent monsters and monstrosities. Then they seem less monstrous themselves. When they get blind-drunk, cheat, steal, beat their wives, starve an old woman, when they kill a trapped fox with an axe or riddle the last existing unicorn with arrows, they like to think that the Bane entering cottages at daybreak is more monstrous than they are. They feel better then. They find it easier to live.[12]

Strigas and necrophages might seem emblematic of our ideas of monstrosity. Obviously, these kinds of creatures are metaphysical aberrations of humankind. For Geralt, the *real* explanation for why things like strigas and necrophages are viewed as monsters par excellence is more complicated. Unable or unwilling to face up to how much evil in the world is caused by human agents, human beings project their worst natures on to biological deformities. This cognitive practice plays an essential role in not just constructing the categorial distinction between "human" and "monster," but also in reproducing that cultural activity. Projecting our worst natures onto biological deformities may itself function as a coping mechanism for dealing with absolute and horrific breaches of vulnerability and established morality. Indeed, the effort to properly come to terms with the sheer scale and type of humankind's inhumanity toward fellow human agents, as well as humanity's cruelty toward nonhuman animals and the natural world, is psychologically straining. On this point, it's worth reflecting on what Michel de Montaigne (1533–1592) writes:

> If I had not seen it I could hardly have made myself believe that you could find souls so monstrous that they would commit murder for the sheer fun of it; would hack at another man's limbs and lop them off and would cudgel their brains to invent unusual tortures and new forms of murder, not from hatred or for gain but for the one sole purpose of enjoying the pleasant spectacle of the pitiful gestures and twitchings of a man dying in agony, while hearing his screams and groans. ... As for me, I have not even been able to witness without displeasure an innocent defenseless beast which has done us no harm being hunted to the kill.[13]

What strengthens Montaigne's point about moral monstrosity is how moral monsters are often ordinary, even to the point of being mediocre, people. As Hannah Arendt (1906–1975) famously put it in her book about the trial of the Nazi bureaucrat Adolf Eichmann, the "banality of evil" reveals how sickening and despicable actions are often committed by everyday human folk.[14] This is a very frightening discovery, to the point of even shattering our delusion that only vividly monstrous souls are capable of monstrous deeds. As a way of coping with recognizing the banality of evil, we produce that bifurcating ideology and habituate ourselves into repeated practices of projecting our worst natures onto biological deformities.

"Magic doesn't work on me. Silver does, though"

Both Montaigne and Geralt focus on cruelty to animals as illustrative of moral monstrosity. In the opening episode of the Netflix series, "The End's Beginning," young Marilka talks in a cheerfully nonplussed manner about killing rats in a very violent manner and how she sold her family's dead dog for coin.[15] This further evinces the dialectics of monstrosity: she displays no shame, no hint of regret, and little to no self-awareness of how cruel she comes across. Her speech and behavior are unsettling.

Marilka's hostility toward nonhuman animals is not exhaustive of the callous viciousness that moral monsters tend to exhibit. Most of her fellow villagers of Blaviken treat Geralt cruelly and without any kindness. From the very moment he enters the inn to find the town's alderman and formally complete his witcher contract, Geralt receives visibly hostile gazes, fearful looks, and derogatory comments. His very existence is viewed by many of the inn's patrons as aberrant, not least because "mutant," a term ordinary human beings regularly use to refer to witchers, is intentionally abusive: witchers are construed as "diabolic creations, filthy degenerates born of Hell." As such, Geralt experiences the pain of misrecognition through being "othered" because of his mutagenic nature and abilities. The first vaguely positive experience he has in the inn is with the hostess Isadora, who does not have a distorted perception of him: she politely and warmly asks him what he would like to drink and eat, extending Geralt norms of courtesy. Geralt's "rehumanization," though, is cut short, as his conversation is interrupted by the rude and aggressive innkeeper who menacingly tells Geralt, "We don't want your kind here, witcher." Indeed, the scene is jarring not only because the innkeeper's violent speech punctures the warmth of Isadora, but also because the innkeeper threatens Geralt with execution if he refuses to leave the inn. Such language and behavior are typical of people wedded to ideologies invested in a culture of cruelty and othering—the practices of moral monsters, in other words.

Geralt's second positive experience at the Blaviken inn happens with Renfri, who not only appears respectful to Geralt but also pressures the innkeeper to serve Geralt some refreshment. Renfri is seen sympathetically by the audience because she, like Isadora, has no distorted perception of Geralt. More than that, Renfri is unique in her experience of the ubiquity of moral monstrosity and the banality of evil: "More and more, I find monsters wherever I go." She offers a nuanced critical observation about humanity, one which resonates with the challenge to the bifurcating ideology. However, as we later learn, Renfri's life, to date, is saturated by intense and barbaric violence, so much so that she is obsessed with revenge against Stregobor, to the point where she can only think and act violently. She is also manipulative and deceitful, tricking Geralt into sincerely believing she heeded his advice about letting go of her hatred for Stregobor. Perhaps the most compelling evidence for thinking of Renfri as a moral monster comes from her own tragic self-identification with monstrosity: "Magic doesn't work on me. Silver does, though."

If Renfri may be deemed a moral aberration, then there is a good reason to think Stregobor is one as well. In his way of talking about Renfri to Geralt (referring to her as "it"), in his casting of an illusion in which he is surrounded by passive, silent nude women, in his espousal of the Curse of the Black Sun discourse, and in his cruel experimentation on other alleged Daughters of Lilit, he tries to justify his unhinged, misogynistic dehumanizing acts in the name of science. There is a radical contrast between Stregobor's callous enthusiasm for performing an autopsy on Renfri's corpse and the way Geralt delicately lays Renfri on the ground after killing her in combat, expressly insisting on preserving her dignity in death.

Yet the episode "The End's Beginning" also shows that Geralt's moral and psychological complexity bends toward the dialectics of monstrosity. Geralt's iconic "Evil Is Evil" speech ends darkly, when Geralt confesses he's reluctant to make moral choices between lesser and greater evils. In effect, he is saying that he does not want to pick a side and get his hands dirty. For Bernard Williams (1929–2003), refusing to pick a side and get one's hands dirty is "more than likely to mean that one cannot seriously pursue even the moral ends of politics."[16] Not only that, reluctance to make moral choices between lesser and greater evils may well appear to be demonstrative of a radically uncaring disposition: it is what enables evil to fester and to flourish. The further fact that Geralt, later in the episode, describes the killing blows he delivered to his "first monster"—a rapist—as "spectacular" is unnerving, even though Geralt was justified in regarding a rapist as a (moral) monster.

"Monsters are born of deeds done. Unforgivable ones"

The opening episode of season 2 of the Netflix series is also a fertile ground for the dialectics of monstrosity. First, while the audience and Geralt both initially focus on his current beast-like physical appearance, Nivellen's rape of a priestess years before gives the viewer a more compelling reason to think of Nivellen as a monster. As he puts it to Ciri, "[m]onsters are more than just horrid looks and claws and teeth. Monsters are born of deeds done. Unforgivable ones."

Second, Tissaia is visibly distressed and traumatized following the Battle of Sodden: the Nilfgaardian army, though defeated, slaughtered many mages. During her interrogation of the captured high-ranking Nilfgaardian commander, Cahir, Tissaia buckles under intense strain. The interrogation degenerates into torture:

'Tis not in my nature ... to be cruel. But you have taken someone from me. Someone I care about deeply. So now I will take your knowledge, your memories,

your very being, and leave you cold and helpless, trapped in the eternal darkness of your own mind. I know. I know you want to scream. But it's too soon.
It's too soon because I haven't even started yet. ... If evolution has traced any
groove at all in your brain, I will plough it somewhat deeper. And then you
will know what a scream can really be!

Tissaia internalizes the Battle of Sodden's objectively horrifying conditions. She comes to view Cahir as the embodiment of Nilfgaardian pitiless-
ness and cruelty. Unmade and devastated by Nilfgaard's cruelty, Tissaia
loses her grip on her own humanity by failing to heed Friedrich Nietzsche's
(1844–1900) famous warning that "[w]hoever fights monsters should see
to it that in the process he does not become a monster. And if you gaze long
enough into an abyss, the abyss will gaze back into you."[17]

In "The End's Beginning," a telling conversation occurs between Geralt
and Stregobor. The witcher asks the mage "What kind [of monster needs
killing]?" The mage replies "The worst kind. The human kind." Stregobor's
answer reveals something else about the dialectics of monstrosity: that
conceptual space not only blurs the distinction between "monster" and
"human," but it prioritizes focusing on being alert to and combatting
everyday human moral monsters and the ways in which such agents are
cruel through and through, disparaging of vulnerability, and contemptuous
of compassion.

Notes

1. Stephen Mulhall, *On Film* (New York: Routledge, 2016), 12.
2. Jacques Derrida, *Of Grammatology*, trans. Gayatri Spivak (Baltimore: The Johns Hopkins University Press, 1998), 5.
3. Colin N. Milburn, "Monsters in Eden: Darwin and Derrida," *MLN* 118 (2003), 603.
4. Visit https://www.facebook.com/codeghost07/videos/witcher-3-wild-hunt/932274620632831 for a video of the in-game conversation.
5. Axel Honneth, *The Struggle for Recognition: The Moral Grammar of Social Conflicts*, trans. Joel Anderson (Cambridge, MA: MIT Press, 1996), 92.
6. Axel Honneth, *Reification: A New Look at an Old Idea* (Oxford: Oxford University Press, 2008), 74.
7. Honneth, *Reification*, 60, cf. 79.
8. Honneth, *Reification*, 58.
9. Judith N. Shklar, "Putting Cruelty First," *Daedalus* 111 (1982), 17.
10. Raymond Geuss, *The Idea of a Critical Theory* (Cambridge: Cambridge University Press, 1981), 50.
11. For further about unmaking, see Elaine Scarry, *The Body in Pain: The Making and Unmaking of the World* (Oxford: Oxford University Press, 1985). See Jay M. Bernstein, *Torture and Dignity: An Essay on Moral Injury* (Chicago: The University of Chicago Press, 2015).

12. Andrzej Sapkowski, *The Last Wish*, trans. Danusia Stok (London: Gollancz, 2008), 90.
13. Michel de Montaigne, *The Complete Essays*, trans. Michael A. Screech (London and New York: Penguin, 1993), 484.
14. See Hannah Arendt, *Eichmann in Jerusalem: A Report on the Banality of Evil* (New York: Penguin, 1964). Eichmann's trial took place in Jerusalem from April 11 to August 15, 1961. It was centered on his role in helping deport and transport Jews to concentration camps and to death camps as part of the Third Reich's Final Solution, an industrial genocide program that murdered 6 million Jews. For Arendt, however, Eichmann was not a horrifying and psychotic monster, but rather an almost comically pathetic ordinary man who had lost his ability to think and reflect. As much as I think Arendt's position is compelling, I think she makes a serious error in articulating a conception of monstrosity that appears insensitive—or even blind—to the dialectics of monstrosity.
15. Marilka effectively tells Geralt that she killed the dog, too.
16. Bernard Williams, "Politics and Moral Character," in Stuart Hampshire ed., *Public and Private Morality* (Cambridge: Cambridge University Press, 1978), 62.
17. Friedrich Nietzsche, *Beyond Good and Evil*, trans. Walter Kaufmann (New York: Vintage, 2002), 146, 69.

Index

The Witcher and Philosophy: Toss a Coin to Your Philosopher, First Edition.
Edited by Matthew Brake and Kevin S. Decker.
© 2025 John Wiley & Sons, Inc. Published 2025 by John Wiley & Sons, Inc.